B&B

Australia
Accommodation Guide
The B&B Book – 2015

Great places to stay • Great things to do

*"The difference between a hotel and a B&B . . .
you don't hug the hotel staff when you leave."*

Edited by Carl Southern

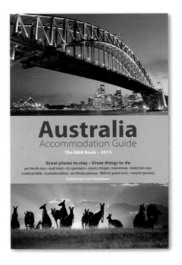

Editor: Carl Southern
Cover and internal design: Russell Jeffery: Emigraph, Sydney
Typesetting: Bookhouse, Sydney
Maps: Carto Tech Services, Adelaide
Printing: Asia Pacific Offset

Distribution
Australia: Peribo. Gordon and Gotch
UK and Europe: Vine House Distribution
Paper: Printed on paper produced from Sustainable Growth Forest

Published 2014

Inn Australia Pty Ltd
PO Box 330, Wahroonga, NSW 2076, Australia
Email: info@BBBook.com.au
Web: www.BBBook.com.au

27th Edition
Copyright © 2014 Inn Australia Pty Ltd

Every effort has been made to ensure that the information in this book is as up to date as possible at the time of going to press. All Listing Information including contact details, room rates and accommodation facilities has been supplied by the hosts and B&B associations. The publishers have provided the listing information in good faith and will not be liable for any errors nor will they accept responsibility arising from reliance on any contents in the book.

Includes Index
ISBN: 978-0-9875756-1-6

We welcome your comments and suggestions

Contents

"B&B Book hosts treat you as a special guest from the moment you arrive until the moment you leave."

Acknowledgements

Good accommodation starts with great hospitality and the 2015 edition of the Australia Accommodation Guide – The B&B Book 2015 includes wonderful accommodation options each offering unique accommodation.

International tourism visits to Australia continue to rise and the many operators included in our guide play a significant part in offering specialised accommodation, much different from the established offerings of large international brands.

I wish to thank all who have contributed in many ways to support this book – the 27th edition.

The many wonderful hosts included
Jim & Janet Thomas, *The New Zealand Bed & Breakfast Book*
Liz Pryor, Hosted Accommodation Australia (HAA)
Nigel Wells, Apec Internet
Russell Jeffery, Emigraph
Simon Paterson, Bookhouse
Penny Crocker, Asia Pacific Offset
Michael Coffey, Peribo
Chris Davies, Gordon and Gotch
Pauline Gosden, Vine House (UK)
Lex Laidlaw, Power Retail Pty Ltd
Sarah Palmer and Kit Zimmerman, Faladons Accountants
Moh Tang and May Koh, B-Sealed
Jan and Fred Howell, James Pierce, Eva, Alex, Seb, Joan, Jane, Alan, Ian and Jared Southern
St Edmund's School

Finally I thank you, the readers of the *Australia Accommodation Guide – The 2015 B&B Book*, who visit the accommodation included. We rely entirely upon your support to continue publishing our guide. So when you find your accommodation in the book, please tell your hosts, "I found you in The B&B Book."

Carl Southern, Editor

With photographs supplied by the hosts and descriptions written by themselves you will discover the special features of the accommodation through their own eyes.

Australia
Accommodation Guide
The B&B Book – 2015

Great places to stay • Great things to do

Stay where the activity is . . .

Go horse riding, canoeing, deep sea fishing, cycling or hot air ballooning

Take your pets on holiday to a wonderful B&B

Enjoy a Romantic Getaway at a rural retreat

Get away to a lovely apartment in the city or by the sea

Holiday with your family at a wonderful cottage in the country

Stay at a holiday home by the sea or on a farm

Stay eco-friendly and enjoy food as nature meant it to be

Pamper yourself in a small hotel with a spa

Wake up to a wonderful day in the wine regions

Go to the theatre in one of our major cities

Stay in a home with a beautiful garden

Australia Accommodation Guide

The B&B Book 2015

Great places to stay • Great things to do

Welcome to the 2015 edition of the *Australia Accommodation Guide – The B&B Book* featuring Wonderful Accommodation and Generous Hospitality. Hosts included in the *Australia Accommodation Guide* welcome guests from Australia and overseas to enjoy wonderful accommodation, fine hospitality and good value.

Last year was a great year for tourism in Australia with more overseas visitors than ever before. 2015 seems it will be even better. The niche accommodation businesses included in the *Australia Accommodation Guide* and not the hotel chains which abound in Australia and overseas. So we encourage you to step beyond the sameness of the chains and sample to varied and charming styles included in this year's guide. The *Australia Accommodation Guide* features small businesses run by hosts who take an interest in their guests to ensure they receive the best experience during their stay. From the welcome smile, the local knowledge, the fine accommodation, with comfortable beds, crisp sheets, a good bathroom you will find a place where you can relax and wake up refreshed and prepared for the next day.

Today, you can find no better value than in the hosted accommodation sector than ever before. Most properties in the *Australia Accommodation Guide* include breakfast in their tariff and often it is a generous breakfast. Many include extras such as a drink on arrival, an after dinner drink or complementary parking. Some offer great value meals or free internet access.

The *Australia Accommodation Guide* features a variety of styles from the fabulous to the simple, the quirky and funky, and the homely and well lived. Many welcome pets, most welcome children and some specialise in romantic getaways. You will find B&Bs, guesthouses, farmstays, cottages, holiday homes, apartments and small hotels all over Australia.

The *Australia Accommodation Guide* receives wonderful feedback from guests and hosts. They value your comments far more than the ticks and checks that inspectors make when assessing properties. Many guests visiting the accommodation featured in the book add their comments to the hosts' guest book or online at www.BBBook.com.au.

When staying at accommodation featured in the *Australia Accommodation Guide* ". . . the only surprises you will experience will be pleasant surprises!"

Markdale Homestead, Crookwell

A Quick Guide

This guide will help you to get the most from the many accommodation choices featured in the book. To help you choose your next place to stay, each entry includes a full colour photograph or photographs with a description of the accommodation, a detailed list of features and facilities and full contact details.

How to find a place to stay

The chapters are arranged alphabetically by state, then location. Some accommodation may be featured under a region others under a town or city. To locate a particular accommodation you might need to search first under the town then the region according to how 'well known' they are.

Accommodation featured in the book is indicated on the maps at the beginning of each chapter and in an index at the end of each chapter. Following the index we have included a directory listing of other recommended accommodation. The listing includes member accommodation from the major B&B Association around Australia: HAA, BBFNSW-ACT, BNBNQ and QTIC who have similar quality standards to the *Australia Accommodation Guide*. An index by accommodation name is included at the end of the book.

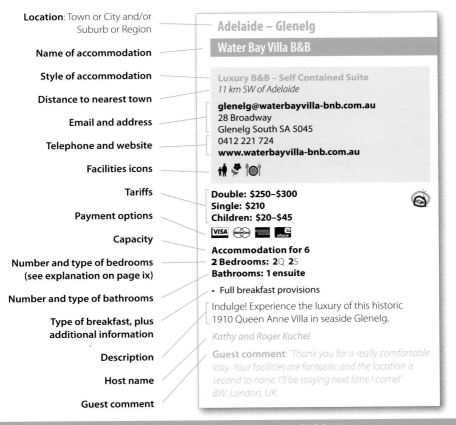

Location: Town or City and/or Suburb or Region

Name of accommodation

Style of accommodation

Distance to nearest town

Email and address

Telephone and website

Facilities icons

Tariffs

Payment options

Capacity

Number and type of bedrooms (see explanation on page ix)

Number and type of bathrooms

Type of breakfast, plus additional information

Description

Host name

Guest comment

Adelaide – Glenelg
Water Bay Villa B&B

Luxury B&B – Self Contained Suite
11 km SW of Adelaide

glenelg@waterbayvilla-bnb.com.au
28 Broadway
Glenelg South SA 5045
0412 221 724
www.waterbayvilla-bnb.com.au

Double: $250–$300
Single: $210
Children: $20–$45

Accommodation for 6
2 Bedrooms: 2Q 2S
Bathrooms: 1 ensuite

• Full breakfast provisions

Indulge! Experience the luxury of this historic 1910 Queen Anne Villa in seaside Glenelg.

Kathy and Roger Kuchel

Guest comment: *'Thank you for a really comfortable stay. Your facilities are fantastic and the location is second to none. I'll be staying next time I come!'* BW, London, UK.

Accommodation

The *Australia Accommodation Guide* includes many different accommodation styles including: Small Hotels, City Apartments, Country Cottages, Rural Retreats, Family Farmstays, Beachside Holiday Homes, Eco Friendly Getaways, Pet Friendly Stays, B&Bs For Garden Lovers, Romantic Getaways, Traditional B&Bs and Stays in Wine Regions.

Whatever the style, accommodation featured in the *Australia Accommodation Guide* offers unique characteristics with the common feature being *'Generous Hospitality'*. Your host or owner has created a special place to stay when your comfort and enjoyment is paramount. Some properties offer grand suites or luxurious self contained facilities others offer simple and homely B&B accommodation.

If you choose a cottage or apartment, you will be completely self-contained with your own private facilities. If you choose a small hotel guesthouse or traditional B&B, you will have your own comfortable and private bedroom, usually with a private or ensuite bathroom. Breakfast is usually included in your room rate unless otherwise indicated.

Styles

Cottages and Apartments: Private self-contained accommodation with kitchen, living and dining areas. Some entries have properties in different locations.

Separate Suite: Private accommodation which may include living and dining areas.

Bed & Breakfast: Guests usually share a dining room and living room with other guests but not with hosts.

Homestay: Guests may share some areas with hosts such as living or dining rooms.

Guesthouse or Small Hotel: Accommodation, often with a restaurant and the warm hospitality found in B&Bs.

Farmstay: Accommodation on a working farm with farm activities.

Luxury: Higher quality accommodation, often including quality furnishings, bed linen and toiletries.

Fothergills of Fremantle

Activities

One of the pleasures of travel is the opportunity to slow down and enjoy new experiences. The *Australia Accommodation Guide* is more than a collection of Great Places to Stay, there are also Great Things to Do. There are more options than ever to enjoy being involved in new activities at your chosen accommodation or close by, whether you stay in a B&B or a cottage or take you pets or children with you. You can stay in a winery, experience horse safaris, deep sea fishing, go skiing, hot air ballooning, canoeing, cycling, play golf, go bird watching or hiking, visit beautiful gardens, enjoy great food, be pampered and indulged in spas, see whales migrating, enjoy art studios, galleries and museums, farm animals and farm life.

Accommodation Description

Each listing entry and photograph in the guide has been provided by the hosts themselves through which you will discover the uniqueness of the accommodation.

Breakfast

Your breakfast is included in the accommodation featured in the *Australia Accommodation Guide* unless otherwise indicated. One of the delights of staying away is a great breakfast and you can be sure your B&B host will prepare a generous meal, whether it is a traditional country breakfast of country bacon and farm fresh eggs or a platter of seasonal fruits, home made bread and preserves.

Continental

A non-cooked breakfast, usually includes cereals, bread or toast, fruit or fruit juice, tea or coffee. Some hosts may offer a Gourmet, Tropical or Full Continental, which may include several choices from cold meats, cheeses, pastries, tropical fruits and fresh juices.

Full

A continental style breakfast plus a cooked course.

Special

Some hosts offer varied options for B&B or Self Contained Accommodation. Some hosts offer gourmet style breakfasts or cater for special diets.

Breakfast Provisions

Breakfast supplies or *Welcome Basket* provided. ie Supplies sufficient for a Continental Breakfast or Full Breakfast. Some hosts offer breakfast for the first night others offer breakfast for the duration of your stay and replenish breakfast supplies each day.

Accommodation Only

Some accommodation, usually Self Contained, does not provide breakfast or offers breakfast for an additional charge.

Additional Meals

Some rural stays, farmstays or guesthouses offer additional meals. Others offer barbecue packages or picnic hampers. You may need to request meals in advance or by arrangement (B/A).

Beds and Bedrooms

Entries show the number and size of beds, bedrooms and guests that can stay.

S = *Single*: Beds for 1 person (1 bed)

T = *Twin*: Beds for 2 persons (2 beds)

KT = *King Twin*: Beds for 2 persons (2 large single beds)

D = *Double*: Bed for 2 persons (1 bed)

Q = *Queen*: Bed for 2 persons (1 bed)

K = *King*: Bed for 2 persons (1 large bed)

Bathrooms

Most accommodation provides ensuite or private bathrooms for your exclusive use. Older or historic places may offer private bathrooms for your exclusive use but off the hallway. Some accommodation offer luxurious bathrooms – some with spas.

Ensuite: Exclusive use with access from your bedroom

Private: Exclusive use usually with access off the hallway

Shared: Bathroom shared with other guests.

"We received the greatest hospitality, slept in the most wonderful bed and enjoyed the best breakfast in a long, long time. We will return!"

Reservations

- We recommend that you book well in advance to confirm your accommodation.
- Book directly with your host by email or telephone or mail.
- Advise dates of arrival and departure, time of arrival, the room/s you require, how many guests in your party and any special requirements.
- Many properties now welcome children or pets , but please mention this when booking.
- Some accommodation has minimum stays during peak periods.
- You may need to pay a deposit in advance. Ask how much is due, when full payment is required.
- Check the cancellation policy. Owners of businesses may be unable to relet the accommodation if you cancel your reservation.
- A travel insurance policy can cover you for unforseen cancellations.
- Most hosts accept credit cards, many accept payment by eftpos and all accept cash.
- The *Australia Accommodation Guide* promotes small accommodation businesses, so when you book please tell your host, "*I saw you in the B&B Book.*"

Tariff

Accommodation included in the *Australia Accommodation Guide* offers great value accommodation, particularly as your breakfast is usually included. Rates shown include GST and are valid for the current year but are subject to change. If the quoted rate is higher, tell you hosts you saw them advertised in the B&B Book at a better rate.

Rates are for two persons (double) or 1 person (single) and vary according to the quality of the accommodation, the location, the facilities offered and seasonal variations. Low season or midweek bookings can offer good value particularly in popular tourism destinations. Confirm rates when booking. Some hosts offer discounts for extended stays. Some can put another bed in the room, for an extra person for a small additional charge.

Check-In

Check-in times are usually from 1.00–2.00 in the afternoon with check-out 10.00–11.00 in the morning. Hosts are usually flexible with check-in and check-out times. So ask when booking if you need a earlier check-in or a later check-out. You may be able to vary the time if your room is ready or there are no guests checking-out that same day.

Conditions of Stay

Hosts welcoming guests to stay at their accommodation aim to provide not only you but subsequent guests similar experiences of wonderful accommodation and great hospitality. Most hosts keep their terms and conditions to a minimum; some may invite you to 'sign-in' on arrival and agree to their 'Conditions of Stay'. This could cover you as well as the host in case of an unforseen incident. Moreover it guarantees all guests that the accommodation will always offer the finest standards.

Hospitality

Your hosts want you to enjoy your stay as much as you do. If you experience any concerns, problems or complaints tell your host as soon as possible so they can be addressed immediately.

Icons

♿ **Easy Access**: Suitable for less able or non ambulant guests.

⛹ **Children Welcome** (Check details with hosts)

Pets Welcome (Check details with hosts)

Facilities for horses: i.e. agistment close by

Accommodation for Couples: Some accommodation is designed for couples or romantic getaways. Other properties may be unsuitable for children due to hazards such as unfenced water

Accommodation with Outstanding Gardens

Special Location

Winery/wineries or Wine Activities close by or a short drive

Restaurant/restaurants close by

Eco Tourism: Accommodation complying with or supporting Eco tourism

Onsite Activities available

Swimming Pool

Tennis Court

Function facilities

Weddings catered for

Internet Access: Maybe cable or Wifi

Cable or satellite television

Day Spa. Some properties also have spa treatments.

⊘ **No Smoking on Property**: All properties are now non smoking inside. Non smoking properties are smoke free zones across the property.

Member of National or State B&B Association

AAA Tourism
★★★ **AAA Tourism Assessed**: The stars! Complying with AAA Tourism at time of publication

Tourism Accredited: The green tick issued by Australian Tourism Accreditation Association

Recommended Accommodation

Each entry in the Guide has contributed a small fee to be included so please support these businesses when booking your next place to stay.

Many belong to state or national industry associations, AAA Tourism, business accreditation or the local tourism association. We included at the end of each chapter a list of recommended accommodation from Australian B&B Associations: HAA, BBFNSW-ACT, QTIC and BNBNQ.

Please Mention The B&B Book

Today many people use a variety of sources to locate their accommodation. We hope that this guide helps you in finding the right accommodation to suit your needs. Whether you telephone, use our website, please tell your hosts, "We found you in The B&B Book."

The Website – BBBook.com.au

You may wish to view your accommodation choice online before you book. You can find all entries included in the *Australia Accommodation Guide* on our comprehensive website at BBBook.com.au. You will find more information on each accommodation, more photographs and direct links to each B&B hosts own website. You can book directly with the property or complete an online booking form.

Tell your hosts, "I found you in *The B&B Book*!"

Book Orders

Order a copy of the *Australia Accommodation Guide* or the *New Zealand Bed & Breakfast Book* as a gift **Only $19.95**.

You can buy books from bookstores or newsagents or order directly from:

Inn Australia
PO Box 330
Wahroonga
NSW 2076
Info@BBBook.com.au

Quality Assurance

Accommodation included in the *Australia Accommodation Guide* offer a Commitment to Generous Hospitality. Below are details of the minimum standards you can expect. Put simply, *"The only surprises you will experience will be pleasant surprises!"*

Housekeeping

The property is well maintained internally and externally.

Absolute cleanliness in all guest areas, kitchen, refrigerator and food storage areas.

All inside rooms are non-smoking.

Hospitality

Hosts are present to welcome and farewell guests (unless advised in self-contained accommodation)

Guests are treated with courtesy and respect

Guests are offered hosts' contact details if hosts leave the premises.

Room rates, booking and cancellation policy are advised to guests.

Local tourism and transport information is available.

Bedrooms

Bedrooms solely dedicated to guests.

Quality bed linen, sound floor coverings, bedding, pillows and furnishings

Bedroom heating and cooling appropriate to the climate with fans and heating or reverse cycle air-conditioning

Bedding and pillows appropriate to the climate, with extra available

Bedside lighting for each guest

Blinds or curtains on all windows where appropriate

Adequate clothing and storage space

Adequate sized mirror

Bathrooms

Sufficient bathroom and toilet facilities for all guests

Bath or shower, hand basin and mirror

Waste bin in bathroom

Adequate supplies for each guest: toiletries, soap, towels, bathmat, facecloths

Towels changed or dried daily for guests staying more than one night

Privacy lock on bathroom and toilet doors

Meals

Breakfast: A generous breakfast is provided (unless advised otherwise)

Meals: Available for guests for additional charge in some accommodation

Drinks: water, tea and coffee offered or available

General

Roadside identification of property

An honest and accurate description of listing details and facilities

Hosts accept responsibility to comply with government regulations

Description includes if hosts' pets and young children are sharing a common area with guests

Adequate Public and Product Liability under a B&B Insurance Policy

Extras

Many accommodation places provides a number of additional extras including:
Lock on guest rooms or secure storage facilities

Air-conditioning, particularly in hotter areas

Laundry facilities

Fresh flowers, magazines, books

Fresh fruit, complimentary drinks

B&B World App

Download Bed and Breakfast World App to **iPhone and iPad**

• pet friendly stays • small hotels
• city apartments • country cottages
• rural retreats • family farm stays
traditional B&Bs • beachside
holidays • eco friendly getaways
• B&Bs for garden lovers
• romantic getaways

Search Bed and Breakfast-World

Download from Apple

New South Wales

NSW

NSW is a great place for any type of holiday at any time of the year with great adventure holidays and plenty of things to see and the chance to try new adventures. You'll find beautiful art at the many fine galleries, museums and cultural events and enjoy gourmet food and wine tasting across NSW. You can ski one weekend and surf the following weekend anywhere along the coast at beaches from Byron Bay to Eden.

Tibooburra

Bourke

Wilcannia

Cobar

Broken Hill

Menindee

Ivanhoe

Hillston

Mildura

Hay

30

Balranald

Deniliquin

Tocumwal

Albury

9

Murwillumbah

53

Tenterfield

Lismore

Moree

27

Grafton

Lightning Ridge

Walgett

Armidale

Coonabarabran

Tamworth

Port Macquarie

Dunedoo

Narromine

Dubbo

Range

Parkes

Newcastle

Blue
Mountains

Sydney

Dividing

Wollongong

Yass

Bowral

ga Wagga

Canberra

SOUTH

PACIFIC

OCEAN

Great

Cooma

Bega

Eden

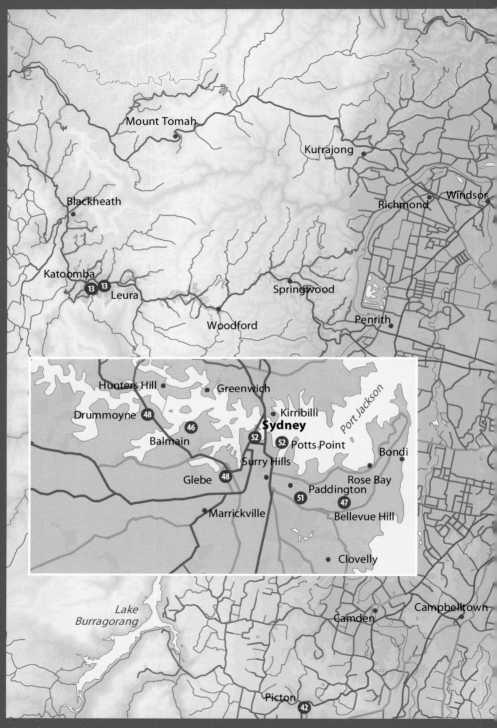

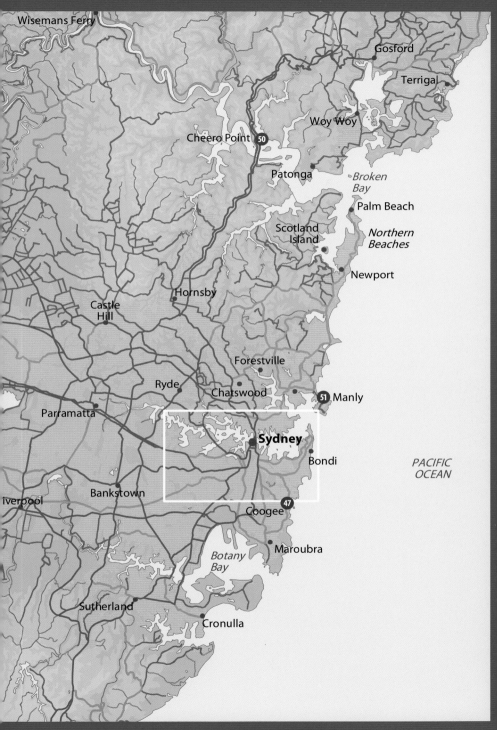

Wisemans Ferry

Gosford

Terrigal

Woy Woy

Cheero Point 50

Patonga

Broken Bay

Palm Beach

Northern Beaches

Scotland Island

Newport

Hornsby

Castle Hill

Forestville

Ryde

Chatswood

51 Manly

Parramatta

Sydney

Bondi

PACIFIC OCEAN

Bankstown

iverpool

47

Coogee

Maroubra

Botany Bay

Sutherland

Cronulla

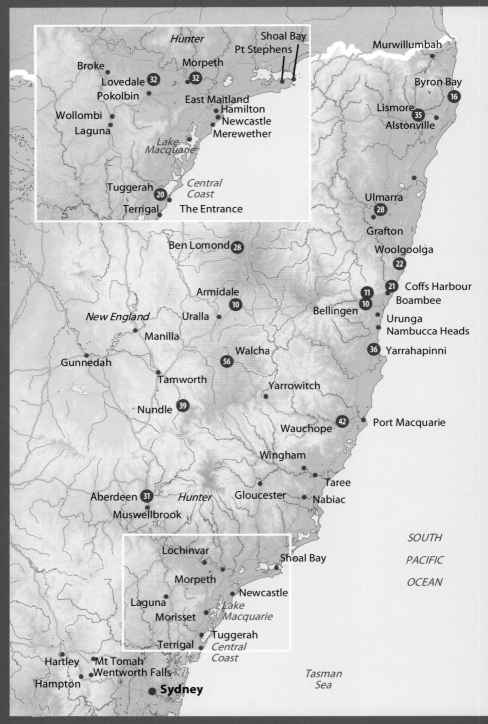

Reynella Homestead

B&B and Guest House and Lodge Style B&B
9 km E of Adaminaby

reynella@activ8.net.au
'Reynella' 699 Kingston Road
Adaminaby NSW 2629
(02) 6454 2386 or 1800 029 909
www.reynellarides.com.au

AAA Tourism
★★★

Single: $125
Children: On application
$125pp (Lodge). Homestead horse riding $95pp
Dinner: Full three course dinner included

VISA · MasterCard · AMERICAN EXPRESS · eftpos

Accommodation for 50
19 Bedrooms: 4K 1Q 2D 10T 23S
Lodge style accommodation/shared bathrooms
Bathrooms: 5 guest share

• Full breakfast

Lodge accommodation on working sheep
and cattle property of approx 6000 acres –
opportunities for some involvement. Largest horse
trekking operation in Kosciuszko National Park.
3 day/4 night or 5 day/6 night Safaris. First and last
night at the Homestead. With 2 two nights out
camping or 4 nights out camping in the Kosciuszko

National Park. Operating from October to May. Stay
at The Homestead $125 per night, horse riding an
extra $95 per day. We require minimum of 4 people
riding to take day rides. Stay at the Ski Lodge in the
winter only $125 per adult, discount for families,
includes 3 course dinner and full breakfast. Ideal
base for Skiing Accommodation. Discounts for
direct bookings on ski accommodation. Superb
food and BYO.

Also cottage available for rent, sleeps 14. Local
fishing, bush walking, riding instruction. (Summer).
Original operators for 40 years. Visit our website for
dates and rates for treks.

Roslyn and John Rudd

Albury

Briardale B&B

B&B
5 km N of Albury

briardale@exemail.com.au
396 Poplar Drive
Lavington NSW 2641
(02) 6025 5131 or 0407 254 368
www.briardalebnb.com.au

Double: $145–$190
Single: $139–$139

Dinner may be booked when reserving your suite.
Dinner: Simple and fresh dinner menu available with
24 hrs notice.

Accommodation for 6
3 Bedrooms: 3Q
Bathrooms: 3 ensuite
The Heathwood Spa Suite features a two-person
corner spa

- Full breakfast

Affectionately known as the 'Lairds Manor'
Briardale, Albury's finest Bed and Breakfast, has
three delightfully appointed spacious suites. Each
features ensuite bathroom, Queensize brass bed
with deluxe mattress and fine quality linen, comfy
doonas and electric blankets in winter, beautiful
antique dressing table, individual air-conditioning,
LCD television, USB charger sockets and wardrobe.
All Suites have views over the old cottage gardens
and Heathwood Park. Each ensuite has a large
shower, heated towel rail and ceiling heat lamps.
Briardale is a short 1.5km walk to major shopping
centres, two hotels, numerous cafés and restaurants
and North Albury Sports Club.

Robert and Robyn Clarke

Adaminaby

Selwyn is the perfect place to learn
to ski or snowboard with it's gentle,
progressing terrain and caring
mountain staff. Our family friendly
atmosphere will make you and
your family feel right at home. In
summer you can go horse trekking
in the Kosciuszko National Park.

Roslyn Rudd
Reynella Homestead

Armidale

Armidale Boutique Accommodation

Self Contained Cottages (2)
0.5 km S of Armidale Town Centre

Tracy@ArmidaleBnB.com.au
c/ – 134 Brown Street
Armidale NSW 2350
(02) 6772 5276 or 0402 058 504
www. ArmidaleBnB.com.au

Double: $155–$165
$60 per extra person per night

VISA MasterCard

Accommodation for 6
3 Bedrooms: 2Q 1D
Camellia Court: 2B/R; The Elms: 1B/R
Bathrooms: 1 private
One in each cottage

• Breakfast provisions first night

Two very stylish self-contained properties, situated in the heart of Armidale. Our aim is to offer you beautiful, comfortable accommodation while maintaining the ethos of 'value for money'. 'Camellia Court' is contemporary in design and style, complete with leather lounges and a fabulous north-facing deck – wheelchair friendly too. 'The Elms' is charmingly private with its own small, protected garden and is perfect for a single or couple. Close to shops, restaurants, the Regional Art Gallery, and University.

Tracy and David Everett

Bellingen

Rivendell

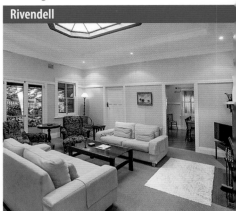

B&B
0.1 km E of Bellingen

info@rivendellguesthouse.com.au
10–12 Hyde Street
Bellingen NSW 2454
(02) 6655 0060 or 0403 238 409
www.rivendellguesthouse.com.au

AAA Tourism
★★★★

Double: $155–$165
Single: $135–$145

VISA MasterCard eftpos

Accommodation for 8
4 Bedrooms: 3Q 2T
Bathrooms: 3 ensuite, 1 private

• Full breakfast

In the heart of historic Bellingen, Rivendell is a beautifully decorated Federation home. Luxurious rooms furnished with antiques, fluffy bathrobes, open to shady verandahs and picturesque gardens. Take a refreshing dip in the freshwater pool, or in winter, relax by the log fire. After dinner enjoy complimentary port and chocolates. TV, stereo, books, games, magazines and tea/coffee making is provided in the guest lounge.

Janet Hosking

Guest comment: *'Lovely stay, fab food and cosy accommodation – we will be back! Thank you' Justin and Caroline UK.*

Bellingen

CasaBelle Country Guest House

Luxury and Guest House and Romantic B&B
1.2 km N of Bellingen

enquiries@casabelle.com
Gleniffer Road
Bellingen NSW 2454
(02) 6655 9311
www.casabelle.com

 AAA Tourism
★★★★✦

Double: $245
Dinner: By prior arrangement

VISA MasterCard eftpos

Accommodation for 6
3 Bedrooms: 1K 2KT 2Q
Bathrooms: 3 ensuite
2 rooms with spa baths

• Full breakfast

CasaBelle an award winning B&B invites you to enjoy a very special accommodation experience.

Step into a tranquil Tuscan courtyard with vibrant bougainvillea and bubbling fountain. Enjoy acres of forest and garden views from your beautifully appointed room furnished with all luxury comforts including TV/DVD, hairdryer, bath robes, imported French toiletries, fresh flowers, bowls of fruit and nuts, filter coffees and home-made cakes. Candlelit spa baths, log fires, complimentary port and chocolates, a library of books, CD/DVD's and games. Sumptuous breakfasts served until noon overlooking gardens filled with birdlife. Just off the Pacific Highway midway between Sydney and Brisbane.

Suzanne and Fritz

Bellingen – Gleniffer

Cottonwood Cottage – Luxury in the Country

Luxury Charming French-style Cottage with Kitchen *10 km N of Bellingen*

info@cottonwoodfarm.com.au
71 Gordonville Road
Gleniffer NSW 2454
0432 272 973 or 0428 864 333
www.cottonwoodfarm.com.au

Double: $300
Single: $300
2 night minimum stay

VISA MasterCard AMERICAN EXPRESS

Accommodation for 2
1 Bedroom: 1K
Super King size, superb quality bed.
Bathrooms: 1 ensuite
Inside cottage – large en suite bathroom, 2 person shower with waterfall shower head.

• Full breakfast provisions

Luxurious, stylish, 5 star, purpose built. Perfect for discerning couples and honeymooners. Set on 61 private acres and boasting panoramic mountain views, fine furniture and luxurious textiles… cottonwood is the ultimate luxury escape.

Inside, an all-white light filled space, exquisitely detailed and styled, with a rustic gentility and an abundance of thoughtful and welcoming touches, including heated floors, wood fired heater, air conditioning, hidden flat screen TV, extensive movie library and Bose sound system. Outside, a private courtyard, established gardens, outdoor bath and breathtaking views. Get ready to experience a new level of silence. You wont want to leave!

Suzi and Daniel Maher

Bellawongarah at Berry

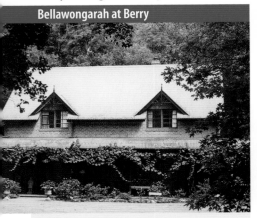

Heritage Listed Luxury B&B and Cottage
8 km SW of Berry

deb@accommodation-berry.com.au
869 Kangaroo Valley Road
Bellawongarah NSW 2535
(02) 4464 1999
www.accommodation-berry.com.au

Double: $250–$260

VISA MasterCard

Accommodation for 4
2 Bedrooms: 2Q
Queen beds
Bathrooms: 2 ensuite

• Full breakfast

A luxurious B&B country retreat set in rain forest on Berry Mountain, offering a choice of accommodation for couples. The 1868 Old Mountain Church provides a romantic cottage with a kitchenette for one couple or enjoy the luxurious Loft suite with double spa in the main house. Full country breakfast each morning plus afternoon tea on arrival. 2 night minimum stay. Close to Berry and Kangaroo Valley. Tranquil gardens, abundant native wildlife, mountain scenery and surrounding national parks for bushwalking, bird watching or just relaxing peace and quiet.

Deb Mitchell

Blue Mountains

Looking for some peace and relaxation? Or maybe some adventure and exhilaration? Stunning scenery, great tea rooms and spas, then bushwalks, adventure abseiling and canyoning for the energetic. The famous Three Sisters and Blue Mountains national park has it all, and what a great escape from the busy world.

Blue Mountains – Katoomba

Melba House

Luxury B&B
0.5 km E of Katoomba

stay@melbahouse.com
98 Waratah Street
Katoomba NSW 2780
(02) 4782 4141 or 0439 251 488
www.melbahouse.com

AAA Tourism
★★★★✦

Double: $130–$280
Single: $130–$180
Mid week rate available: Indulgence Packages available

VISA ⬤ ⬤ ⬤

Accommodation for 6
3 Bedrooms: 1K 1KT 2Q
Bathrooms: 3 ensuite
2 Spa Ensuites and 1 Shower Ensuite

• Full breakfast

Imagine your own log fire and spa, central-heating, electric blankets, large comfortable suites with own sitting and dining areas, sumptuous breakfasts, that's historical 4.5* Melba House. Quiet and secluded yet close to many restaurants, galleries, antique and craft shops and walking tracks. Also, close to the best-loved attractions of Katoomba and Leura. See our website www.melbahouse.com.

Sue Handley

Guest comment: *'Of the B&Bs around the world we have stayed, this is our best experience, it's exquisite.' (W. Dallas Texas).*

Blue Mountains – Leura

Broomelea

Luxury B&B
0.5 km S of Leura

info@broomelea.com.au
273 Leura Mall
Leura NSW 2780
(02) 4784 2940
www.broomelea.com.au

AAA Tourism
★★★★✦

Double: $165–$225
Single: $140–$190

VISA ⬤ ⬤ ⬤ ⬤ ⬤

Accommodation for 10
4 Bedrooms: 1KT 3Q 2S
Bathrooms: 4 ensuite

• Full breakfast

A beautiful 1909 mountain home for guests who would like more than simply a bed and a breakfast. We offer spacious ensuite rooms with 4 poster beds, open fires, lounges, TV, Video, CD Players, a freshly prepared gourmet breakfast each morning and most importantly local knowledge. Broomelea is perfectly located in the Living Heritage precinct of Leura just a 10 minute stroll to famous cliff top walks with great views or our beautiful village with numerous restaurants and galleries.

Bryan and Denise Keith

Blue Mountains – Leura

Leura's Magical Manderley

Luxury Self Contained Apartments
0.3 km E of Leura

manderleys@bigpond.com
157 Megalong Street
Leura NSW 2780
(02) 4784 3252 or 0417 286 533
www.manderley.com.au

Double: $180–$250
Single: $150–$180
Stay 4 nights midweek, pay 3

Accommodation for 4
2 Bedrooms: 1K 1Q
Bathrooms: 2 private
2 double hydro spas and showers

• Full breakfast provisions

Experience the Magic of Manderley – Peace, Privacy and Luxury – right in the heart of historic Leura. Two stunning, self-contained and elegant garden apartments, each accommodating one couple in ultimate luxury. Guests enjoy the idyllic and secluded setting just a stroll to popular Leura village. After a day exploring, pour a glass of champagne, relax and rejuvenate the body and mind in your private, double 36 jet Hydro Spa. Tariffs include aperitifs, champagne, chocolates, Molton Brown spa products.

Robyn Piddington

Guest comment: *'The secret to this beautifully presented property is luxury and elegance. Nothing is overlooked and no expense is spared to ensure each guest feels indulged.' Bruce Elder,* Sydney Morning Herald.

Blue Mountains – Leura

The Greens of Leura

B&B
0.1 km E of Leura

stay@thegreensleura.com.au
24–26 Grose Street
Leura NSW 2780
(02) 4784 3241
www.thegreensleura.com.au

AAA Tourism
★★★★✦

Double: $175–$220
Single: $155–$200

Accommodation for 12
5 Bedrooms: 1K 3Q 1T
Bathrooms: 5 ensuite
3 rooms with double spa

• Full breakfast

Accommodation, Location and Value, The Greens offers the best combination in Leura and the Blue Mountains. Set in the heart of Leura just a minutes walk from the chic shops and restaurants, The Greens enjoys a tranquil yet convenient setting.

Enjoy the open fire and extensive range of books from the library before retiring to one of our comfortable rooms for a good nights sleep.

Awake to our generous full cooked breakfast that will set you up for a days' exploring! Foxtel. Free Internet access. Spa rooms available.

Jacky and Claudio Palamara

Blue Mountains – Leura

Megalong Manor

B&B (Heritage Listed)
0.15 km E of Leura

stay@megalongmanor.com
151–153 Megalong Street
Leura NSW 2780
(02) 4784 1461 or 0418 261 470
www.megalongmanor.com

  AAA Tourism
★★★★✓

Double: $190–$215
2 night minimum stay weekends

Accommodation for 7
3 Bedrooms: 1K 1KT 1Q 1S
Bathrooms: 3 ensuite

• Full breakfast provisions

Heritage Listed building, built in 1913 as the Literary and Arts Institute. Noted as a fine example of Federation architecture in NSW.

One of the Blue Mountains most renowned and desired holiday retreats. Three luxury self contained suites provide privacy with a special old world charm. All have ensuites, sitting/dining areas, central heating, gas log fires plus fully equipped kitchenettes.

An easy one block stroll from Leura village shops, restaurants and railway station.

David Sim and Kathy Hamilton

Boorowa – Rye Park – Yass

The Old School Country Retreat

Self Contained Country House
20 km SE of Boorowa, 40 km N of Yass

theoldschool@bigpond.com
76 Yass Street
Rye Park NSW 2586
(02) 4845 1230 or 0418 483 613
www.theoldschool.com.au

 AAA Tourism
★★★✓

Double: $190
Single: $160
Children: $30

Accommodation for 12
5 Bedrooms: 1K 2Q 1D 1T 2S
2 suites, 3 rooms each, ensuite
Bathrooms: 2 ensuite, 1 family share, 1 private
Orchard Wing suite has a bath

• Special breakfast

Warm fires, good books and a piano make this retreat a return to life's simple pleasures. Set on four acres amidst trees, roses, gardens and ponds an atmosphere is created that encourages relaxation.

An ideal retreat in the country where a group of friends can gather and enjoy self contained accommodation in a large country house.

The Old School is an award winning property.

Rye Park is half an hour north of Yass.

Margaret Emery

Luxury Villas
Byron Bay

escape@thevillasofbyron.com.au
19–23 Gordon Street
Byron Bay NSW 2481
(02) 6685 6746 or 0419 490 010
www.thevillasofbyron.com.au

Accommodation for 18

- Breakfast by arrangement

Double: $595–$895
Extensive in-villa pamper menu available
Dinner: in-villa dining with private chef from $135 pp

10 Bedrooms: 8K 2Q
2 × 1 bedroom Villas, 3 × 2 bedroom Villas
Bathrooms: 6 ensuite
Each villa features: Double bath/shower, private
outdoor rain shower, private heated pool and spa

You are assured absolute privacy and freedom
in your own Balinese inspired villa. Luxuriously
appointed, your every need is catered for. The

award winning Villas offer the very finest in luxury accommodation truly setting a fresh new standard for 5 star accommodation in Byron Bay. The unique design artistically blends both modern and traditional elements offering you relaxed and casual luxury with a hint of Bali and a dash of Byron, plus all the comforts of home.

The heated marble floors and detailed workmanship all add to the charm and character of the villas which has a decidedly romantic atmosphere. The perfect setting for a honeymoon or romance at any age.

Each villa has its own heated pool and spa set in tropical Zen gardens. Private outdoor rain shower, king size beds, TV/DVD/iPod and surround sound, pay TV, heated marble floors, Wi-Fi, ceiling fans, air-conditioning, gourmet kitchen with espresso machine, handcrafted Balinese furniture soothing water features throughout the gardens, laundry and private off street parking.

The Villas are located only a short 5 minute stroll from Byron's famous beaches and the CBD, and almost adjacent is The Arts Factory Village.

Sein and Taliah Lowry

Luxury Lodge
Byron Bay

enquiries@bayhavenlodge.com
16 Shirley Street
Byron Bay NSW 2481
(02) 6680 7785 or 0417 794 441
www.bayhavenlodge.com

Double: $145
Children: by arrangment

VISA

Accommodation for 14
7 Bedrooms: 7Q
Deluxe, Garden, Superior and Grand Suites
Bathrooms: 7 ensuite, 1 guest share
Heated Swim Spa or private bath in some suites

• Special breakfast

Bay Haven Lodge is a fully renovated and modernised traditional whaler's cottage. Set in a brilliant location, it is the closest B&B to Byron's buzzing town centre and stunning beaches so there's really no need to bring the car! Adjacent to 'The Wreck,' one of Byron's most famous surf breaks, Bay Haven Lodge is a very comfortable 150 metre stroll to the heart of town and, it is the only one of its kind offering guest accommodation in Byron Bay. A must see for those in search of a relaxing and memorable holiday. This beautifully appointed property has warmth, character and charm, with a fresh, modern and relaxed feel.

Choose from Garden, Deluxe, Grand or Superior Suites, all featuring beautiful decor with eye-catching prints by local artists, Garden and Deluxe Suites feature high-set ceilings, polished teak floorboards, natural stone ensuite with choice of shower heads and all with tea and coffee making facilities. They also contain all the modern fixtures one would expect, including reverse cycle air conditioning, remote control ceiling fans, dimmable down lighting, large mirrors, 3D compatible LCD screen TVs and DVD players with MP3 connection.

Some suites the added luxury of a bubbling, heated swim spa, Wi-Fi (Grand and Superior Suites) and on-site parking. Basic Kitchenette facilities are also available to guests booking the Grand or Superior Suite.

David Willis

Candelo – Bega Valley

Bumblebrook Farm Motel

Farmstay and Self-Contained Apartment
20 km SW of Bega

stay@bumblebrook.com.au
Kemps Lane
Candelo NSW 2550
(02) 6493 2238 or 0411 041 622
www.bumblebrook.com.au

Double: $110–$130
Single: $90
Children: Under 13 free. Extra adult $20/night.
$20 surcharge for 1 night stay Mid week specials and
long stay specials

Accommodation for 14
4 Bedrooms: 1K 1KT 3Q 4S
Bathrooms: 4 ensuite

• Full breakfast provisions

A 100 acre property with magnificent views and
lovely bush walks, fronting Tantawangalo Creek.

We have four well equipped self-contained units.

Breakfast is a 'cook-your-own' from our fresh
farm eggs.

Children are welcome and can often help feed the
farm animals. A BBQ is provided in playground near
the units. Beaches and National Parks nearby.

Pets welcome with prior arrangement.

Alan and Wendy Cross

Byron Bay

Byron Bay is one of Australia's
most popular holiday destinations.
Attracting a colourful array
of people seeking alternative
lifestyles, relaxation and natural
beauty since the 60's. Its
spectacular beaches and lush
rainforests make it the perfect
place to visit.

Central Coast

The Central Coast is a holiday playground with trendy markets, al fresco cafés and classy boutique shops. Take a scenic drive through the lush valleys and feel the natural beauty of the hinterlands.

Greenacres B&B

Self Contained Suites
1 km SW of Tuggerah

greenacres-bb@tpg.com.au
8 Carpenters Lane
Mardi NSW 2259
(02) 4353 0643 or (02) 4353 0309
www.greenacres-bb.com

Double: $125–$145
Single: $120–$135
Extra Person: $20 each per night

Accommodation for 7
2 Bedrooms: 2Q
Lounge has folding double bed
Bathrooms: 2 ensuite

• Full breakfast provisions

Greenacres B&B is a tranquil private retreat set on 3.5 evergreen acres, only 4 minutes to Westfield Tuggerah and a short drive to Tuggerah Lakes, Gosford, The Entrance and Shelly Beach. Two fully self contained air-conditioned suites with luxury queen beds, sofa beds, TV and DVD. Guests have use of the games room with billiard table, air hockey and home movie theatre, free in house movies, 14 metre swimming pool, Bali style gazebos, extensive landscaped gardens with ponds, fountains, waterfalls, bushwalking, row boating on dam and campfires in winter. Enjoy hand feeding our Silver Perch fish. Pets by arrangement.

Elizabeth and John Fairweather

Coffs Harbour – Arrawarra Headland

Headlands Beach Guest House

B&B and Guest House
5 km N of Woolgoolga

info@headlandsbeach.com.au
17 Headland Road
Arrawarra Headland, Woolgoolga NSW 2456
(02) 6654 0364 or 0417 249 500
www.headlandsbeach.com.au

AAA Tourism
★★★★

Double: $160–$200
Single: $130–$180
Refreshments on arrival

VISA

Accommodation for 6
3 Bedrooms: 3Q
Well appointed reverse cycled air conditioned ensuited bedrooms with TV/DVD, clock/radio, ceiling fans.
Bathrooms: 3 ensuite

• Full breakfast

Absolute beach frontage B and B overlooking the Pacific Ocean with northerly views of the beach, ocean, headlands and the Solitary Islands National Marine Park. Situated halfway between Sydney and Brisbane, the perfect stop for your overnight rest. 15 minutes north of Coffs Harbour and 5 mins from the seaside village of Woolgoolga.

The B&B occupies the lower level of the property offering guests spacious surrounds.

Three well appointed reverse cycle airconditioned ensuite bedrooms with queen beds, TV/DVD, clock radio, electric blankets and fans.

Valerie and Terry Swan

Coffs Harbour – Woolgoolga

At Woolgoolga you can sit on the beach and watch pods of migrating humpback whales as they make their way up and down the beautiful Mid-North Coast between May and November.

Denise Hannaford
Solitary Islands Lodge

Coffs Harbour – Woolgoolga

Solitary Islands Lodge

Luxury B&B
25 km N of Coffs Harbour

denise@solitaryislandslodge.com.au
3 Arthur Street
Woolgoolga NSW 2456
(02) 6654 1335 or 0419 248 081
www.solitaryislandslodge.com.au

AAA Tourism
★★★★

Double: $160–$200

Accommodation for 6
3 Bedrooms: 3K
King size beds or long singles
Bathrooms: 3 ensuite
1 room has bath

• Continental breakfast

Ocean views from all rooms makes Solitary Islands Lodge unique – just two minutes stroll to the beach and cafés. Located just 25km north of Coffs Harbour in the seaside village of Woolgoolga making it a perfect stopover. Solitary Islands Lodge overlooks the Pacific Ocean with spectacular northerly views of the ocean, mountains and Solitary Islands Marine Park. Three unique rooms provide ample space and comfort with king beds, ensuite bathrooms, television, DVD, radio, bar fridge also tea/coffee making facilities. A large deck with ocean views is also available for guests. Airport transfers from Coffs Harbour can be arranged.

Denise and John Hannaford

Crookwell

Crookwell is nestled on top of the Great Dividing Range, an hour from Canberra, great for Abercrombie and Wombeyan Caves. Autumn is a blaze of colour – winter sees rolling hills blanketed in white powdery snow. Masses of exquisite blossoms, bulbs and flowers herald spring and a gentle summer allows you to escape the harsh heat and humidity of coastal regions.

Mary and Geoff Ashton
Markdale Homestead

Crookwell

Markdale Homestead

Heritage Listed Farmstay and Cottage with kitchen   *40 km NW of Crookwell*

g_ashton@bigpond.com
462 Mulgowrie Road
Binda NSW 2583
(02) 4835 3146 or (02) 8212 8599
www.markdale.com

Double: $50–$230
Single: $25–$205
Children: Under two no charge
Phones and Wi-Fi Free
Dinner: $25 to $40

VISA MasterCard

Accommodation for 24
12 Bedrooms: 2Q 3D 7T
2 and 4 Bedroom Stone Houses, 6 Bedrooms
Shearers Quarters
Bathrooms: 1 ensuite, 4 guest share
1 or 2 in Stone Houses, 2 in Shearers' Quarters

- Breakfast by arrangement

Food for the soul. A stunning landscape, 6000 acres
to walk over, solar heated pool and all weather
tennis. See availability, get quote and book online.

The Markdale Homestead and Garden combine
the talents of two Australian Icons; Edna Walling,
garden designer, and Professor Wilkinson, architect.
Live in two adjoining, self contained, beautifully
renovated, stone houses. Both have central
heating, open fire, sitting room, kitchen, laundry,
satellite TV, CD Player, free phones and broadband
internet access. Or stay in the comfortable Shearers'
Quarters at cheaper rates.

Geoff and Mary Ashton

Dubbo

Lying on the banks of the
Macquarie River in the heart of the
Western Plains of NSW is the city of
Dubbo, where country hospitality
is second to none and proud to
be home to the famous Taronga
Western Plains Zoo.

Kem Irvine
Pericoe Retreat B&B, Dubbo

Dubbo

Pericoe Retreat B&B

Luxury B&B
12 km NE of Dubbo

pericoe@pericoeretreat.com.au
12R Cassandra Drive
Dubbo NSW 2830
(02) 6887 2705 or 0407 896 828
www.pericoeretreat.com.au

AAA Tourism
★★★★★

Double: $245–$300
Single: $170
Dinner: Evening meals available from an a-la-carte menu

Accommodation for 12
4 Bedrooms: 4Q
Bathrooms: 4 ensuite
2 with Spas

• Full breakfast

Experience the wonderful seclusion and relax in 5 star luxury airconditioned suites.

Featuring spa ensuites, open fires, billiard room and bar, TV room, sunroom with deck, swimming pool and tennis court.

Enjoy full cooked breakfast, afternoon tea and sumptuous evening meals, served in a variety of settings. Pericoe Retreat is set on 25 acres with meandering gardens, an abundance of wildlife and birds, and magnificent views over the Talbragar Valley.

Our exclusive, personalised service and attention to detail will ensure your stay is one to remember.

Kem and Ross Irvine

Dubbo – Central West

Walls Court B&B

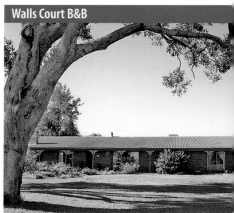

Farmstay and Private Cottages
12 km S of Dubbo

wallscourt@bigpond.com
11L Belgravia Heights Road
Dubbo NSW 2830
(02) 6887 3823 or 0407 226 606
www.wallscourt.com.au

AAA Tourism
★★★★

Double: $160
Single: $130
Children: $25
Extra person $30
Dinner: Dinner and/or picnic basket lunch by arrangement

Accommodation for 8
2 Bedrooms: 1K 1Q 4S
2 private cottages
Bathrooms: 2 private

• Full breakfast

Relish the tranquillity and comfort of your Walls Court suite as you laze on the veranda with a drink observing the birds in the garden. See your children's joy as they feed the chooks, pat dogs and gather eggs. Gain more from your visit to the zoo; we are volunteer guides. Revel in crowd free shopping precincts or savour the tastings at nearby wineries. Explore attractions yourself or take advantage of our familiarity with the area. Your pet is welcome by arrangement. Learn a new craft – make a pair of silver earrings for a small additional cost.

Neil and Nancy Lander

Dunedoo – Central West

Redbank Gums B&B

Self Contained Units
Dunedoo

grahamls@bigpond.com.au
41 Wargundy Street
Dunedoo NSW 2844
(02) 6375 1218 or 0428 751 218
www.redbankgums.com.au

AAA Tourism
★★★✦

Double: $85–$95
Single: $65
Family $135–$145
Dinner by arrangement

VISA MasterCard eftpos

Accommodation for 10
3 Bedrooms: 1K 1KT 1D
Bathrooms: 3 ensuite

• Full breakfast provisions

Welcome to Redbank Gums B&B which is an ideal base when touring the central west. Spacious 3 bedroom unit or 3 separate units with kitchen, laundry and lounge with television and DVD. Relax in the shady garden and enjoy a barbeque. We are in a quiet area with off street parking opposite the Golf Course and are within walking distance to most amenities. Dunedoo is a friendly, hospitable town along the Golden Highway, set alongside the Talbragar River and is well known for the annual Bush Poetry Festival. Redbank Gums accepts pets by prior arrangement.

Sue and Lloyd Graham

Dunedoo – Central West

Dunedoo is a pretty country town in central west NSW, adjacent to the Talbragar River and is the southern gateway to Warrumbungle National Park. It is well located to Dubbo and to the wine growing region of Mudgee.

Sue Graham
Redbank Gums B&B, Coonabarabran VIC

Eden

Historic Eden is a popular whale watching destination with Southern Right and Humpback whales migrating between May and October. Throughout-the-year cruises to see Bottlenose dolphins, seals and penguins are popular.

Gail and David Ward
Cocora Cottage B&B

Cocora Cottage B&B

B&B (Heritage Listed)
Eden

info@cocoracottage.com
2 Cocora Street
Eden NSW 2551
(02) 6496 1241 or 0409 961 241
www.cocoracottage.com

Double: $150–$165
Single: $120–$130

VISA MasterCard eftpos

Accommodation for 4
2 Bedrooms: 2Q
Bathrooms: 2 ensuite

• Full breakfast

This Heritage listed accommodation was the original Police Station in Eden. It is located in a quiet area close to Eden's famous Killer Whale Museum, the Wharf and restaurants. Breakfast is served upstairs with spectacular views down to the Wharf and across Twofold Bay to the foothills of Mt Imlay. Both bedrooms have a Queen sized bed, an ensuite with a spa, a television and free wireless internet. The front bedroom features the original open fireplace while the back bedroom offers bay views.

There are 2 large outdoor deck areas, one is undercover in the garden. Both have great views.

Gail and David Ward

Glen Innes

Cherry Tree Guesthouse

First Class Self Contained Country Guesthouse   *5 km S of Glen Innes*

info@cherrytreeguesthouse.com.au
86 Winters Road
Glen Innes NSW 2370
0448 804 030
www.cherrytreeguesthouse.com.au

Double: $225
2 night minimum stay. Twin or Queen rooms from $100 per night when booked with King room.

VISA MasterCard

Accommodation for 6
3 Bedrooms: 1K 1Q 1T
Bathrooms: 1 private
• Breakfast by arrangement

This beautiful self-contained country guesthouse is situated on Bettina and Philip Lynn's organic farm where you can enjoy the pleasures of first class modern country living with endless privacy and tranquillity. Experience the rural lifestyle by taking a walk through the surrounding area or simply watch the stock graze from the comfort of the ideally positioned sunroom.

The guesthouse is only a short drive to local cafés, restaurants, wineries, shops, services and tourist attractions. Glen Innes is home to the Australian Celtic Festival, World Heritage rainforests and renowned fossicking sites.

You may rent the whole guesthouse or simply rent the king room and still have exclusive use of all living areas.

Bettina and Philip Lynn

Glen Innes

The Australian Standing Stones at Glen Innes are based on the first solar aligned megalithic stone circles erected thousands of years ago during the peak of Celtic civilisation. This area is rich in minerals: sapphires, topaz and quartz crystals.

Glen Innes Visitor Information Centre

Glen Innes – Ben Lomond

Silent Grove Farmstay B&B

B&B and Homestay and Farmstay and Self Contained Cottage *38 km N of Ben Lomond*

silentgr@activ8.net.au
698 Maybole Road
Ben Lomond NSW 2365
(02) 6733 2117 or 0427 936 799
www.silentgrovefarmstay-bandb.com.au

AAA Tourism
★★★✦

Double: $90
Single: $50
Children: $15
$100 per night for S/C Cottage, 2 Adults, 3 Children
Dinner: $18

Accommodation for 6
3 Bedrooms: 1Q 1D 2S
Bathrooms: 2 guest share

• Full breakfast

Enjoy country hospitality in a peaceful rural setting, short detour by sealed road from the New England Highway. Working sheep and cattle property. Farm activities. 4WD tour (fee applies). Panoramic views, scenic walks, yabbying (seasonal), tennis court, fishing, occasional snow fall.

Easy access to New England, Gibraltar Range, Washpool National Parks. Glen Innes Australian Stones Celtic Festival held 1st weekend May. Smoking outdoors. Winner of 2001 Big Sky Regional Tourism Hosted Accommodation.

Campervans welcome. Take the time to detour you will be pleased you did.

John and Dorothy Every

Grafton – Ulmarra

Rooftops Bed and Breakfast

Luxury B&B and Guest House
10 km N of Ulmarra

rooftopsulmarra@bigpond.com
6 Coldstream Street
Ulmarra NSW 2462
(02) 6644 5159 or 0427 072 734
www.rooftops.com.au

AAA Tourism
★★★★

Double: $110–$130
Single: $90
Children: A small child can stay with mum and dad for free
Dinner: Can be arranged by prior arrangement

Accommodation for 8
4 Bedrooms: 2Q 2D
Bathrooms: 2 ensuite, 1 guest share

• Full breakfast

At Rooftops Bed and Breakfast your comfort is our priority. We are conveniently located just off the Pacific Highway in the Heritage listed Village of Ulmarra NSW. Main street frontage, River views, Off Street Parking. Yummy alfresco Breakfast on the balcony. Quiet rooms AC mod cons included. We have a house cat named Dusty.

Sandra Grogan

Grenfell

The Garden Room

Stand-alone B&B
Grenfell

mardie.3@bigpond.com
42 Warraderry Street
Grenfell NSW 2810
0427 437 156
www.grenfell.org.au

Double: $120
Single: $115

Accommodation for 2
1 Bedroom: 1Q
super bed
Bathrooms: 1 ensuite
A great shower

• Full breakfast

You will be greeted with a warm welcome and every endeavour will be made to ensure your visit to Grenfell is memorable. After all, one remembers locations but never forgets the hospitality. In a quiet location, only 2 blocks from the shops and finalist in the Weddin Shire Business Awards, 2014.

Included also, egg cooker, sandwich maker, plunger and instant coffee specialising in local produce. Card and board games. Moroccan theme décor. Peaceful location with garden outlook and off-street parking. Events through out the year in Grenfell: Henry Lawson Festival of Arts; two Race meetings; Guinea pig races; Go-karts; Carriage riving; Grenfell Show; Bird watching; The Grenfell Muster; Tennis, Bowling and Golf Competitions.

Mardie Bucknell

Grenfell – Central West

Wondiligong B&B

B&B and Separate Suite
1.5 km E of Grenfell PO

pippacol2@hotmail.com
Hilder Road
Grenfell NSW 2810
(02) 6343 1106
www.grenfell.org.au

Double: $120
Single: $90
Children: By arrangement.

Accommodation for 5
2 Bedrooms: 1Q 1T
1 Queen, 2 Singles, 1 Divan.
Bathrooms: 2 ensuite

• Continental provisions supplied

A warm welcome awaits you at 'Wondiligong' – a restful spot with views of the Weddin Mountains and off street parking at your door. Each bedroom has an ensuite, door onto verandah and another into sitting room with kitchenette. Grenfell is a friendly heritage town in an historic goldmining and farming area. Henry Lawson, the poet, was born on the goldfields and Ben Hall, the bushranger, rode the district with his gang. Weddin Mountains National Park is nearby, many bird trails to follow and the Henry Lawson Festival of Arts is held annually on the June long weekend.

Pip and Colin Wood

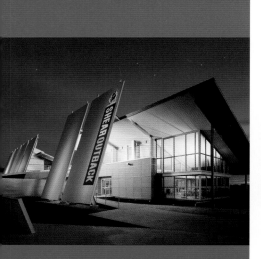

Hay

Hay is the home of Shear Outback, The Australian Shearers' Hall of Fame and has five amazing Museums. Discover the powerful stories of the Dunera Museum, where 6600 German, Italian and Japanese Internees and Italian and Japanese POW's were in 3 camps in Hay from 1940–1946.

You can wander the main street to see Hay's historic buildings or experience the beauty of the Murrumbidgee River.

Hay is the centre of some of the flattest country on Earth, where you can see spectacular sunsets and is the perfect place to see the stars in all their glory.

Sally Smith
Bank B&B

B&B
Hay Central

ttsk@tpg.com.au
86 Lachlan Street
Hay NSW 2711
(02) 6993 1730 or 0429 931 730
www.users.tpg.com.au/users/ttsk

Double: $140
Single: $100

Accommodation for 4
2 Bedrooms: 1K 1T
2 luxurious rooms equipped to make your stay relaxing
Bathrooms: 1 private

• Full breakfast

This National Trust classified mansion was built in 1891 to house the London Chartered Bank, one of the historic buildings restored to its original condition in Lachlan Street. The residence consists of a large dining room complete with period furniture and décor. The cedar staircase leads to the guest suite of two bedrooms and a fully modernised bathroom (complete with spa).

The guest sitting room opens onto the balcony overlooking the main street. We look forward to you experiencing the hospitality of Hay with us.

Sally Smith

Craigmhor Mountain Retreat

CRAIGMHOR

B&B and Luxury Homestay B&B, Suite and Apartment *48 km E of Aberdeen*

bnb@craigmhor.com.au
2120 Upper Rouchel Road
Upper Rouchel NSW 2336
(02) 6543 6393
www.craigmhor.com.au

AAA Tourism
★★★★

Double: $135–$200
Single: $77–$100
Children: $387.50–$50
4WD tours from $100
Dinner: $33–$55 served with Upper Hunter Wines

VISA

Accommodation for 10
4 Bedrooms: 3Q 1T 2S
Bathrooms: 2 ensuite, 1 guest share

• Full breakfast

Total contrast to city living – country hospitality, seclusion, splendid views, crisp mountain air in foothills of Barrington Tops. Peace and tranquillity assured – just you, your host, 1000 ha Australian bush and all its wildlife. Homestay; B&B; Self-Catered; Mix and Match to suit. Possible activities: doing absolutely nothing, picnicking by mountain streams, bush walking (50 km of forest trails), mountain biking, fishing stocked dams, Lake Glenbawn, 4-WD touring (optional extra), exploring Upper Hunter Country – magnificent horse studs, historic towns, wineries, National Parks.

Gay Hoskings

Hunter Valley – Upper Hunter Country

Fine Foods and Wine, Wilderness and Wildlife, Spectacular Scenery, Thoroughbred Horses and Racing, Bushwalking and Cycling. Sample the laidback country lifestyle with six National Parks, six Golf Courses, Lake Glenbawn for top fishing and boating), local produce of cheese, olives and wines, country pubs and cafés.

Gay Hoskings
Craigmhor Mountain Retreat

Hunter Valley – Lovedale – Pokolbin

Hill Top Country Guest House

Homestay and Villas, Guest House and Farmstay *17 km N of Cessnock*

stay@hilltopguesthouse.com.au
288 Talga Road
Rothbury NSW 2320
(02) 4930 7111
www.hilltopguesthouse.com.au

Double: $90–$250
VISA

Accommodation for 22
11 Bedrooms: 1K 5KT 4Q 1D 4T
Bathrooms: 9 ensuite, 2 private
Spa baths

• Special breakfast

An Australian Country Experience, staying in the colonial homestead or modern Villas. Situated on the Molly Morgan Range with spectacular views of the Hunter Valley and Wine Country. Go, horse riding and encounter abundant native wildlife of kangaroos, wombats, echidnas, possums roaming in their natural environment. Farm animals. Hay rides and picnics. Winery tours leave daily. The charming guest house offers Spa Suites, wood fires, 10' billiard table, Grand Piano, delicious meals, massages, beauty treatments, sauna and air-conditioning. The guest house is ideal for couples and family and friends gatherings. The Romantic Villas are ideal for couples.

Margaret Bancroft

Hunter Valley – Morpeth

Bronte Guesthouse

Guest House
10 km E of Maitland

reservations@bronteguesthouse.com.au
147 Swan Street
Morpeth NSW 2321
(02) 4934 6080
www.bronteguesthouse.com.au

AAA Tourism
★★★★

Double: $150–$240
VISA

Accommodation for 12
6 Bedrooms: 4K 2Q
Bathrooms: 6 ensuite
One room has a bath

• Full breakfast

Set in historical township of Morpeth, this guesthouse in extremely comfortable and warming with extra special attention to detail. All rooms are well appointed with private ensuites with all toiletries provided, individually controlled air conditioning, tea and coffee making facilities in room, LCD TVs, DVD and CD players plus wireless broadband. There are two guest lounge areas with open fire places and a selection of books, games and DVD's for your entertainment. Your fully cooked gourmet breakfast is served on the guesthouses balcony overlooking the township with glimpses of the Hunter River. Located in the heart of Morpeth, with fabulous eateries and restaurants, wine tasting, art galleries and loads of boutiques and speciality shops.

Lisa Simmonds-Webb

Sandholme Guesthouse

Luxury B&B Guesthouse
1 km S of Huskisson on Jervis Bay

guesthouse@sandholme.com.au
2 Jervis Street
Huskisson NSW 2540
(02) 4441 8855
www.sandholme.com.au

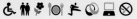

AAA Tourism
★★★★★

Double: $200–$240
Children: under 15 not catered for
Guest kitchen available

Accommodation for 8
4 Bedrooms: 4K 2S
Bathrooms: 4 ensuite
4 with Spa

- Continental breakfast

Sandholme Guesthouse; luxury Bed and Breakfast
(May to mid Dec) / self-contained Holiday Rental
(mid Dec to end April) in Huskisson on Jervis Bay,
offers a spacious couples retreat in a friendly coastal
setting. Enjoy luxurious Spa guest rooms each with
en-suite and Spa, guest Lounge and Games Room
(separate from your Hosts), wide veranda and
delicious espresso coffee, a place to relax and revive
from the stress of a busy life. Just 200 meters from
the water and a short walk to great restaurants,
Sandholme is only 2½ hours from Sydney and
2¼ hours from Canberra via Nerriga Road.

Alan and Christine Burrows

Jervis Bay

Jervis Bay is one of nature's secrets;
crystal clear waters and white
sandy beaches, a place where
Whales rest and Dolphins live
year round.

Image Jervis Bay Tourism
www.jervisbaytourism.asn.au

Kangaroo Valley

Kangaroo Valley Views

B&B
Kangaroo Valley

info@kangaroovalleyviews.com.au
194 Moss Vale Road
Kangaroo Valley NSW 2577
(02) 4465 1990
www.kangaroovalleyviews.com.au

Double: $175–$210
Children: $25–$35
Additional adult $40–$60

Accommodation for 14
5 Bedrooms: 1KT 2Q 1D 1T
Roll away beds available
Bathrooms: 3 ensuite, 2 private

• Full breakfast

Kangaroo Valley Views B&B is surrounded by
Barrengarry Mountains and Morton National
Park in the historic and picturesque village of
Kangaroo Valley.

Your accommodation includes Queen-size beds
with ensuite in the main bedroom with single beds
and family accommodation also available.

Kangaroo Valley Views offers 6.8 acres of award
winning gardens and bushland surrounds, large
indoor and outdoor living areas, bushwalking,
bicycle riding, horse riding, canoeing, golf and
tennis Indoor activities include TV, VCR and CD
players, board games, billiards with other sporting
equipment on request. Animals are welcome by
prior arrangement.

Margaret and Darrel Boys

Kiama

Kiama, a beautiful seaside town
famous for its blowholes, pristine
beaches and natural beauty
of a magnificent hinterland
with its historic dry stone walls.
Visit Minnamurra Rainforest or
the Illawarra Fly Tree Top Walk,
Jamberoo Action Park, vineyards
and wineries.

Kiama

Seashells Kiama

Luxury Self Contained Cottage
0.5 km SW of Kiama PO

dianne@seashellskiama.com.au
72 Bong Bong Street
Kiama NSW NSW 2533
(02) 4232 2504 or 0414 423 225
www.seashellskiama.com.au

Double: $230–$440
Children: Children's and Babies rates available
2 nights min booking. Seasonal rates apply.

Accommodation for 6
3 Bedrooms: 1Q 1D 2S
+ 1 porta cot
Bathrooms: 3 private
includes bath and separate WC

• Accommodation only

Unwind . . . Relax . . . and experience the delights
of Kiama from this thoughtfully renovated 1960s
bungalow. The spacious living area with sweeping
town and ocean views is sunroom by day and
cosy living room by night. Neat as a pin and full of
light this retro-styled home has all the amenities
you would expect and more . . . best of all, has
personality. Whether looking for a weekend away
or a longer stay Seashells Kiama is ideal for a
summer holiday or winter retreat – the perfect
getaway for couples, families and friends. Illawarra
Tourism Award Winner.

Dianne Rendel

Lismore – Clunes

PJ's

B&B
16 km N of Lismore

pjsbb@bigpond.com
152 Johnston Road
Clunes NSW 2480
(02) 6629 1788 or 0412 996 243
www.pjsretreat.com

Double: $150
Single: $125

Accommodation for 6
3 Bedrooms: 3K
Bathrooms: 3 ensuite

• Full breakfast

PJ's looks over some of the most beautiful
countryside in NSW. All guest rooms have
panoramic views that are spectacular. The stylishly
purpose built B&B which features three elegant
and spacious bedrooms all with the usual comforts
including complimentary port, chocolates and local
coffee. A personalised country breakfast is served.
PJ's is the ideal spot from which to experience
the many wonders of the Northern Rivers. Or just
simply relax by the saltwater pool or your own
private courtyard and soak up the view. Quality
accommodation at an affordable price.

Terry and Susan Hurst

Macksville – Yarrahappini

Take the time to explore a piece of paradise on the NSW Mid North Coast. Tourist Drive 14 is 26km sealed road scenic drive around the base of Yarrahapinni Mountain. Visit the Macleay River estuary at Stuarts Point, Grassy Head and Middle Head beaches, Yarriabini National Park, its lookout and picnic areas, Scotts Head and returning to the Pacific Highway.

Kevin Wilson
Yarrahapinni Homestead

Yarrahapinni Homestead

Luxury B&B
7.5 km SW of Stuarts Point

yarrahome@bigpond.com
340 Stuarts Point Road
Yarrahapinni NSW 2441
(02) 6569 0240 or 0418 225 810
www.yarrahome.com.au

Double: $155–$180
Single: $130–$155
Dinner by arrangement

VISA MasterCard **eftpos**

Accommodation for 6
3 Bedrooms: 3Q
Large with en-suite and verandah
Bathrooms: 3 ensuite

• Full breakfast

Luxury B&B accommodation located on 10 parkland acres between mountain rainforests and sparkling white beaches on the NSW Mid North Coast. A romantic getaway In easy reach of Stuarts Point, Macksville, Nambucca Heads and South West Rocks. Yarrahapinni Homestead is an ideal location to stay and relax whilst driving the Legendary Pacific Coast Touring Route. Large rooms with en-suite and verandah, flat screen TV, DVD and refrigerator. Utility room including washing machine and microwave. Tariff is inclusive of refreshments on arrival morning and afternoon teas and a sumptuous breakfast from our extensive menu. Discounted two and three night packages.

Kevin and Glenda Wilson

Merimbula

Robyn's Nest Guest House

Luxury BnB and Self Contained Apartments
2 km N of Merimbula

enquiries@robynsnest.com.au
188 Merimbula Drive
Merimbula NSW 2548
(02) 6495 4956
www.robynsnest.com.au

 AAA Tourism
★★★★★

Double: $175–$275

Accommodation for 58
27 Bedrooms: 10K 10KT 7Q 6T
BnB 6 rooms, self contained cottages one or
two bedrooms
Bathrooms: 27 ensuite
Some Cottages have spa baths

• Full breakfast

Robyn's Nest is a 5* multi-award winning luxury
BnB set amid 100 acres of bushland with 25 acres
of Absolute Lake Frontage with water views
from every room. Halfway between Sydney
and Melbourne on the coastal route, 2hrs from
Canberra and 2hrs from the snowfields. Facilities:
heated pool, spas, sauna, tennis court, jetty/boat
and mooring into prime fish breeding grounds.

3mins from the town centre that has 20 restaurants,
pristine beaches, whale watching, bushwalking,
deep sea and rock fishing. Romantic Indulgence
packages available.

Robyn Britten

Narooma – Tilba

Pub Hill Farm

B&B and Farmstay and Self Contained Cottage
8 km SW of Narooma

pubhill@bigpond.com
566 Wagonga Scenic Drive
Narooma NSW 2546
(02) 4476 3177
www.pubhillfarm.com

Double: $130–$155
Single: $120–$130

Accommodation for 10
5 Bedrooms: 2KT 2Q 1D
4 bedrooms B&B, 1 bedroom cottage
Bathrooms: 5 ensuite

• Full breakfast

Pub Hill Farm is a small farm, sitting high on a hill
overlooking the beautiful Wagonga Inlet and
with 2 kilometres of water frontage. The birdlife is
abundant and the extreme quiet makes it an ideal
place to bird watch. Small mobs of kangaroos
live on the property. All rooms have water views,
private outdoor areas and private entrances, plus
ensuites, microwaves, fridges, TV, and tea and coffee.
We welcome guests' pets. The gardens are fully
fenced for their safety. If you prefer self contained
accommodation, Karibu Cottage is gorgeous. Just
for two, with mezzanine bedroom and fabulous
views over Wagonga Inlet, Karibu sits in a secluded
garden where you can enjoy water views in
complete privacy. There is a cosy wood fire for winter.

Micki and Ian Thomlinson

Guest comment: *'Quite the best B&B we have ever
stayed at, anywhere. Superb hospitality' J and PJ,
Woodham, Surrey, England.*

Narromine

Camerons Farmstay

B&B and Homestay and Farmstay and Cottage with Kitchen   *6 km SW of Narromine*

cameronsfarmstay@bbbook.com.au
Nundoone Park, 213 Ceres Road
Narromine NSW 2821
(02) 6889 2978
www.bbbook.com.au/cameronsfarmstay.html

AAA Tourism
★★★↗

Double: $120–$140
Single: $90
Children: welcome
Self Contained Cottage from $120
Dinner: B/A

Accommodation for 12
5 Bedrooms: 3Q 2D 1T
Bathrooms: 1 ensuite, 1 guest share

• Full breakfast

Our home, 30 minutes west of Dubbo. We offer 4 star S/C cottage and B&B. Our house is modern and spacious with reverse cycle air-conditioning with each bedroom having a fan/heater; guest lounge has television, video, books, tea/coffee making facilities, fridge etc. It is surrounded by large gardens and all weather tennis court. Ian and Kerry run a successful Border Leicester Sheep stud – see lambs, shearing, haymaking, cotton growing and harvesting (seasonal), tour cotton gin. Visit: Dubbo Zoo, Iris Farm, Aviation Museum and Gliding Centre.

Ian and Kerry Cameron

Guest comment: *'Excellent, comfortable accommodation and great hospitality. So good to come back.' P&G, Belgium.*

Nundle

In the picturesque foothills of the Great Dividing Range, is the historic gold mining village of Nundle. Take some time to be active or just relax and enjoy the rural surroundings.

Marie and Jim Aspinall
The Birches B&B

Nundle

Birches B&B at Nundle

Luxury B&B
60 km SE of Tamworth

edleweiss@bigpond.com
71 Gill Street
Nundle NSW 2340
(02) 6769 3227 or (02) 6769 3222
www.nundleaccommodation.com/welcome.html

AAA Tourism
★★★★

Double: $165–$225
Single: $165–$225
Children: By arrangement

Accommodation for 6
3 Bedrooms: 2Q 1T
2 Queen Spa Bedrooms and 1 Twin Accessible Room
Bathrooms: 3 ensuite
Two Ensuites have a Spa Bath and I Ensuite is Wheelchair Accessible

• **Continental breakfast**

Birches B&B is a 4 Star luxury style B&B located in the centre of Nundle. There are two Queen Rooms with spa bath and a Twin Accessible Room with shower. There is a Guest Lounge and wide verandah at the front to sit and enjoy the views across the village and surrounding hills. All rooms have ensuite bathrooms, reverse cycle airconditioning for year round comfort, refrigerators, tea and plunger coffee making facilities, cookies, crockery, cutlery, selection of glasses, microwave, jug, toaster, DVD players, HD Televisions. A lovely place to do as little or as much as you like.

Marie and Jim Aspinall

Orange

Cleveland B&B

B&B and Homestay
Orange Central

stay@clevelandbnb.com.au
9 Crinoline Street
Orange NSW 2800
(02) 6362 5729 or 0408 306 349
www.clevelandbnb.com.au

Double: $150
Single: $100

Accommodation for 15
4 Bedrooms: 4Q 3S
Bathrooms: 4 ensuite
1 bathroom with spa

• **Full breakfast**

Our guest book is full of praise for our comfortable beds. We are ex farmers so that means good old country hospitality with a warm welcome and a hot cuppa on arrival. The House is heated throughout, the beds have electric blankets for that little extra warmth. We have evaporative cooling for the summer but summers are very pleasant. All rooms have fridges, digital television, wi-fi and there is off street parking. We are 3 minutes from the CBD and we can pick you up from the airport, station or Visitor Information Centre.

Sue and Neil Skinner

Parkes

Parkes is centrally located in the Central West, easily accessible for an overnight stay. Visit our Australian icon – the world famous CSIRO Radio Telescope, "The Dish" and explore the world of astronomy.

Helen and Mal Westcott
Kadina B&B

Kadina B&B

Luxury B&B
1.5 km E of Parkes CBD

kadinabb@bigpond.net.au
22 Mengarvie Road
Parkes NSW 2870
(02) 6862 3995 or 0412 444 452
www.kadinabnb.com

AAA Tourism
★★★★✦

Double: $140
Single: $105
Children: Under 12 $20, Under 16 $30
Dinner: 2 courses $35 pp dinner by arrangement

Accommodation for 7
3 Bedrooms: 2Q 1T 1S
The twin room has a King Single Deluxe trundle bed and a bathroom, no ensuite.
Bathrooms: 2 ensuite, 1 private

• Full breakfast

Come and enjoy the tranquillity and ambience of this lovely modern spacious home. Watch TV, listen to music, play piano, read or just soak in the views. Dine in our traditionally furnished dining room, patio or secluded back garden. Mal is involved in cereal growing farming. Guests may visit when convenient. Come and see 'The Dish'. Relax in our luxurious therapeutic Hot Tub.

Come and visit the Henry Parkes Centre, new Tourist Information, Elvis collection, Vintage Cars and Historical Museum, all in one place. Parkes is a great place to base yourself and explore the wonders of the Central West.

Helen and Malcolm Westcott

The Old Parkes Convent B&B

Self Contained Apartments
0.5 km E of Parkes PO

parkesconvent@bigpond.com
33 Currajong Street
Parkes NSW 2870
(02) 6862 5385 or 0428 625 385
www.parkesconvent.com.au

Double: $190
Single: $150
Children: $25–$40. Extra adult $40.
$170 per night for 2 nights or more

VISA | | | | eftpos

Accommodation for 11
3 Bedrooms: 1Q 4D 1S
2 apartments each with 1 double bed and
1 double sofabed
Bathrooms: 2 ensuite

• Full breakfast provisions

Experience spacious living in one of our exclusive apartments. You'll enjoy your own private lounge, bathroom, kitchen, and air conditioned comfort before awaking to a full and delicious breakfast. Outside you can enjoy a heated spa with barbecue area. Stay a night or a few days. Built in 1923 and set on half an acre of land in the centre of town, The Old Parkes Convent was once home to the Sisters of Mercy and girl, student boarders. The Old Parkes Convent B&B is only a short stroll to the shops, clubs, hotels, and restaurants.

Judy and Colin Wilson

Picton

Mowbray Park Farmstay

Farmstay, B&B, Cottages and Lodges
9 km SW of Picton

mowbray@farmstayholidays.com.au
745 Barker's Lodge Road
Picton NSW 2571
(02) 4680 9243
www.farmstayholidays.com.au

Double: $170
All inclusive $168–$188 per adult, $45–$99 per child. Self-cater (Minimum 4 persons) $102 per adult, $55–$59 per child.
Dinner: Included in the all inclusive packages.

VISA

Accommodation for 28
17 Bedrooms: 14D 10T
Bathrooms: 12 ensuite
2 deluxe rooms with spas

• Full breakfast

Welcome to our slice of paradise. Come and enjoy the peace and watch your children delight in the wide open spaces at one of the most popular family holiday destinations in NSW. Mowbray Park is a working farm and farmstay where you can experience all aspects of country life in a relaxed setting with all the comforts you would expect. Children can take a hayride for a real 'hands on' farm experience, helping with the farm chores, feeding the livestock and cuddly nursery animals. Guests can choose from the deluxe ensuite rooms of the main Homestead to the colonial warmth of Majellan Lodge with its wide sweeping views and ensuite guest rooms to classic Country Lodges.

Port Macquarie Hinterland – Wauchope

Auntie Ann's B&B

B&B
0.5 km SW of Wauchope PO

auntyannsbnb@virginbroadband.com.au
19 Bruxner Avenue
Wauchope NSW 2446
(02) 6586 4420
www.bbbook.com.au/auntieanns.html

AAA Tourism
★★★✦

Double: $99
Single: $66

VISA

Accommodation for 6
3 Bedrooms: 2D 1T
Bathrooms: 1 guest share

• Full breakfast

Wauchope is the gateway to Port Macquarie's Hinterland. Within easy driving are several national parks, nature reserves and vineyards as well as one of the largest single drop waterfalls in the Southern Hemisphere. Overlooking the golf course, Auntie Ann's is close to clubs, restaurants and shops. Visit Timbertown Heritage Park, art, pottery and furniture galleries or just relax by the pool with some locally made fudge.

Also available: Air-conditioning, TV room, BBQ, tea/coffee making facilities, heaters or air conditioner in each room.

Ann Pereira

Snowy Mountains – Tumut

Elm Cottage

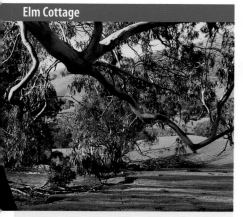

Luxury Self Contained Cottages
10 km SE of Tumut

info@elmcottage.com.au
3/722 Little River Road
Tumut NSW 2720
(02) 6947 5818 or 0428 482 778
www.elmcottage.com.au

AAA Tourism
★★★★✦

Double: $225–$420
Extra person $40 per night

VISA MasterCard eftpos

Accommodation for 21
11 Bedrooms: 4K 1KT 3Q 6S
Bathrooms: 2 ensuite, 4 family share

• Breakfast by arrangement

Pet Friendly. Stunning river and valley views. Set on 62 acres Elm Cottage is located halfway between Sydney and Melbourne. Our luxury 2, 3 and 4 bedroom, fully self-contained luxury cottages, have 180 degree views of the River. Well spaced apart the cottages offer quality furnishings with every facility to make your stay memorable. From your balcony you can and watch the sheep and cows wander past, take a walk along the two miles of river bank, fish for trout, swim at our private sandy beach, and enjoy stargazing through crystal clear skies, before curling up to sleep with the sounds of the river below. Elm Cottage typifies the best in Tumut pet friendly accommodation and provides an atmosphere that can help you create magical moments.

David and Deborah Sheldon

Sofala

Tanwarra Lodge

4½ Star rated Luxury Accommodation and Restaurant   *3 km SW of Sofala*

tanwarralodge@bigpond.com
324 Hill End Road
Sofala NSW 2795
(02) 6337 7537
www.tanwarralodge.com

AAA Tourism
★★★★✦

Double: $135–$160
Full cooked breakfast available for additional charge
Dinner: Pizzas available by request

VISA MasterCard eftpos

Accommodation for 10
3 Bedrooms: 3Q
Plus 2 sofa beds
Bathrooms: 3 ensuite

• Continental breakfast

Tanwarra Lodge is a hidden treasure in the Australian bush just 3 kilometres from our country's oldest surviving gold town, Sofala in NSW, and is Sofala's only officially Star Rated Accommodation.

Tanwarra Lodge presents affordable luxury accommodation with all the comforts of home in a spacious landscape surrounded by 176 acres of crown land situated a comfortable three and a half hour drive from Sydney. The cabin/rooms offer queen size beds, some with an additional option of a double sofa bed, a living area, kitchen (cabin only), ensuite bathroom, air conditioning, television and a large covered deck with BBQ facilities and an outside spa. All this overlooking the picturesque Turon River.

Warren and Sue Hill

Chelsea Park and Arcadia House

Menabillie Manor

B&B and Country Style Home
2.5 km S of Bowral

chelsea@hinet.net.au
589 Moss Vale Road
Burradoo NSW 2576
(02) 4861 7046 or 0414 468 860
www.chelseapark.com

Double: $150–$195
Single: $150
Arcadia House: 2 nts midweek $850. 2 nts weekend
$1150. 7 nts $1300.
Dinner: Candlelight supper weekend package $340.

VISA MasterCard

Accommodation for 17
3 Bedrooms: 1KT 2Q
Arcadia House 5 bedrooms
Bathrooms: 1 ensuite, 2 private
2 Private Chelsea Park. 2 Bathrooms in Arcadia House

• Special breakfast

Chelsea Park 'Hollywood Mansion in the Highlands'
is a glamorously restored Art Deco mansion. Three
delightfully restored and decorated rooms include
the Mayfair with award-winning 1930s furniture,
the Chelsea with lush soft furnishings and the
elegant Japanese themed Shibumi. Unwind in
the spa bath, relax in the woodland garden or
enjoy a game of billiards in the guest lounge.
Arcadia House is a two storey country-style home
located close to the heart of Bowral. Delightfully
renovated its spacious modern interior offers fully
self-contained accommodation with 5 bedrooms,
doonas, quality linen, electric blankets. Large family
room with gas-log fire, TV/DVD/VCR.

Alex and Davidia Williams

B&B
1 km SW of Bowral

jdbw@bigpond.net.au
3 Merilbah Road
Bowral NSW 2576
0439 600 000
www.menabillie.com.au

Double: $265–$295
VISA MasterCard AMERICAN EXPRESS

Accommodation for 4
2 Bedrooms: 2Q
spacious suites
Bathrooms: 2 ensuite
Modern deluxe bathrooms

• Full breakfast

A sumptuous country residence with two luxury
spacious residential wings having excellent
furnishings and fixtures, modern private
bathrooms. Cable TV, tea/coffee/bar fridge facilities,
several private lounges for quite relaxation, wood
fire setting for complimentary refreshments
upon arrival, billiard room, grand piano, 1½ acre
garden, superb cooked breakfast with local
farm products, every comfort catered for – a
memorable experience.

John and Susy Williams

Chorleywood B&B

B&B and Self Contained Cottage
2 km S of Bowral

suehawick22@gmail.com
86 Burradoo Road
Burradoo NSW 2576
(02) 4861 3617
www.highlandsnsw.com.au

Double: $110–$140
Single: $90–$100
Children: Baby in own cot only
Discount for 3 nights or more

VISA MasterCard eftpos

Accommodation for 4
2 Bedrooms: 1Q 2T
Cottage includes ensuite bathroom with queen or twin beds. Guest room has queen bed.
Bathrooms: 1 ensuite, 1 private

• Full breakfast provisions

Chorleywood B&B is 2km South of Bowral in the beautiful locality of Burradoo. The cottage offers a garden setting, privacy and peace. The bathroom is ensuite and TV DVD and Wi-Fi are provided. Heating is well provided for in the cooler climate of the Southern Highlands of NSW. Guests are welcome to relax in the garden. Breakfast is served in the dining room or ingredients are provided for self-catering. Bowral has wonderful places to see. It is surrounded by natural beauty spots such as Fitzroy Falls and picnic places like Lake Alexandra. Attractions include historic towns like Berrima, antique shops and restaurants, Bradman Museum and several art galleries.

Sue Hawick

Sydney

Sydney rightly remains the top destination in Australia and Sydney Harbour is the focus for many visitors. The harbour is alive with boats and ferries twelve months of the year. Take a trip to one of the islands for a picnic lunch.

Sydney – Balmain

An Oasis In The City

B&B
2 km SW of Sydney

anoasis@optusnet.com.au
20 Colgate Avenue
Balmain NSW 2041
(02) 9810 3487 or 0408 476 421
www.babs.com.au/oasis

Double: $195
Single: $185
2 night minimum. Additional person $30. Christmas AU$230 7 night min. New Year AU$230 7 night min. Christmas and New Year AU$230 10 night minimum.

Accommodation for 3
1 Bedroom: 1Q 1S
Large cathedral room with harbour view
Bathrooms: 1 ensuite

• Continental provisions supplied

Located in one of Sydney's most historic and charming inner suburbs, Balmain Village, An Oasis offers a very large, sun-filled room with views over Sydney Harbour. The suite is completely private, with own bathroom and entrance. We offer a substantial Continental breakfast. Included in the room are a fridge, electric kettle, toaster and hairdryer, 82cm LCD television and DVD player and reverse cycle air-conditioner. There is a hot outdoor spa available to our guests with complimentary spa towels. An Oasis is a walk away from restaurants, cafés, pubs and bars. Public transport is also minutes away and include ferries and buses into Sydney. Dog friendly parks are also close by.

Elisabeth Prax

Sydney – Balmain

Friends in Balmain

Separate Suite
2 km SW of Sydney

ak@chord.com.au
4 Waterview Street
Balmain NSW 2041
0412 824 898 or 0407 104 708
www.bbbook.com.au/friendsinbalmain.html

Double: $160–$175

Accommodation for 2
1 Bedroom: 1D
Bathrooms: 1 ensuite

• Continental breakfast

Friends in Balmain is a self containted apartment within our home. There is a double bedroom, luxurious ensuite bathroom and private sitting room with TV, DVD and tea, toast and coffee making facilities. Friends in Balmain is ideally situated to take advantage of the vibrant village life of Balmain and the spectacular City of Sydney. Beyond your front door a great selection of wonderful cafés is located within minutes walk of the cottage. You can enjoy great food, fine coffee, great pub fare and the passing parade that is the essential ingredient of life in Balmain. Attractions such as Circular Quay, The Rocks, Darling Harbour and the Opera House are a ten to fifteen-minute ferry ride away.

Andrew and Michelle

Sydney – Bellevue Hill – Rose Bay

Syl's Sydney Homestay B&B

B&B and Self Catering Apartment
6 km E of Sydney

sylviaure@me.com
75 Beresford Road
Bellevue Hill near Rose Bay NSW 2023
(02) 9327 7079 or 0411 350 010
www.sylssydneyhomestay.com.au

Double: $160–$180
Single: $110–$140
Children: Under 5 free. 5–10 $20. Over 10 or extra adult $50
Apartment $210 for 2 persons 7 night minimum stay fr Christmas to New Year.

Accommodation for 8
2 Bedrooms: 2K 1Q 1D 4S
Bathrooms: 1 guest share, 1 private

• Continental breakfast

Rose Bay is one of Sydney's most beautiful harbourside suburbs and hospitality and friendliness are the essence of our modern, spacious family B&B with bush and harbour views, pet dog and that real home away from home atmosphere. We are a short stroll from cafés, restaurants, tennis, golf, sailing and the most beautiful harbour in the world and on excellent bus and ferry routes to the City, Opera House and Bondi Beach. Syl and Paul will share their local knowledge and hospitality in a relaxed informal setting. So if formality is what you seek, then Syl's is not for you! All rooms have TV and the self contained garden apartment is ideal for families.

Sylvia and Paul Ure

Sydney – Coogee

Dive Hotel

Hotel
In town

thedive@bigpond.net.au
234 Arden Street
Coogee NSW 2034
(02) 9665 5538
www.divehotel.com.au

Double: $170–$270
Family Frienly 3 bedroom annexe also available

Accommodation for 32
16 Bedrooms: 9K 7Q
3 rooms with Ocean Views
Bathrooms: 16 ensuite

• Continental breakfast

Dive is a small family run hotel smack on Coogee Beach.

Dive has 16 rooms, 3 with spectacular ocean views. It's 20 minutes' drive from Sydney airport and the City. It's a door-to-door bus ride away to the City, Opera House, NSW University, Randwick Racecourse, Aussie Stadium and Cricket Ground. And it's a Frisbee throw away to parks and pools, cliff top walks and Coogee's thriving restaurant, pub, club and café, culture. Featured in Travel and Leisure USA, Conde Nast Traveller, NY Times, Time Out, Lonely Planet, London Observer and Guardian.

Terry Bunton and Mercedes Mariano

Sydney – Drummoyne

Eboracum

B&B and Homestay
5 km SW of Sydney

mjyork@bigpond.com
18A Drummoyne Avenue
Drummoyne NSW 2047
(02) 9181 3541 or 0414 920 975
www.bbbook.com.au/eboracum.html

Double: $150
Single: $120
Dinner: B/A

Accommodation for 4
2 Bedrooms: 1KT 1Q
Bathrooms: 1 family share, 1 private

• Full breakfast

Charming water frontage home by the Parramatta River, amid beautiful trees, with glorious views. Boatshed and wharf at waters edge. Handy to transport, short stroll to the bus or Rivercat ferry wharf, off street under cover parking. Ideal central location for business or pleasure, 5km to Sydney CBD, Darling Harbour, Opera House, museums, theatres and sporting venues. Many restaurants and clubs, nearby . . . Enjoy the hospitality of Jeannette and Michael, with their two cats and the ambience of their comfortable home.

Jeannette and Michael York

Sydney – Glebe

Bellevue Terrace

B&B and Homestay
2.3 km NW of Sydney Central

bellevuebnb@iinet.net.au
19 Bellevue Street
Glebe NSW 2037
(02) 9660 6096 or 0406 383 061
www.bbbook.com.au/bellevueterrace.html

Double: $120–$160
Single: $100–$160
Children: 12 yrs or over

Accommodation for 6
3 Bedrooms: 1Q 1D 1T
Bathrooms: 2 guest share

• Continental provisions supplied

My spacious, elegant townhouse is situated on a quiet residential street in the inner city suburb of Glebe, where you will find a great variety of restaurants, boutiques, galleries, pubs, and the Sydney University campus.

Walk to Darling Harbour, Chinatown, Paddy's Market and the Powerhouse Museum, or take a bus to the City centre (just 2.3 kms away) or Coogee Beach.

We are happy to supply maps, brochures and ideas for things to see and do in Sydney.

Rob and Heather

Sydney – Glebe

Cathie Lesslie B&B

Homestay
3 km SW of Sydney CBD

cathielesslie@gmail.com
18 Boyce Street
Glebe NSW 2037
(02) 9692 0548
www.cathielesslie.net

Double: $130–$140
Single: $90–$100
Children: $25

VISA MasterCard eftpos

Accommodation for 8
4 Bedrooms: 3D 2S
Bathrooms: 2 guest share

• Full breakfast

Quiet leafy inner city, close to transport, cafés, cinemas, universities and Darling Harbour. Large comfortable room with digital TV, fridge and tea and coffee facilities. Hot 'bacon and eggs' breakfast, your choice including fruit, juiced oranges and freshly baked croissants. We want you to feel welcome and at ease. Please phone first for bookings.

Cathie Lesslie

    Easy access

    Children welcome

    Pets welcome

    Facilities for horses

    Couples or adults

    Outstanding garden

    Special location

    Winery nearby

    Restaurant nearby

    Eco friendly

    Onsite activities

    Swimming pool

    Tennis court

    Function facilities

    Wedding facilities

    Internet access

    Cable or satellite TV

    No smoking

Above the Hawkesbury

River View Cottage
5 km NE of Brooklyn

ath@inn.com.au
15 Milloo Parade
Cheero Point NSW 2083
(02) 9487 5560 or 0414 327 545
www.abovethehawkesbury.com.au

Double: $225–$395
Children: Extra person $30
Seasonal rates apply. Weekend and Holiday Specials
available

Accommodation for 5
2 Bedrooms: 1Q 1D 1S
Queen room, plus double with single above.
Bathrooms: 1 private
Petite with shower

- Accommodation only

The View . . . magnificent . . .

Beautifully renovated cottage, stylishly decorated
and enjoying 180 degree water views down the
lower Hawkesbury River. Located on a quiet road
across from the waterfront reserve with bush steps

down to a private jetty and pontoon where you
can moor your boat or picnic beside the water.

Furnishings are soft, contemporary and Asian
inspired. Large sliding picture windows open to a
tiny Juliet-style balcony overlooking the reserve.
The Cottage includes everything for a relaxed and
comfortable stay including a small dining room/
kitchen with quality appliances, air-conditioning in
each room, ceiling fans, comfortable leather sofa,
arm chairs, large LCD television, CD player with iPod
dock. A barbecue area with views over the cottage
to the river is reached by a spiral staircase behind
the cottage.

Eva and Carl

Sydney – Manly

Manly Harbour Loft

Luxury B&B
0.5 km SW of Manly

info@manlyloft.com.au
1/12 George Street
Manly NSW 2095
(02) 9949 8487 or 0411 898 550
www.manlyloft.com.au

Double: $120–$300
Single: $100–$230

VISA (MasterCard)

Accommodation for 4
2 Bedrooms: 1K 1Q
High ceilings, spacious, plenty of natural light, en suite, quiet and private
Bathrooms: 2 ensuite
Modern wet-room with shower, toilet and basin.

• **Breakfast by arrangement**

Manly Harbour Loft is one of Sydney's finest B&Bs. This luxury accommodation offers the best of both worlds. 'Visit Sydney and Stay in Manly'. Designed for a comfortable and memorable stay your accommodation is spacious, bright and airy with private entrance, high ceilings and your own balcony with views of Sydney Harbour and Manly. Enjoy your breakfast on the balcony. Features include King size bed, lounge, TV, CD, DVD, fridge, reverse air-conditioning, computer with broadband, wireless access, free Wi-Fi, reading lamps, hair-dryer, iron with ironing board, tea and coffee facilities, crockery and cutlery, books and games.

Sally and Lee Burnes

Sydney – Paddington

Harts of Paddington

Homestay
2.8 km E of Sydney Central

paddington91@bigpond.com
91 Stewart Street
Paddington NSW 2021
(02) 9380 5516
www.bbbook.com.au/harts.html

Double: $150–$170
Single: $100–$160
High season rates apply.

Accommodation for 4
2 Bedrooms: 1Q 1T 1S
Bathrooms: 1 ensuite, 1 guest share, 1 private

• Special breakfast

Conveniently located 19th Century Cottage in Sydney's Historic Paddington, courtyard garden, two minutes from Oxford Street and the bus service to the CBD, Sydney Harbour, Circular Quay, The Rocks, The Opera House, Botanical Gardens, Sydney Casino, Chinatown, and Bondi Beach.

Nearby Centennial Park, Fox Studios, Aussie Stadium, Sydney Cricket Ground, Art Galleries, Antique Shops, Pubs, Restaurants, Fashion Boutiques, Cinemas, Paddington Markets. All rooms with T.V, clock radios, electric blankets and feather quilts.

Ironing facilities, varied breakfasts, fruit platters. One Abyssinian cat.

Katherine Hart

Sydney – Potts Point

Simpsons of Potts Point Boutique Hotel

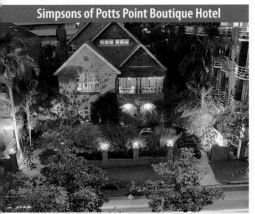

B&B and Boutique Hotel
2 km E of Sydney City

hotel@simpsonshotel.com
8 Challis Avenue
Potts Point Sydney NSW 2011
(02) 9356 2199
www.simpsonshotel.com

Double: $235–$350

VISA

Accommodation for 28
12 Bedrooms: 5K 5Q 2T
All individually decorated with modern conveniences
Bathrooms: 12 ensuite
2 King-bed rooms also have bath-tub

• Continental breakfast

An intimate 12-room hotel, in a restored 1892 Victorian mansion. Simpsons is located in leafy tree-lined Potts Point, a vibrant and cosmopolitan neighbourhood, with many interesting restaurants, bars, galleries and cafés nearby. Just a 20 minute stroll into the City, via the beautiful Botanic Gardens and then on to the Opera House and historic Rocks area.

Each room is different with its own character, yet all the modern creature comforts to make for a relaxed and pleasant stay.

All rooms have private en-suite bathrooms, air-conditioning, fans, tea and coffee making facilities, fridges, flat screen TVs, direct dial phones, Wi-Fi, as well as windows that open.

Keith Wherry, Marie Harland, Ree Daly

Sydney – The Rocks

Russell Hotel

B&B and Heritage Listed Hotel
The Rocks

manager@rh.wdshotels.com.au
143a George Street
Sydney NSW 2000
(02) 9241 3543
www.therussell.com.au

AAA Tourism
★★★✦

Double: $159–$309
Children: Extra person rate of $30 applies to children over four years

VISA MasterCard eftpos

Accommodation for 68
30 Bedrooms: 5KT 24D 1S
Bathrooms: 20 ensuite, 4 guest share
Bathrooms shared with 2–3 rooms

• Continental breakfast

Found in the heart of the rocks, The Russel Hotel has been a longstanding accommodation of choice for travellers. The hotel's unparalleled location near the best of Sydney's sites and attractions means you won't have to travel far – we're an easy walk from Sydney Harbour, the Sydney Opera House, Circular Quay, the Sydney Harbour Bridge, great shopping and restaurants.

The Russel Hotel Bed and Breakfast offering provides our visitors with a unique opportunity to experience our attentive hospitality in the heart of The Rocks the birthplace of Australia. Our genuine Bed and Breakfast Sydney accommodation is provided in an unparalleled location near the best of Sydney's sites and attractions.

Louise Marshall

Tenterfield

Stannum House

Luxury B&B
0.5 km S of Tenterfield

info@stannumhouse.com.au
114 Rouse Street
Tenterfield NSW 2372
(02) 6736 5538
www.stannumhouse.com.au/

Double: $180–$235
Single: $120–$135
Children: 5–12 yo $35pp
Extra adults $50 pp. Please book online on our website.

Accommodation for 15
4 Bedrooms: 1K 3Q 1D 5S
Julius Caesar Room 1K and 1Q, Reid Room 1Q and 2S,
Napoleon Room 1Q and 1S, Josephine Room 1D and 2S.
Bathrooms: 1 ensuite, 3 private
If all 4 rooms are booked, we utilise one downstairs
bathroom.

- Full breakfast

Come and enjoy old-fashioned hospitality at
its best in this beautifully restored Italianate
Victorian-era villa. Stannum is a showcase for the
opulence of a former era. The ground floor display
rooms are packed with antiques. Upstairs is a
magnificent cedar spiral staircase.

Each bedroom has a private bathroom, and there's
a large kitchen and TV room for your use. We also
have a fully-licenced Thai restaurant, open Thursday
to Sunday. Your hosts are brothers-in-law Paul
O'Connell and Rob Deshon.

Rob Deshon and Paul O'Connell

Tenterfield

The perfect setting for an
adventure, Tenterfield is home to
amazing national parks, beautiful
rivers, waterfalls and creeks, as well
as historical sights, attractions and
museums, wineries and delicious
food. Enjoy mild alpine summers,
sunny winter days and crisp winter
nights, blazing red autumns
and bright wildflower springs
in Tenterfield.

Image credit: Paul Foley and Destination NSW

Bimblegumbie Mountain Lodge

B&B, Self Contained Lodge, Cottages and Apartment   *9 km SW of Jindabyne*

holiday@bimblegumbie.com.au
942 Alpine Way
Crackenback NSW 2627
(02) 6456 2185 or 0412 484 966
www.bimblegumbie.com.au

AAA Tourism
★★★✈

Double: $162–$259
Single: $95–$180
Children: $10 to half price depending on age
Breakfast $19.50

Accommodation for 22
10 Bedrooms: 2K 2KT 6Q 2T
Luxury colourful bedding, feather topped beds,
brilliant queen/king beds, individually decorated
rooms, TVs etc.
Bathrooms: 2 ensuite, 2 guest share, 3 private
1 has bath

• Full breakfast

Self Contained Cottages and Apartment, B&B and Self
Contained Big House on 155 Acres. Pets welcome,
yummy homemade breakfasts available in Big
House. Peaceful, private and relaxing, award winning
wonderful gardens with individual sculptures,
colourful birdlife and wildlife. Interesting eclectic
artistic décor. A collector's delight of wide variety.
Very resident friendly dogs. 150 acres mountain virgin
bush walks and paths, close to ski fields, horse riding,
trout fishing, Lake Jindabyne. Relax, recuperate,
rejuvenate, reflect, respond, remember, return.
A place to discover and really relax. Once visited
always remembered and a lingering desire to return.

Prudence Parker

Tilba

The National Trust villages of
Central Tilba and Tilba Tilba are
well known for its cheese, gold
mining past, gardens, heritage
and indigenous culture. Close
to Narooma and Bermagui,
with pristine coastline and
secluded beaches.

Stuart Absalom
Green Gables

Tilba Tilba – Narooma

Green Gables

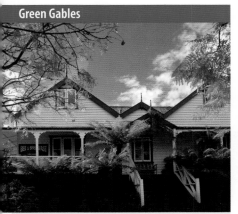

B&B
16 km S of Narooma

relax@greengables.com.au
271 Corkhill Drive
Tilba Tilba NSW 2546
(02) 4473 7435 or 0419 589 404
www.greengables.com.au

AAA Tourism
★★★★

Double: $170–$230
Single: $120–$150
Children: $20–$40
Dinner: $40 B/A

Accommodation for 7
3 Bedrooms: 3Q 1T
Bathrooms: 2 ensuite, 1 private

• Full breakfast

With mesmerising views, this stylish eco-sensitive accommodation features generous hospitality, fine food and endless relaxation at any time of the year. Set in lush gardens there are three large bedrooms with ensuite/private bathrooms and an inviting guest sitting room. Dinner is available by arrangement either served on the verandah or in the private dining room. Meals often feature vegetables from the productive garden as well as local produce. What better way to experience the natural beauty of the unique Tilba heritage area with its irresistible combination of mountains and unspoilt ocean beaches.

Stuart Absalom and Philip Mawer

Tumut

Russellee B&B

B&B and Private Ranch Style Country Home
4 km N of Tumut

russeldr@bigpond.com.au
462 Wee Jasper Road
Tumut NSW 2720
(02) 6947 4216 or 0427 474 216
www.russellee.com.au

Double: $120–$160
Children: $15, extra adult $30, pets $10
Full breakfast for additional cost.

Accommodation for 12
6 Bedrooms: 3K 2Q 1T
4 private 1–3 bedroom units
Bathrooms: 4 ensuite

• Full breakfast provisions

Russellee B&B is a relaxing and tranquil environment set amongst a parkland garden and located in the picturesque Tumut Valley minutes from town. Be welcomed by fresh flowers in four different accommodation options: the three bedroom Blue Wren suite, the large Rosella studio, the Kookaburra cabin. Enjoy your breakfast hamper alfresco overlooking the countryside and gardens or stay in the Finch room with breakfast served in your own living area. We offer two day Scrapbooking, Patchwork and Quilting Retreats several times a year. Learn new skills, meet new friends and be waited upon for a great relaxing weekend at the foothills of the Snowy Mountains and the Kosciuszko National Park.

Dorothy and Tony Clee

Wagga Wagga

Dunn's B&B

B&B
2 km S of Wagga Wagga PO

kate@dunnsbedandbreakfast.com.au
63 Mitchelmore Street
Wagga Wagga NSW 2650
(02) 6925 7771 or 0435 043 079
www.dunnsbedandbreakfast.com.au

Double: $140
Single: $130

VISA MasterCard eftpos

Accommodation for 4
2 Bedrooms: 2D
Bathrooms: 2 ensuite

• Full breakfast

Dunn's B&B is an elegant Federation home where we combine country hospitality with elegance and comfort. The three spacious bedrooms feature brass beds and modern ensuites. They are equipped with television, refrigerator, tea/coffee making facilities and independent heating/cooling. Breakfast is served in the dining room at a magnificent mahogany table. We offer free wireless internet, undercover parking and a private entrance. Other facilities include guest sitting room, balcony, maps, complimentary homemade afternoon tea and vintage car ride. Be Our Guest!

Les and Kate Dunn

Walcha

Anglea House B&B

Apartment with Kitchen
Walcha

angleahouse@bbbook.com.au
Cnr Thunderbolt Way and Hill Street
Walcha NSW 2354
(02) 6777 2187 or 0428 605 459
www.angleahouse.com.au

Double: $140
Extra person $35.00 per night

Accommodation for 3
1 Bedroom: 1Q
Plus single sofa-bed in living area.
Bathrooms: 1 ensuite

• Continental provisions supplied

Anglea House Bed and Breakfast is a self-contained apartment for up to 3 guests in the north west wing of historic Anglea House located in the beautiful and very productive New England Tablelands region of New South Wales and is easily accessible by the very scenic Thunderbolts Way, (north-south) and the Oxley Highway (east-west).

Facilities include ensuite and separate living area is within walking distance of eateries and shops Separate guest entrance and off street undercover parking which ensures privacy no matter how long your stay.

Guests are free to enjoy our large garden or just relax, rest and revitalise. It's the perfect place to-soak up clean country air.

Liz and Tony

Wellington

Carinya B&B

B&B
0.5 km S of Wellington

carinya@well-com.net.au
111 Arthur Street (Mitchell Highway)
Wellington NSW 2820
(02) 6845 4320 or 0427 459 794
www.bbbook.com.au/carinyabb.html

AAA Tourism
★★★✦

Double: $115–$115
Single: $115–$115
Children: $12–$15. Porta cot available

VISA MasterCard

Accommodation for 8
3 Bedrooms: 1K 2Q 2S
3 Large including 1 family room
Bathrooms: 2 guest share
• Full breakfast

Carinya is an old homestead set in a lovely award winning garden. Carinya Bed and Breakfast has been operating successfully since 1994. Helen and Miceal O'Brien enjoy welcoming friends and families. You will find a cool swimming pool for the summer months, a billiard table and tennis court for the more energetic and cozy slow combustion fire during winter months. Off street secure parking a big attraction.

The southern verandah is to die for in the summer months where you can sip that champagne or have breakfast on a lovely cool morning.

Miceal and Helen O'Brien

Wellington

Mackay's Rest

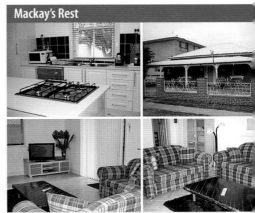

Cottage with Kitchen
0.5 km S of Wellington

carinya@well-com.net.au
120 Arthur Street (Mitchell Highway)
Wellington NSW 2820
(02) 6845 4320 or 0427 459 794
www.bbbook.com.au/mackaysrest.html

AAA Tourism
★★★✦

Double: $115–$115
Single: $115–$115
Children: Children welcome
Minimum stay 2 nights or 2 rooms

VISA MasterCard

Accommodation for 9
4 Bedrooms: 3Q 1T 1S
3 Large and 1 small twin room
Bathrooms: 2 private
1 full bathroom, 1 seperate toilet, 1 seperate shower/ laundry
• Breakfast provisions first night

Mackays' Rest offers 3 large queen bedrooms, two bathrooms, a laundry, separate dining and fully equipped kitchen and can sleep nine with comfort.

There is a large TV family entertainment area at the back of the renovated and historic house. Bookings for two nights or two rooms minimum.

The cottage has proved a great attraction for family reunions. Use of the swimming pool and tennis court at 'Carinya B&B' is welcome. Many attractions make Wellington a must stopover including Caves, Golf Course, Botanic Garden, Burrendong Dam and day trips to Mudgee, Parkes and Dubbo.

Miceal and Helen O'Brien

Wellington

Yahgunyah Cottage

Cottage with Kitchen
1.5 km S of Wellington

carinya@well-com.net.au
30 Maxwell Street
Wellington NSW 2820
(02) 6845 4320 or 0427 459 794
www.bbbook.com.au/15963.html

Double: $115–$115
Single: $115–$115
Children: Children welcome
Minimum stay: 2 nights or 2 rooms

VISA

Accommodation for 9
4 Bedrooms: 3Q 3S
4th bedroom is either 1 king + 1 single, or 3 singles
Bathrooms: 2 ensuite, 1 guest share

• Breakfast provisions first night

Very new, tiled living area and hall, and beautifully carpeted bedrooms. Most walls and ceilings in original part of the house are lined in wunderlich Beautiful fret work in hall and on the outside front verandah. Lovely old timber vernacular cottage from yesteryear. Very convenient and close to everything. A lovely roomy and private space.

Great for family gatherings, weddings and visits to retired family members. Bring your folks down and cook them dinner and have your privacy.

Laundry Open plan kitchen living – dining room BBQ available. Off street parking Undercover space for 1 vehicle or 4 motor bikes.

Helen O'Brien

Young – Cootamundra

Old Nubba Schoolhouse

Self-Contained Farm Cottages
3 km N of Wallendbeen

nubba1@bigpond.com
Old Nubba
Wallendbeen NSW 2588
(02) 6943 2513 or 0438 432 513
www.bbbook.com.au/oldnubbaschoolhouse.html

Double: $120
Single: $75–$95
Children: $20
2 night minimum stay

Accommodation for 13
7 Bedrooms: 2Q 2D 6S
Bathrooms: 3 private

• Full breakfast provisions

Old Nubba is a sheep/grain farm between Cootamumdra and Young, 3½ hours Sydney, 1½ hours Canberra.

The Schoolhouse, Killarney Cottage and Peppertree Cottage are all fully self-contained and have slow-combustion heating, reverse cycle air-conditioning, electric blankets and linen/towels provided. They sleep 4–8 and are set in their own gardens thru the trees from the homestead.

Farm attractions include peace and quiet, bush walks, birdlife, bike riding, fishing and olive picking. Well behaved doggies and cats welcome.

Many local tourist attractions nearby.

Fred and Genine Clark

Recommended Accommodation

Canberra – Deakin

Gates Cottage B&B
72 Buxton Street, Deakin
(02) 6161 4163
gatesbandb@grapevine.net.au
gatesbandb.com.au

Canberra – Macgregor

Ginninderry Homestead
468 Parkwood Road, via Macgregor
(02) 6254 6464
info@ginninderry.com.au
ginninderry.com.au

Adaminaby – Snowy Mountains

🐾 **Reynella Homestead**
699 Kingston Road, Reynella
(02) 6454 2386
reynella@activ8.net.au
reynellarides.com.au

Albury – Lavington

🐾 **Briardale B&B**
396 Poplar Drive, Lavington
(02) 6025 5131
briardale@exemail.com.au
briardalebnb.com.au

Armidale

🐾 **Armidale Boutique Accommodation**
134 Brown Street, Armidale
(02) 6772 5276
Tracy@ArmidaleBnB.com.au
ArmidaleBnB.com.au

Bathurst

Barcoos Farmstays Bathurst
1080 Trunkey Road, Perthville
(02) 6337 2383
info@barcoosbarn.com.au
barcoosbarn.com.au

Bellingen

🐾 **CasaBelle Country Guest House**
Gleniffer Road, Bellingen
(02) 6655 9311
enquiries@casabelle.com
casabelle.com

🐾 **Rivendell**
10-12 Hyde Street, Bellingen
(02) 6655 0060
info@rivendellguesthouse.com.au
rivendellguesthouse.com.au

Fernridge Farm Cottage
1673 Waterfall Way, Bellingen
(02) 6655 2142
judy@fernridge.com.au
fernridge.com.au

Bellingen – Gleniffer

🐾 **Cottonwood Cottage**
71 Gordonville Road, Gleniffer
0432 272 973
info@cottonwoodfarm.com.au
cottonwoodfarm.com.au

Bemboka

Giba Gunyah Country Cottages
224 Polacks Flat Road, Bemboka
(02) 6492 8404
ggunyah@yahoo.com.au
gibagunyah.com.au

Berry

🐾 **Bellawongarah at Berry**
869 Kangaroo Valley Road, Bellawongarah
(02) 4464 1999
deb@accommodation-berry.com.au

Blue Mountains – Katoomba

🐾 **Melba House**
98 Waratah Street, Katoomba
(03) 5565 1380
stay@melbahouse.com
melbahouse.com

Blue Mountains – Leura

🐾 **Broomelea**
273 Leura Mall, Leura
(02) 4784 2940
info@broomelea.com.au
broomelea.com.au

🐾 **Leura's Magical Manderley**
157 Megalong Street, Leura
(02) 4784 3252
manderleys@bigpond.com
manderley.com.au

🐾 **The Greens of Leura**
24-26 Grose Street, Leura
(02) 4784 3241
stay@thegreensleura.com.au
thegreensleura.com.au

🐾 **Megalong Manor**
151-153 Megalong Street, Leura
(02) 4784 1461
stay@megalongmanor.com
megalongmanor.com

Blue Mountains – Mount Tomah

🐾 **Tomah Mountain Lodge**
25 Skyline Road, Mount Tomah
(02) 4567 2111
tomahlodge@ozemail.com.au
tomahmountainlodge.com.au

Boorowra – Rye Park – Yass

🐾 **The Old School**
76 Yass Street, Rye Park
(02) 4845 1230
theoldschool@bigpond.com
theoldschool.com.au

Byron Bay

🐾 **Bayhaven Lodge**
16 Shirley Street, Byron Bay
(02) 6680 7785
enquiries@bayhavenlodge.com
bayhavenlodge.com.au

🐾 **The Villas of Byron**
19-23 Gordon Street, Byron Bay
(02) 6685 6746
escape@thevillasofbyron.com.au
thevillasofbyron.com.au

Candelo – Bega Valley

🐾 **Bumblebrook Farm Motel**
Kemps Lane, Candelo
(02) 6493 2238
stay@bumblebrook.com.au
bumblebrook.com.au

Central Coast – Tuggerah

🐾 **Greenacres B&B**
8 Carpenters Lane, Mardi
(02) 9520 7009
greenacres-bb@tpg.com.au
greenacres-bb.com

Coffs Harbour – Northern Beaches

🐾 **Headlands Beach Guest House**
17 Headland Road, Arrawarra Headland
(02) 6654 0364
info@headlandsbeach.com.au
headlandsbeach.com.au

Coffs Harbour – Woolgoolga

🐾 **Solitary Islands Lodge**
3 Arthur Street, Woolgoolga
(02) 6654 1335
denise@solitaryislandslodge.com.au
solitaryislandslodge.com.au

Crackenback – Jindabyne

🐾 **Bimblegumbie**
942 Alpine Way, Thredbo Valley
(02) 6456 2185
bimblegumbie@bimblegumbie.com.au
bimblegumbie.com.au

Crookwell

🐾 **Markdale Homestead**
462 Mulgowrie Road, Binda
(02) 4835 3146
g_ashton@bigpond.com
markdale.com

Dorrigo

Mount Christopherson Retreat
458 Muldiva Road, Dorrigo
(02) 6657 5333
info@mountchristopherson.com.au
mountchristopherson.com.au

Dubbo

🐾 **Pericoe Retreat B&B**
12R Cassandra Drive, Dubbo
(02) 6887 2705
pericoe@pericoeretreat.com.au
pericoeretreat.com.au

🐾 **Walls Court B&B**
11L Belgravia Heights Road, Dubbo
(02) 6684 7047
wallscourt@bigpond.com
wallscourt.com.au

Dunedoo – Central West

🐾 **Redbank Gums B&B**
41 Wargundy Street, Dunedoo
(02) 6375 1218
grahamls@bigpond.com
redbankgums.com.au

Eden

🐾 **Cocora Cottage**
2 Cocora Street, Eden
(02) 6496 1241
info@cocoracottage.com
cocoracottage.com

Glen Innes

🐾 **Cherry Tree Guesthouse**
PO Box 150, Glen Innes
0448 80 40 30
bettina@cherrytreeguesthouse.com.au
cherrytreeguesthouse.com.au

Recommended Accommodation

Glen Innes – Ben Lomond

☙ **Silent Grove Farmstay B&B**
698 Maybole Road, Ben Lomond
(02) 6733 2117
silentgr@activ8.net.au
silentgrovefarmstay-bandb.com.au

Gloucester

Villa Medici B&B
100 Gloucester Tops Rd, Gloucester
0414 923 479
bookings@villamedici.com.au
villamedici.com.au

Grafton – Ulmarra

☙ **Rooftops**
6 Coldstream Street, Ulmarra
(03) 9751 2464
rooftopsulmarra@bigpond.com
rooftops.com.au

Grenfell

☙ **The Garden Room**
42 Warraderry Street, Grenfell
0427 437 156
mardie.3@bigpond.com

☙ **Wondiligong**
Hilder Road, Grenfell
(02) 6343 1106
pippacol@hotmail.com

Hay

☙ **Bank B&B**
86 Lachlan Street, Hay
(07) 4927 4984
ttsk@tpg.com.au
www1.tpg.com.au/users/ttsk

Hunter Valley – Aberdeen

☙ **Craigmhor Mountain Retreat**
Upper Rouchel Road, Upper Rouchel
(02) 6543 6393
bnb@craigmhor.com.au
craigmhor.com.au

Hunter Valley – Lovedale

☙ **Hill Top Country Guest House**
288 Talga Road, Rothbury
(02) 4930 7111
stay@hilltopguesthouse.com.au
hilltopguesthouse.com.au

Hunter Valley – Morpeth

☙ **Bronte Guesthouse**
147 Swan Street, Morpeth
(02) 4934 6080
info@bronteguesthouse.com.au
bronteguesthouse.com.au

Jervis Bay – Huskisson

☙ **Sandholme Guesthouse**
2 Jervis Street, Huskisson
(02) 4441 8855
guesthouse@sandholme.com.au
sandholme.com.au

Kangaroo Valley

☙ **Kangaroo Valley Views**
194 Moss Vale Road, Kangaroo Valley
(02) 4465 1990
info@kangaroovalleyviews.com.au
kangaroovalleyviews.com.au

Kiama

☙ **Seashells Kiama**
72 Bong Bong Street, Kiama
(08) 8762 0259
dianne@seashellskiama.com.au
seashellskiama.com.au

Lismore – Clunes

☙ **PJ's**
152 Johnston Road, Clunes
(03) 5237 6555
pjsbb@bigpond.com
pjsretreat.com

Macksville South West Rocks – Yarrahapinni

☙ **Yarrahapinni Homestead**
340 Stuarts Point Road, Yarrahapinni
(02) 6569 0240
yarrahome@bigpond.com
yarrahome.com.au

Merimbula

☙ **Robyn's Nest Guest House**
188 Merimbula Drive, Merimbula
(02) 6495 4956
enquiries@robynsnest.com.au
robynsnest.com.au

Moama

Morning Glory River Resort
Gilmour Road, Moama
(03) 5869 3357
morningg@iinet.net.au
morninggloryriverresort.com.au

Narooma – Tilba

☙ **Pub Hill Farm**
566 Scenic Drive, Narooma
(02) 4476 3177
pubhill@bigpond.com
pubhillfarm.com

Narromine

☙ **Cameron's Farmstay**
Nundoone Park, 213 Ceres Road, Narromine
(02) 6889 2978

Newcastle – Hamilton

☙ **Hamilton Heritage**
178 Denison Street, Hamilton
(02) 9949 1984
colaine@iprimus.com.au
accommodationinnewcastle.com.au

Nundle

☙ **Birches B&B at Nundle**
71 Gill Street, Nundle
(02) 6769 3227
edleweiss@bigpond.com

Orange

☙ **Cleveland B&B**
9 Crinoline Street, Orange
(02) 6362 5729
stay@clevelandbnb.com.au
clevelandbnb.com.au

Parkes

☙ **Kadina B&B**
22 Mengarvie Road, Parkes
(02) 6862 3995
kadinabb@bigpond.net.au
kadinabnb.com

☙ **The Old Parkes Convent**
33 Currajong Street, Parkes
(02) 6657 2573
parkesconvent@bigpond.com
parkesconvent.com.au

Picton

☙ **Mowbray Park Farm Holiday**
745 Barker's Lodge Road, Picton
(02) 4680 9243
mowbray@farmstayholidays.com.au
farmstayholidays.com.au

Port Macquarie Hinterland – Wauchope

☙ **Auntie Ann's B&B**
19 Bruxner Avenue, Wauchope
(02) 6586 4420
auntyannsbnb@virginbroadband.com.au

Snowy Mountains – Tumut

☙ **Elm Cottage**
Little River Road, Tumut
(02) 6947 5818
davidsheldon@bigpond.com
elmcottage.com.au

Sofala

☙ **Tanwarra Lodge**
324 Hill End Road, Sofala
(02) 6337 7537
tanwarralodge@bigpond.com
tanwarralodge.com

Southern Highlands – Bowral

☙ **Menabillie Manor**
3 Merilbah Road, Bowral
0439 600 000
jdbw@bigpond.net.au
menabillie.com.au

☙ **Chelsea Park B&B**
589 Moss Vale Road, Burradoo
(02) 4861 7046
chelsea@hinet.net.au
chelseapark.com/

☙ **Chorleywood B&B**
86 Burradoo Road, Burradoo
(08) 8388 1467
suehawick22@gmail.com
highlandsnsw.com.au

Harewood House Luxury B&B
8 Acer Court, Bowral
(02) 4862 5802
suewalker1@mac.com
harewoodhousebandb.com.au

Sydney – Balmain

☙ **An Oasis In The City**
20 Colgate Avenue, Balmain
(02) 9810 3487
anoasis@optusnet.com.au

☙ **Friends in Balmain**
4 Waterview Street, Balmain
0412 824 898
ak@chord.com.au

Waterfront Balmain
9 Longview Street, Balmain
0425 303 331
alicia@wefixcredit.com.au

Recommended Accommodation

Sydney – Bellevue Hill

✤ **Syl's Sydney Homestay B&B**
75 Beresford Road, Bellevue Hill
(02) 9327 7079
homestay@infolearn.com.au
sylssydneyhomestay.com.au

Sydney – Coogee

✤ **Dive Hotel**
234 Arden Street, Coogee
(02) 9665 5538
thedive@bigpond.net.au
divehotel.com.au

Sydney – Drummoyne

✤ **Eboracum**
18A Drummoyne Avenue, Drummoyne
(02) 9181 3541
mjyork@bigpond.com
bbbook.com.au/eboracum.html

Sydney – Glebe

✤ **Bellevue Terrace**
19 Bellevue Street, Glebe
(02) 9660 6096
bellevuebnb@iinet.net.au
babs.com.au/bellevue

✤ **Cathie Lesslie B&B**
18 Boyce Street, Glebe
(02) 9692 0548
cathielesslie@gmail.com
http://cathielesslie.net

Sydney – Manly

✤ **Manly Harbour Loft**
1/12 George Street, Manly
(03) 5465 3282
info@manlyloft.com.au
manlyloft.com.au

Sydney – Paddington

✤ **Harts**
91 Stewart Street, Paddington
(02) 9380 5516
paddington91@bigpond.com

Sydney – Potts Point

✤ **Simpsons of Potts Point Boutique Hotel**
8 Challis Avenue, Potts Point
(02) 9356 2199
hotel@simpsonshotel.com
simpsonshotel.com

✤ **Victoria Court Sydney**
122 Victoria Street, Potts Point
(02) 9357 3200
info@VictoriaCourt.com.au
VictoriaCourt.com.au

Sydney – The Rocks

✤ **Russell Hotel**
143A George Street, The Rocks, Sydney
(02) 9241 3543
manager@rh.wdshotels.com.au
therussell.com.au

Sydney- Hawkesbury River – Brooklyn

✤ **Above the Hawkesbury**
15 Milloo Parade, Cheero Point
(02) 9487 5560
ath@inn.com.au
AbovetheHawkesbury.com.au

Tamworth – Manilla

✤ **Oakhampton Homestead**
1254 Oakhampton Road, Manilla
(02) 4784 1461
belinda@oakhampton.biz
oakhampton.biz

Tenterfield

✤ **Stannum House**
14 Rouse Street, Tenterfield

Tilba Tilba

✤ **Green Gables**
269 Corkhill Drive, Tilba Tilba
(02) 4473 7435
relax@greengables.com.au
greengables.com.au

Tumut

✤ **Russellee B&B**
462 Wee Jasper Road, Tumut
(02) 6947 4216
russeldr@bigpond.com.au
russellee.com.au

Wagga Wagga

✤ **Dunn's B&B**
63 Mitchelmore Street, Wagga Wagga
(02) 6925 7771
kate@dunnsbedandbreakfast.com.au
dunnsbedandbreakfast.com.au

Walcha

✤ **Anglea House**
Cnr Thunderbolt Way & Hill Street, Walcha
(02) 6777 2187
abelder@dodo.com.au
angleahouse.com.au

Wellington

✤ **Carinya B&B**
111 Arthur Street, Wellington
(03) 9877 2737
carinya@well-com.net.au

✤ **Mackay's Rest**
111 Arthur Street, Wellington
(03) 9877 2737
carinya@well-com.net.au

✤ **Yahgunyah Cottage**
30 Maxwell Strret, Wellington
(03) 9877 2737
carinya@well-com.net.au

Young – Cootamundra

✤ **Old Nubba Schoolhouse**
Old Nubba, Wallendbeen
(02) 6943 2513
nubba1@bigpond.com

Northern Territory

Darwin

The Northern Territory is both timeless and as ever-changing as the seasons with a history and culture over 40 000 years old. Rugged yet beautiful, with vibrant colours Alice Springs in the heart of Central Australia presents travellers with a virtual oasis in the Australian Outback. The magnificent MacDonnell Ranges reach up across the landscape in stark reminder of the ancient nature of the place. South west you'll find Uluru in the heart of the Red Centre. In the tropical north you will find Darwin and Kakadu National Park, with amazing wildlife, stunning scenery and a welcome you will remember for ever.

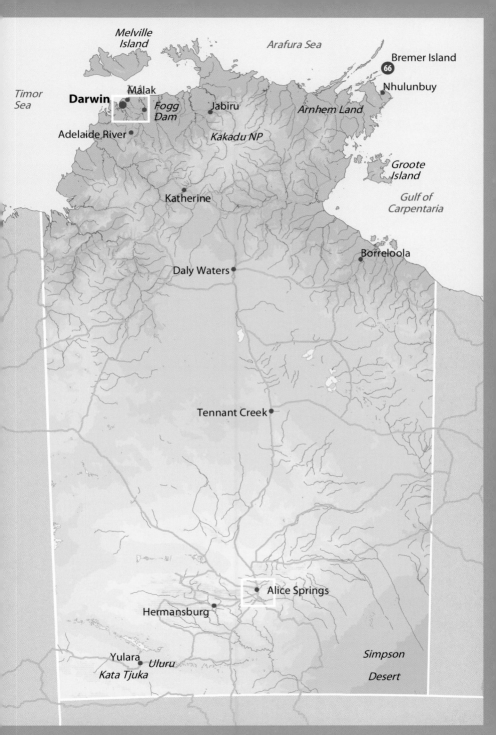

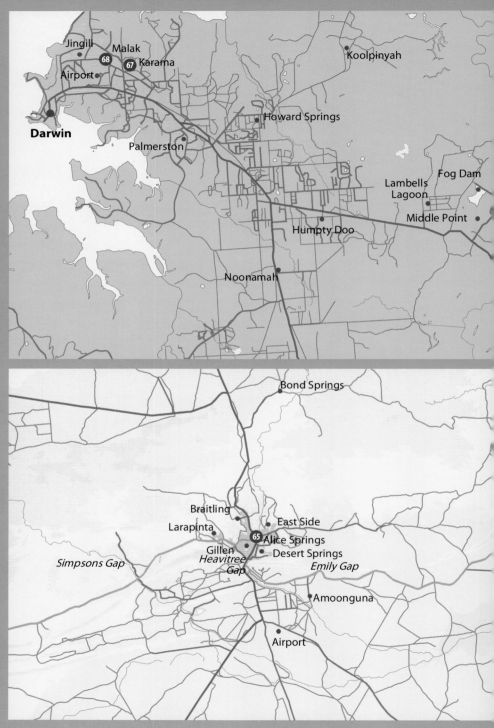

Kathy's Place Bed and Breakfast

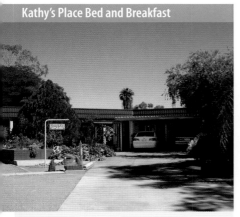

B&B and Homestay and old fashioned customer service   *3 km E of Alice Springs*

kathy@kathysplace.com.au
4 Cassia Court
Alice Springs NT 870
(08) 8952 9791 or 0407 529 791
www.kathysplace.com.au

   AAA Tourism
★★★✓

Double: $140–$140
Single: $80–$80
Children: $10 per child under the age of fifteen
Additional persons in same room $30 each person

Accommodation for 10
3 Bedrooms: 3Q 4S
3 bedrooms in B&B Family Room sleeping five persons.
Bathrooms: 1 ensuite, 1 family share, 1 guest share

• Full breakfast

Friendly Australian homestay. Family room has queen bed, three single beds in room, private shower and toilet. Summer and winter down doonas on all beds. Courtesy arrival pickup is available. Tours arranged and help provided so you can enjoy the treasures 'The Alice' has to offer, taking at least two days to enjoy. Enjoy our swimming pool and garden outdoor area with native birds that come in. Air Conditioning in the summer, plus heaters and fans in the bedrooms and a combustion heater in the main area for the cooler months, providing a cosy atmosphere to chat, read, watch TV tea/coffee available at all times of the day or night. Wireless and exchange library available.

Kathy and Karl Fritz

A Good Rest B&B

Luxury B&B and Self Contained Villa
3 km N of City Centre

agoodrest@bigpond.com
51 Dixon Road
Alice Springs NT 870
(08) 8952 5272 or 0418 652 506
www.agoodrest.com.au

   AAA Tourism
★★★★✓

Double: $180–$270
Single: $180–$200
Dinner by arrangement. Gluten free diets catered for

Accommodation for 7
3 Bedrooms: 3Q 3S
2 Queen bedrooms (or 1 with 2 K/single beds) plus open plan Villa with 1 Queen and 1 K/single
Bathrooms: 1 ensuite, 1 guest share
Private bathroom in Villa

• Full breakfast

Executive, 4.5 star accredited B&B. Quiet, fully self-contained air-conditioned private villa. Features, queen and king single beds, 3DTV, blue ray DVD player stove/oven, fridge, microwave, w/ machine. Plus two well-appointed air-conditioned queen bedrooms with own TV's in residence. Bath robes/slippers in all rooms. Breakfast included and we cater for guests who are gluten and dairy free. Wi-Fi, pool/spa set in beautiful gardens, BBQ, liquor license, secure off street parking, gym equipment, airport transfer and tours can be organized on your behalf, close to Restaurant and Tourist Attractions. Member of TCA.

Margaret Cain and Alf Goody

Molliejay B&B

Banubanu Wilderness Retreat

Apartment and Private Room
In town

molliejay@hotmail.com
2 McKay Street
Alice Springs NT 870
(08) 8952 4795
www.molliejay.com.au

Double: $100–$180
Continental provisions provided in
apartment, accommodation only in suite

Accommodation for 5
2 Bedrooms: 2Q
Single sofa bed also available
Bathrooms: 2 ensuite

• Special breakfast

Molliejay Bed and Breakfast offers self-contained
accommodation within walking distance of the
heart of Alice Springs. Your air conditioned rammed
earth self-contained unit with separate bedroom,
lounge and dining area, boasts a fully equipped
kitchenette and outside paved area with pool and
laundry facilities. Continental breakfast is included.
Undercover off street parking is available. Also
available is a smaller air-conditioned private room,
less expensive and available without breakfast.

We offer an enclosed, pet friendly facility for well
behaved and immunised dogs.

Mollie and Jay Kennedy

Guest Comment: *'Thank you so much for a
wonderful stay in a great pet friendly place! Jessi (the
dog) says thank you!' Mila and Anne Sydney, NSW.*

Eco Wilderness Retreat
Bremer Island

enquiries@banubanu.com
Bremer Island
Bremer Island NT 880
(08) 8987 8085
www.banubanu.com

$310–$480 per person includes 3 meals. An
additional fee of $50 p/p per night is paid to the
Traditional Owners

Accommodation for 14
7 Bedrooms: 3D 4T
2 Cabins, 5 twin share tents
Bathrooms: 3 ensuite, 1 guest share

• Special breakfast

Banubanu is a hosted Beach Retreat that is nestled
into sand dunes on the northern tip of Bremer
Island. The Retreat is surrounded by two beaches
and rocky headlands, all a part of a greater arena
of offshore islands in the Arafura Sea. Banubanu
offers so much for nature lovers, fishermen
and those who just want to chill out and relax.
Accommodation and facilities at Banubanu are
simple but comprehensive for up to 14 people
comfortably with two cabins and four twin share
tents and in keeping with the need to maintain a
minimal ecological footprint in one of Australia's
most pristine areas. A 15 minute charter flight from
Gove Airport in single engine plane or a 40 minute
transfer by boat from the mainland is available.

Helen Martin and Trevor Hosie

Bromeliad B&B

B&B
Karama

carol_darwin43@hotmail.com
26 Copra Crescent
Karama NT 812
(08) 8927 4640 or 0438 644 640
www.bromeliadbandb.com

Double: $150–$220
Single: $150–$220
Children: 1 child share room with parents no extra.
Seasonal rates apply

Accommodation for 5
2 Bedrooms: 1Q 1D
Bathrooms: 2 ensuite

• Continental breakfast

Welcome to the Bromeliad, a fully hosted establishment situated in the quiet Darwin suburb of Karama. Newly renovated and accredited, our home is a restful retreat during your holiday in the Top End. Secure undercover off street parking is available if you have a vehicle.

Breakfast includes a variety of cereal, fresh tropical fruits, yoghurt, dried fruit and a selection of nuts and bread or croissants, spreads including Top End Honey and Rosella Jam. Facilities include swimming pool, Cable TV, laundry, dryer, Iron and ironing board. Complimentary toiletries, chocolates on arrival, coffee and cold drinks.

2014 Brolga Northern Territory Tourism Award - Hosted Accommodation.

Carol and Geoff McKenzie

Darwin

Welcome to Darwin and the Top End of Australia.

We invite you to share our unique tropical lifestyle, enjoy our exotic variety of tropical fruit and vegetables and reflect on our patchwork past that has been shaped by war and cyclones. During your visit meet some of the Larrakia people the Traditional Owners of this land and thank them for sharing their culture with us all.

Carol McKenzie
Photo courtesy Tourism NT Image Library

Darwin's Bed and Breakfast

B&B and Lodge
5 km N of Airport

bealesbedfish@aapt.net.au
2 Todd Crescent
Malak, Darwin NT 812
(08) 8945 0376
www.darwin-bed-and-breakfast-accommodation.com

AAA Tourism
★★★✈

Double: $100–$200
Children: Play areas and cubby house established
Full Day Barra Fishing Trips, 2–6 Day Ext Fishing Safaris
Dinner: Continental Breakfast provisions supplied

VISA MasterCard eftpos

Accommodation for 12
4 Bedrooms: 4Q 12S
With own Ensuites
Bathrooms: 4 ensuite
• Continental breakfast

Darwin's Bed and Breakfast is a dual purpose built establishment. Designed to cater for the B&B traveller and also to the Individuals, Families and Groups that also wish to partake in the adrenalin packed adventure of Barra or Bluewater Fishing in the Northern Territory. It is the home of Darwin's

Barra Base Fishing Safaris, which can cater for all types of fishing, from Barramundi and Bluewater fishing in coastal reefs, rivers and sheltered waters to being able to fish 15 nautical miles to sea to complete adrenalin packed pelagic, sailfish and deep sea game fishing.

Stay 7 days or book any fishing trip – get 10% accommodation discount For more information contact Darwin's Barra Base Fishing Safaris on www.darwinsbarrabase.com.au.

Heather and Allan Beale

Recommended Accommodation

Alice Springs

✿ A Good Rest B&B
51 Dixon Road, Alice Springs
(08) 8952 5272
agoodrest@bigpond.com
agoodrest.com.au

✿ Kathy's Place B&B
4 Cassia Court, Alice Springs
(08) 8952 9791
kathy@kathysplace.com.au
kathysplace.com.au

✿ Molliejay B&B
2 McKay Street, Alice Springs
(08) 8952 4795
molliejay@hotmail.com
molliejay.com.au

Bond Springs Outback Retreat
Stuart Highway, Alice Springs
(08) 8952 9888
bondsprings@outbackretreat.com.au
outbackretreat.com.au

Cavenagh Lodge B&B
4 Cavenagh Crescent, Alice Springs
0414 287 599
cavenaghlodge@ozemail.com.au
cavenaghlodge.com.au

Bremer Island

✿ Banubanu Wilderness Retreat
Bremer Island
(08) 8987 8085
enquiries@banubanu.com
banubanu.com

Darwin

Steeles At Larrakeyah
4 Zealandia Crescent, Darwin
(08) 8941 3636
rustynt@octa4.com.au
darwinbnb.com.au

Darwin – Humpty Doo

At Watties B&B
200 Doxas Road, Humpty Doo
(08) 8988 2878
ade@wattiesbnb.com.au
wattiesbnb.com.au

Darwin – Karama

✿ Bromeliad B&B
26 Copra Crescent, Karama
(08) 8927 4640
carol_darwin43@hotmail.com
bromeliadbandb.com

Darwin – Knuckey Lagoon

Grungle Downs Tropical B&B
945 McMillans Road, Knuckey Lagoon
(08) 8947 4440
sue@grungledowns.com.au
grungledowns.com.au

Darwin – Malak

✿ Darwin's Bed and Breakfast
2 Todd Crescent, Malak
(02) 4353 0643
bealesbedfish@aapt.net.au
darwinsbedandbreakfast.com.au

Darwin – Mcminns Lagoon

While Away Homestay
120 Pheasant Drive, McMinns Lagoon
0417 824 012
info@whileawayhomestay.com
whileawayhomestay.com

Darwin – Palmerston

Palmerston Sunset Retreat
8 Renwick Court, Gray Palmerston
0408 241 950
stay@palmerstonretreat.com.au
palmerstonretreat.com.au

Darwin – Rapid Creek

Lily Pad B&B
4 Waters Street, Rapid Creek
(08) 8985 4293
sandropo@bigpond.net.au
bbfaa.com.au/lilypad.htm

Queensland

Queensland is Australia's most popular holiday state and welcomes visitors from all over the world with its tropical climate, superb beaches and welcoming people. Queensland enjoys warm summers and mild winters and is home to five World Heritage listed sites including The Great Barrier Reef, Fraser Island and the Wet Tropics.

Coral Sea

Weipa

Cape
York
Peninsula

Gulf of
Carpentaria

Great

Cooktown

Cow Bay

Cairns

SOUTH

PACIFIC OCEAN

Burketown

Barrier

Townsville

Reef

Charters
Towers

Airlie Beach

Mount Isa

Cloncurry

Mackay

Winton

Longreach

Rockhampton

99 Yeppoon

Birdsville

Charleville

Brisbane

Cunnamulla

St George

Sydney

© 2012 Carto Tech Services

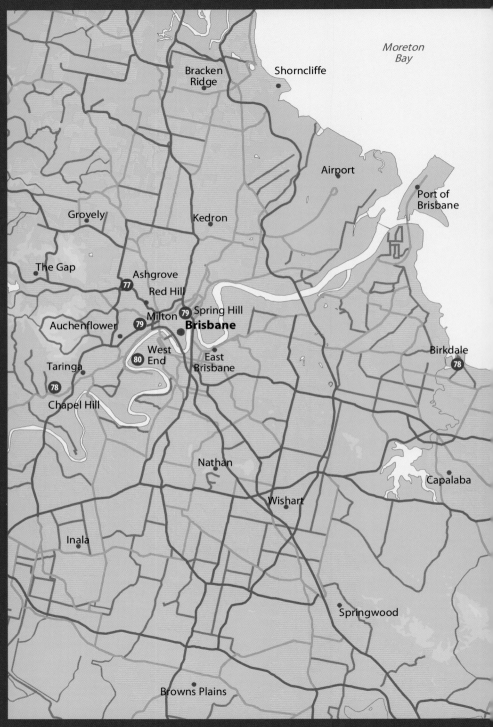

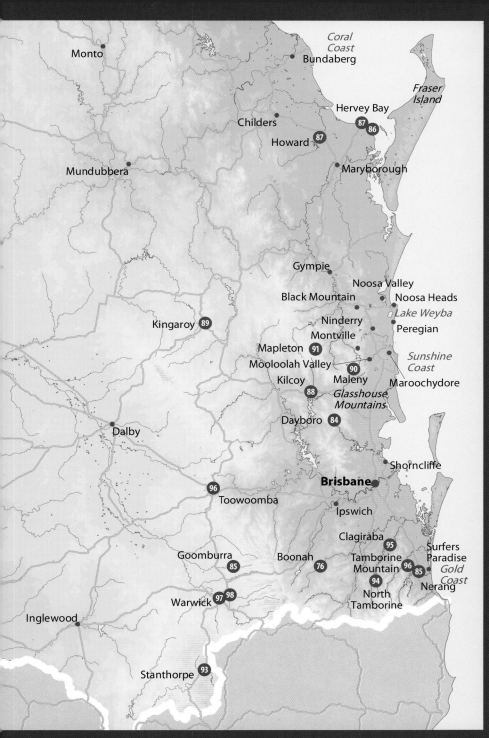

Monto

Coral
Coast

Bundaberg

Fraser
Island

Hervey Bay

Childers

87 86

Howard 87

Maryborough

Mundubbera

Gympie

Noosa Valley

Black Mountain

Noosa Heads

Lake Weyba

Kingaroy 89

Ninderry

Montville

Peregian

Mapleton 91

Mooloolah Valley

Sunshine
Coast

90

Kilcoy

Maleny

Maroochydore

88

Glasshouse
Mountains

Dalby

Dayboro 84

Shorncliffe

Brisbane

96

Toowoomba

Ipswich

Clagiraba

Goomburra

95

Boonah

Tamborine
Mountain

Surfers
Paradise

85

76

96

Gold
Coast

94

85

Warwick 97 98

North
Tamborine

Nerang

Inglewood

Stanthorpe 93

© 2012 Carto Tech Services

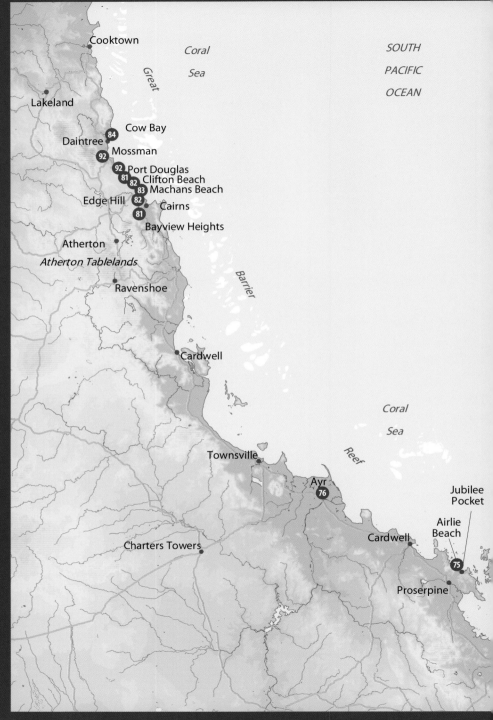

Cooktown

Coral

Sea

SOUTH

PACIFIC

OCEAN

Lakeland

Great

Cow Bay

84 Daintree

92 Mossman

92 Port Douglas

81 Clifton Beach

82 Machans Beach

83

Edge Hill **82** Cairns

81 Bayview Heights

Atherton

Atherton Tablelands

Ravenshoe

Barrier

Cardwell

Coral

Sea

Reef

Townsville

Ayr

76

Jubilee Pocket

Airlie Beach

Cardwell

Charters Towers

75

Proserpine

Whitsunday Moorings B&B

B&B
0.3 km SW of Airlie Beach

info@whitsundaymooringsbb.com.au
37 Airlie Crescent
Airlie Beach QLD 4802
(07) 4946 4692
www.whitsundaymooringsbb.com.au

Double: $150–$195
Single: $150–$165
$40 extra person above two

Accommodation for 3
3 Bedrooms: 2Q 1D
Our regular studios have a queen bed and a double
lounge (pull out) bed
Our Garden Room has a double bed
Bathrooms: 3 ensuite

• Full breakfast

Studio apartments, private terrace, swimming pool,
overhanging Abel Point Marina and Coral Sea.
Spectacular views. Traditional English breakfast,
includes, squeezed juice, tropical fruit, cereals,
choice cooked mains, homemade jams, teas, coffee.
Apartments feature crisp starched linen, daily
servicing, air-conditioning, ceiling fans, satellite
TV, ensuite with shower, hairdryer, 'Gilchrist and
Soames' toiletries, kitchen, refrigerator, microwave,
equipped light meals, clock radio, laundry, guest
computer and free wi-fi. Relax in the pool, a cool
drink, watching the sun setting on boats returning
to Abel Marina below.

Peter Brooks

Whitsunday Heritage Cane Cutters Cottage

Self-contained cottage
7 km SW of Airlie Beach

cottage@whitsunday.net.au
PO Box 59
Airlie Beach QLD 4802
0419 768 195 or (07) 4946 1373
www.whitsundaycottage.com.au

Double: $170
Children: Rollaway or sofabed
available for children
Air conditioned, secluded, breakfast basket 2 people
optional extra

Accommodation for 4
1 Bedroom: 1Q 1D
Main bedroom in cottage, double sofa-bed in
living room
Bathrooms: 1 ensuite
Bathroom has shower, laundry, plenty of towels

• Breakfast by arrangement

This Award Winning 100 year old beautifully
restored Cane Cutters cottage is the Whitsunday's
little hidden gem, perfectly located close to Airlie
Beach but far away enough to experience the
feeling of peace and relaxation of your private
country cottage and tropical gardens. Watch
wallabies and wildlife from the shady verandah,
take a quiet early morning stroll around the tropical
gardens and just soak up the ambience. You may
never want to leave!

Suzette and Adrian Pelt

Ayr – Burdekin

Ayr B&B on McIntyre

Luxury B&B
In town

stay@ayrbnb.com.au
8 McIntyre Place
Ayr QLD 4807
(07) 4783 6401 or 0417 836 401
www.ayrbnb.com.au

AAA Tourism
★★★★

Double: $165–$180
Dinner: Additional charge, on request, with
24 hrs notice

VISA 💳

Accommodation for 6
3 Bedrooms: 1K 2Q
luxury bedrooms
Bathrooms: 1 ensuite, 1 guest share, 1 private
Plunge bath, separate shower

• Full breakfast

Welcome to Ayr Bed and Breakfast on McIntyre, the ultimate accommodation getaway in comfort and country hospitality. Ideally located on an elevated half acre block of landscaped gardens with rural views, only an hours' drive south from Townsville airport. Three guest rooms, one with King bed two with queen beds. Facilities include, reverse cycle air conditioning, Theatre room with large screen TV/DVD, Austar sports, wireless internet, laundry facilities, outdoor heated spa, outdoor pool table, BBQ and off street parking, home-baked afternoon tea on arrival and evening glass of Port. There are no traffic lights to ignite tension, no parking meters and definitely no high rise to spoil the village atmosphere.

Shirley and Ian Mann

Boonah – Kalbar – Scenic Rim

Wiss House B&B

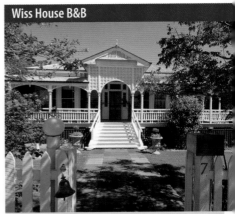

Luxury B&B (Heritage Listed)
8 km N of Boonah

reception@wisshouse.com.au
7 Ann Street
Kalbar QLD 4309
(07) 5463 9030 or 0410 404 641
www.wisshouse.com.au

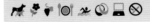

QUEENSLAND
TOURISM INDUSTRY
COUNCIL

Double: $150–$230
Single: $120–$200
VISA 💳

Accommodation for 8
4 Bedrooms: 1K 3Q
Bathrooms: 1 ensuite, 1 guest share

• Full breakfast

Luxury accommodation ten minutes from Boonah in the heart of the Scenic Rim. Treat yourself to the indulgence of a romantic stay at Wiss House Bed and Breakfast. This impressive Heritage Listed home built in 1900 is set on a rise in the rural town of Kalbar overlooking the majestic mountain ranges of Queensland's Scenic Rim. With four individually designed rooms, 3 queen and 1 king you'll be spoilt for choice! Wiss House boasts a high level of contemporary comfort while oozing charm of yesteryear including an ornate Banquet Room with crystal chandelier, fine china and silverware. Guests can dine on a three course meal prepared by our gourmet cook or be served a fully cooked breakfast.

Sara Watson

Brisbane – Ashgrove

Ashbourne House

Self Contained B&B
4.5 km NW of Brisbane CBD

bnb@ashbournehouse.com.au
21 Ashbourne Street
Ashgrove QLD 4060
(07) 3366 6889 or 0414 463 886
www.ashbournehouse.com.au

Double: $130
Single: $115
2 night minimum stay. Extra person $35 per person per night

Accommodation for 4
2 Bedrooms: 1Q 1D
Bathrooms: 1 private
Includes bathrobes, hairdryer and guest toiletries

- **Continental provisions supplied**

Ashbourne House B&B is an original 1920's Ashgrovian home located in the Ashgrove local district. It is vintage quality as it is the oldest house in the immediate vicinity. This B&B nestled in the Avenues, has walking trails that pass the historic Marist College and Glenlyon Drive, yet is only 1 km from Ashgrove shopping precinct with cafés, restaurants and shops, and only 5kms from Brisbane city centre. Private entry, Open and Enclosed Verandah, Lounge with TV, DVD and high speed internet, Dining Room with servery from the kitchen, fully equipped modern kitchen, Laundry with washing machine and clothes dryer, Ducted Air Conditioning throughout. Off street parking.

Kathy and Tony Carr

Brisbane

Brisbane known as the river city with warm its sunny winters and tropical summers which promote lush parks and gardens. Foodies can dine along the river bank at Southbank Parklands, whilst watching the kids frolic in the City Beach. Gateway to the Sunshine and Gold Coasts and to the beautiful Islands of Moreton Bay.

Brisbane – Birkdale

Birkdale Bed and Breakfast

Traditional and private B&B
17 km E of Brisbane CBD

glentrace@bigpond.com
3 Whitehall Avenue
Birkdale QLD 4159
(07) 3207 4442
www.bbbook.com.au/birkdalebb.html

Double: $115
Single: $90
Children: $30

VISA

Accommodation for 8
3 Bedrooms: 2Q 1D 2S
Spacious and private with separate guest entrance
Bathrooms: 2 ensuite, 1 private

• Continental breakfast

Only 20 minutes from Brisbane CBD and airport,
but with a lovely country atmosphere. Set in half
an acre of beautifully landscaped gardens, Birkdale
B&B is a modern English style country home, with
a separate guest wing and separate entrance. All
bedrooms have private facilities and reverse cycle
air conditioning for your comfort. Off street parking.
Enjoy feeding the birds, go whale watching in
nearby Moreton Bay or meet the local koalas.
Qualified Aussie Hosts. Dual Tourism Award Winner.
Corporate and weekly rates.

Geoff and Margaret Finegan

Brisbane – Chapel Hill – Western Suburbs

Chapel Woods B&B

B&B
9 km SW of Brisbane CBD

diannelange1@gmail.com
7 Candlebark Crescent
Chapel Hill QLD 4069
0424 872 745 or (07) 3378 9246
www.chapelwoodsbandb.com

AAA Tourism
★★★★

Double: $160
Single: $120

VISA

Accommodation for 6
2 Bedrooms: 1K 1KT
Bathrooms: 2 ensuite
One room has full bathroom, bath and separate
shower, other one has ensuite shower

• Full breakfast

Chapel Woods in nestled in the foothills of Mt.
Cootha, just 9 km W of Brisbane CBD.

Beautifully appointed with privacy being of utmost
importance, the room has its own entrance
with a secluded sunny patio and barbecue area
overlooking the pool and a beautiful garden. The
tastefully decorated room includes reverse cycle air
conditioning, wi fi, heated bathrooms, bar fridge,
microwave and tea and coffee making facilities. You
can walk to the shops and restaurants. We are 5km
from the Lone Pine Sanctuary and well located for
The Pat Rafter Tennis Stadium, Suncorp Stadium,
St Lucia Golf Course and horse riding centre. Ideal
location for the Bundaleer Wedding Venue, and
Indooroopilly Shopping Centre.

Dianne Lange

Brisbane – Milton – Paddington

Brisbane Milton B&B

B&B
3 km SW of Brisbane CBD

info@brisbanemiltonbedandbreakfast.com.au
12 Haig Road
Milton QLD 4064
(07) 3368 3787 or 0408 437 871
www.brisbanemiltonbedandbreakfast.com.au

AAA Tourism
★★★★✓

Double from $175.00 King from $195.00

VISA MasterCard

Accommodation for 6
3 Bedrooms: 2K 1D
Large airy rooms
Bathrooms: 3 ensuite

• Full breakfast

Brisbane Milton Bed and Breakfast offers quality accommodation in a beautifully restored Queenslander. 3 beautiful rooms with fabulously comfortable Double or King beds, Ensuite Bathroom, Electric Blanket, Reverse Cycle Air Conditioning, Wi-Fi Access, LCD Television with DVD, Clock Radio with iPod Docking Station, Iron and Ironing Board. Summer or winter enjoy breakfast in a sunny spot on the verandah.

Our breakfast menu includes a variety of seasonally influenced fruit dishes as well as your choice of a continental or delicious cooked breakfast.

We constantly update the menu and you can look forward to something absolutely scrumptious.

Philip and Maryanne Rowland

Brisbane – Spring Hill

One Thornbury

Luxury B&B (Heritage Listed)
1 km N of Brisbane

info@onethornbury.com
1 Thornbury Street
Spring Hill QLD 4000
(07) 3839 5334 or 0412 649 404
www.onethornbury.com

Double: $109–$199
Single: $109–$199

VISA MasterCard

Accommodation for 14
6 Bedrooms: 2K 4Q 1T
Bathrooms: 5 ensuite, 1 private
All bathrooms are equipped with quality towels.

• Full breakfast

Contemporary style with individual service. Located in Spring Hill on the doorstep of the CBD in Brisbane Queensland Australia. Choose from King or Queen Superior Rooms with modern stylish en-suite bathrooms, Standard Queen Rooms with original style en-suite bathrooms. Our Heritage Twin or King Room with own separate private bathroom (non-share) across the hall. Also available is our spacious Top-Floor Suite with 1 x King bedroom and 1 x Double bedroom plus private lounge and dining facility. At One Thornbury we offer a tropical-style lounge and breakfast room, equipped with Large Screen TV. A chef-inspired continental breakfast is provided to all guests as well a complimentary all-day espresso (pod) coffee and tea service. A light-meal service is also available at most times.

Geof Harland and Kerrie Conley

Brisbane – West End

Eskdale B&B

B&B
2 km SW of CBD

enquiries@eskdale.com.au
141 Vulture Street
West End QLD 4101
0419 487 393
eskdale.com.au

AAA Tourism
★★★

Double: $130–$150
Single: $80–$100
Children: 1/2 price (fold-out beds available
+$25 child, +$50 adult)
Every 5th night half-price

VISA MasterCard

Accommodation for 10
5 Bedrooms: 1K 2Q 1D 1T
Bathrooms: 1 ensuite, 2 guest share

• Continental breakfast

Eskdale Bed and Breakfast is a typical turn-of-the
century Queensland house close to the restaurant
district of West End. It is 2 km to the city centre
across the Victoria Bridge, and just 1 km from the
Southbank Parklands and the Brisbane Convention
and Exhibition Centre, the Queensland Performing
Arts Centre, Museum and Art Gallery. You will be
close to all the action and still be able to relax on
the back deck and watch the birds feeding on the
Australian native plants in the garden.

Paul Kennedy

Cairns

Whether you love to shop or
enjoy being outdoors soaking
up our beautiful scenery there is
something of interest for everyone
who visits Cairns. The city is perfect
for walking, cycling or swimming at
the lagoon or having a BBQ on the
Esplanade. Discover the delights of
a day trip to the outer Barrier Reef.
Board the historic Kuranda Scenic
Railway and return to Cairns by
Skyrail rainforest cableway. Spend a
day at Cape Tribulation where the
rainforest meets the reef.

Cairns – Bayview Heights

Cairns Reef and Rainforest B&B

Tropical Bungalows
8 km SW of Cairns

info@cairnsreefbnb.com.au
176 Sydney Close
Bayview Heights QLD 4868
0417 771 291
www.cairnsreefbnb.com.au

Double: $145–$165
Single: $125–$135
Minimum 2 night stay. PayPal accepted.

Accommodation for 6
2 Bedrooms: 2Q
Bedrooms and Spa front unique rainforest views
Bathrooms: 2 ensuite, 2 private
Deluxe 2 person spa and shower

• Continental breakfast

Enjoy friendly boutique accommodation at our 'Pavillions in the Rainforest' Cairns bed and breakfast set in a private and pristine rainforest location.

Balinese styled bungalows offering a unique and relaxing Rainforest environment with a private and tranquil brook – yet close to shopping centres, airport and other popular tourist destinations. Room appointments include: Bar Fridge, microwave, Air Conditioning, Spa and En-Suite, Quality King Koil Mattress and linen, Ceiling Fans, Undercover Parking, Plasma Television, Hair Dryer, Iron and Ironing Board, Private Balcony, Tour Desk and personal assistance with your itinerary. Your Gateway to the Wonders of Far North Queensland.

Dianne

Cairns – Clifton Beach

Warrawong Lodge

B&B
Clifton Beach

karen@warrawonglodge.com
20–24 Alexandra Street
Clifton Beach QLD 4879
(07) 4055 3194
www.warrawonglodge.com

AAA Tourism
★★★★

Double: $129–$146
VISA MasterCard

Accommodation for 8
3 Bedrooms: 6Q
Each guest rooms has 2 queen beds.
Bathrooms: 3 ensuite

• Continental breakfast

Luxury Bed and Breakfast with spectacular panoramic view of the Coral Sea and Double Island. The spacious guest rooms each have 2 queen beds, ensuite (bathroom), air-conditioning, TV, ceiling fan and separate entrance. There is a large guest lounge room with 55' HDTV with Austar (cable), next to the kitchen where the continental breakfast is served. Guests enjoy relaxing in the infinity edge pool/spa, which faces the incredible sea view.

Frank Baars and Karen Higgins

South Pacific BnB Clifton Beach

A tropical Haven – Kookas B&B

B&B
24 km N of Cairns

southpacificbnb@gmail.com
18 Gibson Close
Clifton Beach QLD 4879
(07) 4059 0381 or 0412 412 711
www.southpacificbnbcliftonbeach.com.au

Double: $120–$140
Single: $100–$120
Children: Children 5 years to 10 years considered as a child, $20 extra.

Accommodation for 4
2 Bedrooms: 1KT 1Q
King/Twin in separate self contained Cottage. Queen in main house, use of house facilities.
Bathrooms: 1 ensuite, 1 private
King/Twin has an Ensuite. Queen private bathroom.

• Tropical breakfast

South Pacific BnB Clifton Beach Peaceful, Private and so close to the Beach.

Enjoy a walk along the beach or relax with a swim in the fresh water swimming pool. Read a book on the deck or take a bike ride along the Rainforest board walk.

Go for an adventure tour or a dive on the Great Barrier Reef, so much to experience in this Paradise, come and enjoy it.

No Minimum Stays.

Maz and Alan Searle

B&B
6 km N of Cairns

kookas@kookas-bnb.com
40 Hutchinson Street
Edge Hill QLD 4870
(07) 4053 3231 or 0432 287 894
www.kookas-bnb.com

Double: $125–$165
Single: $95–$155
Tropical breakfast

Accommodation for 9
3 Bedrooms: 2K 1Q 1S
Bathrooms: 2 ensuite, 1 private

• Special breakfast

The lush, cool surrounds of Kookas Bed and Breakfast make this the perfect place to enjoy the warm climate of North Queensland. Located in the suburb of Edge Hill, it truly is a snapshot of the tropics. In fact, only a 20 minute walk from Kookas Bed and Breakfast is the acclaimed Flecker Botanic Gardens. All rooms are spacious and tastefully decorated and screening ensures for comfort all year round. Each room features air conditioning, ceiling fans, smoke alarm and separate entry. An inviting, open deck leads you out from the lounge and towards the expansive views of the south. Discover the refreshing pool, a real Australian barbecue, or simply do nothing at all – it's all yours to enjoy.

Marlies Gehrig and Bruno Meier

Cairns – Machans Beach

Machans Beach B&B

Luxury and Separate Suite (Heritage Listed)
Machans Beach

gabrielle.gelly@bigpond.com
167 O'Shea Esplanade
Machans Beach QLD 4878
0405 481 089
www.bnbnq.com.au/machansbeach

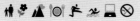

Double: $145
Single: $125
Children: One child can be catered for.
Fees for longer stays can be negotiated

Accommodation for 2
1 Bedroom: 1Q
Bathrooms: 2 ensuite
One ensuite and one outdoor courtyard heritage bathroom

• Continental provisions supplied

Located on absolute waterfront this sparkling new B&B overlooks the Coral Sea. The unit has one large bedroom, living room, and front porch. It is fully self contained, and very private nestled into the lush tropical garden. The salt water swimming pool and elegant décor gives this B&B sophisticated quality. Two bathrooms, one is ensuite and the other in a romantic attached courtyard with a big claw foot bath and champagne is always chilled.

The bedroom is air conditioned, and all rooms have ceiling fans and screens. The living room has TV/DVD and there is a kitchenette for preparing casual meals. The bus stop and two restaurants are within 4 mins walk. We are 8 mins from the airport and 10 mins from Cairns.

Gabrielle Gelly

Daintree – Cow Bay

Holidaying where the Daintree Rainforest meets the Great Barrier Reef: a unique area, unique experiences and unique holiday accommodation. The Daintree Coast combines breathtaking beauty with exceptional biodiversity. The World Heritage Listed Wet Tropics Rainforest and The Great Barrier Reef meet spectacularly along the Daintree Coast and offer an unparalleled richness of rare and primitive flora and fauna.

Marion Esser
Cow Bay Homestay B&B

Daintree

Cow Bay Homestay B&B

B&B
58 km NE of Mossman

marion@cowbayhomestay.com
160 Wattle Close
Cow Bay QLD 4873
(07) 4098 9151
www.cowbayhomestay.com

Double: $210
Single: $160
Children: over 6 years
Extra person $55, Children $45; Special 4 night rate on website !

VISA ⬤⬤

Accommodation for 5
2 Bedrooms: 2Q 1T 1S
Bathrooms: 2 ensuite

• Full breakfast

Cow Bay Homestay B&B is adjacent to two World Heritage Wilderness areas the Daintree Rainforest and the Great Barrier Reef. After a spectacular drive along sandy beaches and through dense rainforest arrive at this unique B&B and wake up to nature: views into vast tropical gardens and rainforest, swim in our fresh water creek, sit under the trees or on the deck spotting birds, stars, butterflies or the goanna. Get active with walks to stunning Cow Bay Beach and big range of guided tours, all showcasing to you the Reef and the Rainforest! Great breakfast. Marion can arrange all your tour bookings. Imagine: Action Packed Relaxation.

Marion Esser

Dayboro

Dayboro Cottages and Llama Walks

Self Contained Cottages
3 km N of Dayboro

dayborocottages@bigpond.com
3229 Mt Mee Road
Dayboro QLD 4521
(07) 3425 2774
www.dayborocottages.com.au

Double: $165–$190
VISA ⬤⬤ eftpos

Accommodation for 10
5 Bedrooms: 4K 1Q
Bathrooms: 5 ensuite

• Accommodation only

Beautifully appointed, fully self-contained and privately located cottages offer stunning views over the Dayboro valley. Each cottage offers large reverse cycle air conditioning, comfortable beds with feather and down doonas and European cushions. Lovely modern bathrooms, luxurious robes, self – catering kitchen, laundry (including washing machine, dryer, iron), spacious living area with a lounge and dining table with a large screen LCD TV, DVD and CD player, private balcony overlooking the beautiful Dayboro valley with an outdoor table, gas barbeque and all BBQ utensils.

Ross and Diane North

Gold Coast – Nerang

Rumbalara B&B

B&B and Apartment with Kitchen
10 km SW of Nerang

denise@rumbalarabnb.com.au
72 Hoop Pine Court
Advancetown QLD 4211
(07) 5533 2211
www.rumbalarabnb.com.au

AAA Tourism
★★★✦

Double: $110
Single: $100
Children: Children are welcome, cot available
Dinner: Evening meal by arrangement

Accommodation for 12
5 Bedrooms: 3Q 2T
3 B&B rooms with tea making facilities and fridge
Bathrooms: 1 ensuite, 1 guest share

• Full breakfast

A Unique Hinterland Experience.

Rumbalara is quiet and peaceful in a semi-rainforest environment but still only 30 minutes to the beaches and tourist attractions. B&B rooms are very comfortable, 2 have access to veranda and have tea and coffee making facilities as well as a small fridge. The Flat is self-contained, but breakfast can be supplied if needed, and it has it's own BBQ and outdoor area which is in the morning sun.

Denise and Alan Ramage

Goomburra

Goomburra Forest Retreat

3 Self Contained Cabins
25 km E of Goomburra

jgmrcairns@iinet.net.au
Forestry Reserve Road
Goomburra QLD 4362
(07) 4666 6058
www.goomburraforestretreat.com.au

AAA Tourism
★★★★

Double: $160–$200
Extra guests $30 per person
Dinner: Ask us about BBQ Dinner Packs

Accommodation for 6
3 Bedrooms: 3Q
2 studio cottages, 1 one-bedroom cottage
Bathrooms: 3 ensuite

• Full breakfast

Enjoy peace and quiet in eco friendly self contained cottages set amongst natural forest and mountains. Goomburra Forest Retreat is beautifully positioned on a 130 acre property on the Southern Downs, nested in the upper Goomburra Valley, on the Great Dividing Range. Three self contained cottages in a beautiful mountain forest provide all the comforts you need with creek frontage and swimming holes within walking distance. Facilities include spacious bathroom with large double shower, lounge room with sofa, full kitchen DVD player and TV, wood fire, balcony with BBQ. Cottages are fully screened with fans inside. There is a covered carport at each cottage.

Margaret and John Cairns

Hervey Bay

Visit World Heritage listed Fraser Island the largest sand island in the world. While you are there make sure you take the scenic flight that takes off and lands on 75 mile beach. From the air you will see much more of the island including beautiful Butterfly Lake.

The Chamomile B&B

B&B
0.5 km NW of Hervey Bay Marina

info@chamomile.com.au
65A Miller Street
Hervey Bay QLD 4655
(07) 4125 1602 or 0408 781 886
www.chamomile.com.au

Double: $135–$160
Single: $110

VISA   MasterCard

Accommodation for 6
3 Bedrooms: 2Q 1T
Bathrooms: 1 ensuite, 1 guest share

• Full breakfast

Relax on the verandah of this multi award winning B&B as you sip a cappuccino. Listen to the calming sound of water spilling over the waterfall in our rainforest gardens and enjoy the peaceful sounds of the birdcalls. It's a birdlover's paradise!! Relish the delicious cooked breakfasts in the morning and afternoon tea upon arrival. Stroll 500m down to the Marina precinct, Boat Club, restaurants and shops and enjoy the sights and colours of the boats and people or visit the nearby Botanical Gardens and nearby beaches. We offer a free booking service for Fraser Island tours, Lady Elliot Island and Whale Watch tours. A very warm welcome awaits you.

Diane Scruton

Hervey Bay – Howard

Montrave House Home and Pet Stay B&B

Villa Cavour B&B

B&B
2 km N of Howard

montrave@bigpond.com
20 Pacific Haven Drive
Howard QLD 4659
(07) 4129 0183 or 0458 090 183
www.montrave.com

Double: $100–$115
Single: $100
Full traditional Aussie or Scottish Breakfast included
Dinner by arrangement. Complimentary cake and
coffee on arrival.

Accommodation for 8
4 Bedrooms: 2Q 1D 1T
Bathrooms: 2 guest share
Spa bath

• Full breakfast

Enjoy the elegance of a bygone era, traditional
Scottish hospitality in the ambiance of a high set
historic Queenslander with modern comforts,
spa bath, wide verandahs and comfortable air
conditioned federation rooms that are individually
and tastefully decorated, in a tranquil atmosphere
on rural acreage with 3 dams. Close to the Burrum
District Golf Club and convenient for golf courses in
Hervey Bay, Maryborough and Childers, boat ramps
for two saltwater rivers and within walking distance
of Howard CBD. Bookings at between 10% to 20%
off advertised prices available for all tours, of Fraser
Island also Lady Elliot Island and Whale Watching
trips out in Hervey Bay as well as vehicle and boat
hire. Central for Hervey Bay and the historic towns
of Maryborough, Childers and Bundaberg.

Jackie and George Adams

B&B
Hervey Bay

reception@villacavour.com.au
15 Banksia Street
Hervey Bay QLD 4655
(07) 4124 5454 or 0421 567 711
www.villacavour.com.au

Double: $150
Single: $135
Children: Additional bed $35
Vegetarian and special diets catered for.
Dinner: Available by request, also lunch.

VISA MasterCard

Accommodation for 8
4 Bedrooms: 3K
1 Queen or 2 singles. 3 upstairs, 1 downstairs
Bathrooms: 4 ensuite

• Special breakfast

Villa Cavour is located on the beautiful Hervey Bay
promontory of Point Vernon. The Queenslander
style home features three spacious, air-conditioned
bedrooms with king beds and ensuites, upstairs
opening to the veranda overlooking the pool. One
room downstairs, opening to the garden, with
Queen bed or two single beds, private ensuite, air
conditioned. Free wireless internet, TV/DVD player,
DVD collection, mini-fridge and tea and coffee
facilities are provided. Rocco is more than happy
to cook some traditional Piemontes specialties and
can also teach you some of the tricks of the trade
with a range of cooking classes. Courtesy pick-ups
and drop-offs are available.

Mara and Rocco

Hervey Bay – Urangan

Bay Bed and Breakfast

B&B and Separate Suite
Hervey Bay

baybedandbreakfast@bigpond.com
180 Cypress Street
Urangan QLD 4655
(07) 4125 6919 or 0420 358 414
www.baybedandbreakfast.com.au

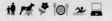

Double: $125–$150
Single: $95–$100
Children: $30.00 per child xtra
extra adult $60.00 in family room

VISA MasterCard

Accommodation for 10
5 Bedrooms: 1K 2KT 3Q 1S
Bathrooms: 2 ensuite, 1 guest share

• Full breakfast

Recommended by the Lonely Planet Qld, Trip Advisor and Le Petit Fute. Quality accommodation in an idyllic tropical setting. Salt water swimming pool, continental and cooked breakfast in our dining room or shady rear terrace. Quality bedrooms with ensuite/shared bathroom or suite with private lounge, bathroom and laundry for that extra touch of privacy. One street from the beach, close to shops, restaurants and clubs. Tours and transfers arranged free of charge. Courtesy pick up from Hervey Bay Airport or Coach Terminal. On Parle Français, oui biensur! Venez nous rendre visite et nous vous offrirons les moments les plus agreable qui existent a Hervey Bay.

Michel and Cheryll Lecointre

Kilcoy – Sandy Creek

Kilcoy Upper Sandy Creek B&B

Self Contained Apartment
75 km SW of Sunshine Coast

pandmc@activ8.net.au
82 Cedarvale Road
Sandy Creek QLD 4515
(07) 5498 1285 or 0409 064 106
www.bbfq.com.au

Double: $120
Additional person $35

Accommodation for 4
1 Bedroom: 1Q
Plus foldout sofa in lounge
Bathrooms: 1 private
Separate toilet

• Breakfast provisions first night

Self contained apartment, comprising queen size bedroom and open-plan kitchen, dining and lounge area. Situated in two acres (fenced) of bushland above a creek with native birds and wildlife. It has private verandahs, undercover parking, gas barbeque and reverse cycle air conditioning/heating. Sleeps up to 4 persons. Wineries are within 10km. Retreat to the bush. Wallabies and birds visit daily.

Paul and Margaret Cortis

Kingaroy

Rock-Al-Roy B&B

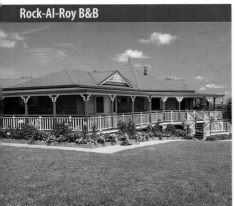

B&B
5 km S of Kingaroy

rockalroybb@burnett.net.au
15 Kearney Street
Kingaroy QLD 4610
(07) 4162 3061
www.rockalroybedbreakfast.com.au

AAA Tourism
★★★✦

Double: $110–$140
Single: $90–$110
Children: $20
Dinner: Yes

 VISA MasterCard

Accommodation for 6
3 Bedrooms: 1Q 1D 2S
Bathrooms: 2 guest share

- Special breakfast

Just five minutes from Kingaroy, this warm modern Queenslander style house set on 7600 m^2 with extensive shrub, gardens and pot plants offers quiet, peaceful surroundings with panoramic views overlooking Kingaroy.

Max and Lyn Lehmann

Guest comments: *'Very welcoming and friendly, even the pets welcomed us.'*

'Great meals.'

'Thank you for making us feel so welcome in your beautiful home.'

Noosa Hinterland

The Sunshine Coast Hinterland has a friendly and sophisticated lifestyle. Experience the peace and tranquillity of this magnificent area, only a short drive from the cosmopolitan village of Noosa, its sun drenched beaches, fine dining restaurants and fabulous boutiques.

Maleny Country Cottages

Fully Self-Contained Country Cottages
8 km SW of Maleny

reception@malenycottages.com.au
347 Corks Pocket Road
Reesville Via Maleny QLD 4552
(07) 5494 2744
www.malenycottages.com.au

AAA Tourism
★★★★

Double: $295–$440
Single: $275–$395
Children: $30–$55
Two nights from $395–$440 Extra adult $30–$55
Dinner: Breakfast hampers B/A. $35 per couple per morning

Accommodation for 4
2 Bedrooms: 1Q 2S
All linen included
Bathrooms: 1 ensuite, 2 guest share

• Breakfast by arrangement

Mountain hideaway on 60 acres of forested property.

Fully self-contained 1 and 2 bedroom air conditioned cottages providing all the necessities needed to make your stay a memorable and relaxing one: linen, spa, fireplace and verandah BBQ.

Our Cottages have been architecturally designed to be in harmony with the environment and the main buildings – and they enjoy similar appointments to those found in the homestead. Abundant wildlife. Several walking tracks meander through the forest.

Claude and Teresa Goudsouzian

Secrets on the Lake, Secrets Gallery and Café on the Deck

Luxury Treehouse Cabins
5 km SW of Montville

aldy@secretsonthelake.com.au
208 Narrows Road
Montville QLD 4560
(07) 5478 5888
www.secretsonthelake.com.au

QUEENSLAND TOURISM INDUSTRY COUNCIL

Double: $360–$455
Rate includes many extras: Chocolates, roses and champagne

Accommodation for 28
14 Bedrooms: 1KT 13Q 2S
Cabins include balcony
Bathrooms: 1 ensuite, 11 private
Sunken double spas

• Special breakfast

Secrets on the Lake offers the perfect opportunity for romance, relaxation and intimate accommodation. Elevated wooden walkways lead you through the rainforest to 10 individually themed treehouses offering total privacy, superb attention to detail and a completely unique world-class experience. Each retreat features carved cedar furniture, double shower, kitchen facilities, special home baked treats, toasty log fire, AC, TV, CD/DVD, sunken double spa and your own balcony with BBQ. What a way to indulge… we provide a stunning view, chocolates, orchids and champagne and includes scones on arrival. All you need to bring is that special someone to share it with.

George and Aldy Johnston

Maleny – Montville – Sunshine Coast Hinterland

Narrows Escape Rainforest Retreat

Luxury Secluded Rainforest Pavilions
4 km SW of Montville

reception@narrowsescape.com.au
78 Narrows Road
Montville QLD 4560
(07) 5478 5000
www.narrowsescape.com.au

AAA Tourism
★★★★✔

Double: $265–$400
Fully licensed
Dinner: BBQ hampers and dinner hampers available

QUEENSLAND
TOURISM INDUSTRY
COUNCIL

VISA MasterCard eftpos

Accommodation for 12
6 Bedrooms: 1Q
1 bedroom per cottage
Bathrooms: 1 ensuite
Spa bath in either lounge or bathroom

- Full breakfast provisions

This award winning boutique resort is the ultimate romantic escape for couples. From the moment you enter, you are aware that something special awaits.

Spoil yourself in your secluded fully self contained pavilion, just minutes from rainforest walks, Lake Baroon and the charming village of Montville with its charming range of restaurants, cafés, shops and galleries. Breakfast hamper provided on arrival with fresh croissants delivered daily. BBQ and dinner hampers available for in pavilion dining.

Mark and Joanne Skinner

Mapleton

Eden Lodge

B&B
1 km S of Mapleton

julie@edenlodge.com.au
97 Flaxton Drive
Mapleton QLD 4560
(07) 5445 7338 or 0414 424 035
www.edenlodge.com.au

AAA Tourism
★★★★✔

Double: $160–$250
Children: Not suitable for children under 13
One of the best experiences that you will ever have!
Dinner: Great tavern or Italian meals in Mapleton

VISA MasterCard AMERICAN EXPRESS eftpos JCB

Accommodation for 9
4 Bedrooms: 4Q 1S
3 ensuite queen bedrooms in the lodge and in the cottage a queen and a single bed.
Bathrooms: 4 ensuite

- Full breakfast

Eden Lodge is a traditional bed and breakfast located within easy walking distance of iconic Mapleton Village. The beautiful quality home, in a great location with sweeping views to the ocean, has a comfortable and functional layout creating a wonderful atmosphere of relaxation. Charlie and Julie Bevan have a passion for customer service, cooking and meeting new people. Mapleton is at the northern end of the Blackall Range in the Sunshine Coast Hinterland. The Village is home to the Mapleton Tavern, coffee shops, restaurants, antique and gift shops with easy access to the scenic beauty of the Mapleton Falls National Park and the Great Walks track.

Charlie and Julie Bevan

Mossman

Mossman Gorge Bed and Breakfast

B&B
1 km SW of Mossman

mossgorg@bigpond.net.au
Lot 15 Gorge View Crescent
Mossman QLD 4873
(07) 4098 2497
www.bnbnq.com.au/mossgorge

Double: $115–$150
Single: $105–$120
Children: Over 10 years $30
Extra person from $25/nt

Accommodation for 6
3 Bedrooms: 2Q 1D
Bathrooms: 3 ensuite

• Continental breakfast

Stunning views in tropical comfort – on the edge of the Mossman Valley, just minutes from Mossman Gorge National park. Experience tropical living in our modern timber tree-top home. Listen for the sounds of green tree frogs, try spotting the rare striped possum or catch a glimpse of blue wrens during breakfast. Bird watchers paradise, 110 species recorded. Take a dip in our pool or watch the sun go down over Daintree world heritage rainforest clad mountains. pets in residence, no smoking indoors. Please phone for directions.

Chris and Mandy Coxon

Port Douglas

Frangipani B&B

Luxury B&B
2 km S of Port Douglas PO

bookings@frangipaniportdouglas.com.au
13 Andrews Close
Port Douglas QLD 4877
0437 410 646
www.frangipaniportdouglas.com.au

Double: $240

Accommodation for 6
3 Bedrooms: 3KT
Bathrooms: 3 ensuite

• Continental breakfast

Luxury B&B accommodation you only dream about. This stunningly luxurious two story villa will truly embrace, and make you feel like you never want to leave. Each room has private balcony, a king bed, or two singles, ensuite. A bar fridge with tea and coffee facilities, iron and board, hairdryer, beach towels, bathrobes, LCD flat screen TV and uninterrupted views to the inviting heated pool and tropical gardens below. There is direct access, no roads to cross, to the pristine sands of Four Mile Beach and the crystal waters of the Coral Sea.

Complimentary bicycles are available for the beach or bike tracks, also a table tennis table, tennis rackets and balls provided.

Leona Brown

Rockhampton – The Range

Hazel Cottage

Self Contained Cottage
4 km S of Rockhampton CBD

lizandcolpatrick@yahoo.com.au
13 Kennedy Street
Rockhampton QLD 4700
(07) 4927 4984 or 0424 846 235
www.bbbook.com.au/HazelCottage.html

Double: $130

Accommodation for 4
2 Bedrooms: 1D 2S
Bathrooms: 1 private

• Continental breakfast

Come and relax at Hazel Cottage.

Fully self contained 2 bedroom cottage, located in residential area 2 km from Capricorn Spire on south side of Rock. Near hospitals, ideal for 2 couples.

4 km from CBD. Rural views and walking track. Adjacent to Yeppen Lagoon.

Within walking distance to Tropic of Capricorn Spire and Botanical Gardens.

Pets welcome if well behaved.

Liz Patrick

Stanthorpe

Honeysuckle Cottages and The Rocks Restaurant

Self Contained Luxury Cottages
2 km N of Stanthorpe

reservations@honeysucklecottages.com.au
15 Mayfair Lane
Stanthorpe QLD 4380
(07) 4681 1510
www.honeysucklecottages.com.au

Double: $150–$230
Single: $130–$225

VISA MasterCard Diners AMEX eftpos

Accommodation for 20
10 Bedrooms: 10Q
2 x 2 bedroom 6 x 1 bedroom
Bathrooms: 8 private

• Full breakfast provisions

Escape to the crisp, clean mountain air, country hospitality and the unique scenery of the Granite Belt. Eight charming cottages with federation era décor nestled amongst thick mountain bushland. One and two bedroom self contained cottages with dual spa bath, log fires, TV and stereo. Choose from one and two bedroom self contained cottages with dual spa bath, log fires, TV and stereo systems. Queen size beds with continental quilts, electric blankets and quality linen will ensure your comfort if you're visiting during the sub-zero winter months. The cottages are all fully insulated, keeping summer heat out and winter warmth in. The Rocks Restaurant is located on site and open for dinner five nights per week serving beautiful a-la-carte dishes. Dinner can also be served in your cottage, course by course. Shops, golf course and galleries are only 3 minutes away.

Rick and Maxine

Tamborine Mountain

Mountain Edge Studios

B&B and B&B chalets and lodge
12 km S of PO

jean@mountainedge.com.au
387 Henri Robert Drive
Tamborine Mountain QLD 4211
(07) 5545 3437 or 0407 453 437
www.mountainedge.com.au

Double: $175–$325
Single: $160–$295
Children: Over 11 yrs or infants under 6 mths
Many packages available
Dinner: Available prebooked

Accommodation for 11
5 Bedrooms: 5Q 1S
The studios are open plan for couples.
Bathrooms: 5 ensuite
3 spa baths, 1 XL bath

• Full breakfast

A beautiful, tranquil escape on Tamborine Mountain which enjoys sensational views across the Gold Coast to the ocean with a spectacular light show at night. Privacy in a romantic, relaxed environment with log fire, ensuite, spa or extra large bath, TV, DVD and CD players, generous kitchenette and patio. The queen bed is on an elevated timber floor to capture the views. The 2 bed, 2 bathroom lodge is designed for 2 couples or extended family to share. All are air conditioned. Breakfast hampers are provided mid week and hot breakfast on weekends. Our super friendly dogs may welcome you.

Jean

Tamborine Mountain

Avocado Sunset B&B

B&B
2 km N of North Tamborine

stay@avocadosunset.com.au
186 Beacon Road
Mount Tamborine QLD 4272
(07) 5545 2365
www.avocadosunset.com.au

 AAA Tourism
★★★★

Double: $165–$250

Accommodation for 8
4 Bedrooms: 4Q
Romantic themed rooms
Bathrooms: 4 ensuite

• Full breakfast

Avocado Sunset Bed and Breakfast is a romantic retreat catering for couples, overlooking the verdant Canungra Valley out to the Great Dividing Range beyond.

There are four themed, queen bedded rooms, and each one is a different experience. At sunset, sip champagne on the deck and watch the sky perform its magic.

In the winter snuggle beside the log fire either in your room or in the beautiful guest lounge.

A massage can be arranged and you can order a Romantic Dinner Platter to enjoy in the privacy of your room.

Relax in the peace and tranquillity of Avocado Sunset – you just won't want to leave but like many of our guests you can come back again and again.

Cheryl and Richard

Tamborine Mountain – Boyland

Clandulla Cottages

Cottages and Farmstay
2 km NW of Boyland

info@clandullacottages.com.au
312 Boyland Road
Boyland QLD 4275
(07) 5543 0990
www.clandullacottages.com.au

Double: $165–$185
VISA MasterCard

Accommodation for 16
5 Bedrooms: 2KT 1Q 1D 2S
Bathrooms: 4 ensuite

• Continental breakfast

Clandulla Cottages and Farmstay features affordable and luxurious holiday accommodation in the heart of the Scenic Rim region. Set in peaceful and private surrounds our fully self-contained cottages combine fresh mountain air and beautiful country views.

A fully equipped kitchen, master bedrooms with en-suites, king, queen or single beds with luxury mattresses and quality linen, large windows and large wide decks. The property features 3 suites (Camelot Suite, Mexicano Suite and Okotoks Suite) and one cottage (Rose Cottage).

The 3 suites can be opened up to make a single joined suite for larger get-togethers. Rates include continental breakfast and free twice-daily animal feeding.

Lorna Butler

Tamborine Mountain – Clagiraba

Fairy Wren Lodge B&B

B&B
Clagiraba

fairywrenlodgebb@gmail.com
24 Henri Robert Drive
Clagiraba QLD 4211
(07) 5533 7427
www.fairywrenlodgebb.com.au

Double: $165–$180
VISA MasterCard eftpos

Accommodation for 6
3 Bedrooms: 3Q
Bathrooms: 1 ensuite, 2 guest share

• Full breakfast

A family operated bed and breakfast in an idyllic bushland setting. One main room with a queen-size bed, private balcony and ensuite. Two separate bedrooms each with queen-size beds and a shared bathroom, also with private balconies.

Fairy Wren Lodge is only 15mins from local wineries, the quaint Tamborine Village and only 25mins from famous Gold Coast beaches. Fantastic for a weekend escape or just stop in for the night. Our family would love to welcome you into our Home to enjoy our hospitality and exquisite surrounds.

Glenda and Wayne Binns

Tamborine Mountain – Eagle Heights

Tamborine Mountain B&B

B&B
35 km NW of Surfers Paradise

info@tmbb.com.au
19–23 Witherby Crescent
Eagle Heights QLD 4271
(07) 5545 3595 or 0418 755 517
www.tmbb.com.au

Double: $160–$220
Full Breakfast: Saturday and Sunday.
Continental breakfast: Monday to Friday

VISA MasterCard *eftpos*

Accommodation for 8
4 Bedrooms: 1K 3Q 1S
Cabin style individual suites with colonial charm and
decks overlooking the lush tranquil gardens with vista
to the coast. Suites contain R/C AC, flat screen TV/DVD,
DVD and book library. Clock radio. Ironing facilities. Tea
and coffee making facilities,
Bathrooms: 4 ensuite

• Continental breakfast

Tony and Pam look forward to sharing this uniquely
Australian Bed and Breakfast accommodation
which is located atop beautiful Tamborine
Mountain, nestled in the Gold Coast Hinterland
just 1 hour from Brisbane and 30 minutes from
the Gold Coast attractions. Situated approximately
500 metres above sea level. Our Bed and Breakfast
has simply the best views from Moreton Bay to the
Gold Coast and beyond. Ideally situated close to
national parks, arts and craft shops, wineries and
restaurants, Tamborine Mountain Bed and Breakfast
is the perfect environment to relax and unwind.
WiFi access is freely provided.

Tony and Pam Lambert

Toowoomba

Beccles on Margaret B&B

Traditional B&B
0.5 km E of Toowoomba

acton1@bigpond.com
25 Margaret Street
East Toowoomba QLD 4350
(07) 4659 9571 or 0427 320 140
www.beccles.com.au

AAA Tourism
★★★★✦

Double: $115–$190
Children: None
Dinner: None

VISA MasterCard *eftpos*

Accommodation for 6
3 Bedrooms: 1K 2Q
Bathrooms: 3 ensuite

• Full breakfast

Beccles on Margaret is a 1938 Queensland
Bungalow possessing a warm and friendly
atmosphere. It is situated on Margaret Street in the
East Toowoomba Heritage Precinct. Included in
the tariff is a Continental or Country Style breakfast
served in the dining room. The spacious rooms
have their own ensuites, air conditioning, tea and
coffee facilities and TV.

Beccles has a choice of King, Queen or twin single
suites. Close to Restaurants, Queens Park, Wineries
and other Toowoomba tourist sites.

Beccles offers off street car parking.

Janette Acton

Warwick – South East Queenlsand

Abbey of the Roses

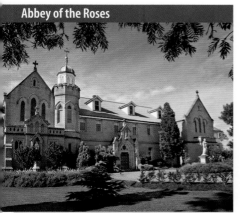

B&B and Guest House (Heritage Listed)
0.5 km S of Warwick

office@abbeyoftheroses.com
8 Locke Street
Warwick QLD 4370
(07) 4661 9777
www.abbeyoftheroses.com

AAA Tourism
★★★★

Double: $190–$295
Children: Couples only unless full house booked by one group
Tennis, bikes, massage, fully licensed.
Dinner: Meals available most nights

Accommodation for 23
11 Bedrooms: 5K 5Q 1T
Each room has a unique style of its own with either private or ensuite bathroom.
Bathrooms: 3 ensuite, 1 family share, 5 private
Attic area has 3 rooms that is rented to one group. It has a shower and toilet, plus a seperate toilet.

• Full breakfast

This 3 storey 1891 Country Manor House, heritage listed sandstone building on 2 acres is an award winning wedding reception venue and B&B in historic Warwick, just under 2 hours from CBD Brisbane. Relax, unwind and step back in time as you marvel at the craftsmanship of our forefathers at this romantic country retreat. Staying at the Abbey B&B is a memorable, unique and unforgettable experience that should be on your bucket list of places to stay.

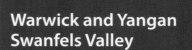

Warwick and Yangan Swanfels Valley

Warwick is just 2 hours south east of Brisbane on the main Melbourne/Sydney to Brisbane road. It is a beautiful city showcasing some of the states finest historic sandstone buildings with streets lined with roses and close to a World Heritage NP. Just a 15 minute drive east is the quaint village of Yangan located in the historic and picturesque hills of the Swanfels Valley. Visit historic buildings, The Lost Pyramid, Double Tops and Mitchell's Peak. Trace the steps of the explorer Allan Cunningham and view the monument celebrating his discovery of the Darling Downs.

Sonia, Abbey of the Roses
Doug and Liz Phillips, R on the Downs B&B

R on the Downs Rural Retreat B&B

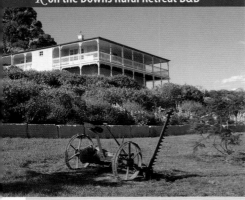

Homestead B&B and Luxury Cottages – Eco Friendly Star Rated   *20 km E of Warwick*

info@r-onthedowns.com
295 Swanfels Road
Yangan QLD 4371
(07) 4664 8587 or 0413 936 056
www.r-onthedowns.com

AAA Tourism
★★★★✩

Double: $160–$245
Single: $150–$235
Beautiful country breakfast hampers for cottages
Dinner: Country meals by arrangement.

VISA MasterCard eftpos

Accommodation for 12
6 Bedrooms: 1K 1KT 5Q
Bathrooms: 6 ensuite
Roomy double spas with beautiful views
• Full breakfast

Savour this award winning Romantic Eco-friendly Escape and Hero Destination. Relax in spacious themed luxury suites in the grand Federation Homestead, or magical Tree-house, or intimate Early Settler's Cottage. Cottages are open planned, spacious, luxurious and include fireplaces, spas and verandahs for those special panoramic views and a romantic restful beautiful bed with high quality linen and mattresses. Surround yourself with panoramic views, beautiful surroundings of the peaceful historic Swanfels Valley, located 15 minutes from Warwick/ Killarney, one hour Toowoomba, or two hours Brisbane. Enjoy your private double spa, perhaps the library, courtyard or Rendezvous garden.

Doug and Liz Phillips

Yeppoon – Capricorn Coast

Set on the Tropic of Capricorn, in Central Queensland, the Capricorn Coast is an undiscovered paradise. Townships along the Capricorn Coast are surrounded by beautiful stretches of coastline where warm waters lap the sands of secluded beaches. Snorkel, dive, trek, fish, shop and dine your way around the Capricorn Coast.

While Away B&B
Capricorn Enterprise
www. CapricornHolidays.com.au

Yeppoon – Capricorn Coast

While Away B&B

Luxury B&B
2.4 km N of Yeppoon

whileaway@bigpond.com
44 Todd Avenue
Yeppoon QLD 4703
(07) 4939 5719
www.whileawaybandb.com.au

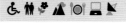

AAA Tourism
★★★★✦

Double: $145–$160
Single: $120

VISA MasterCard eftpos

Accommodation for 8
4 Bedrooms: 1K 1KT 3Q 1T
Bathrooms: 4 ensuite

• Special breakfast

While Away B&B is a purpose built B&B. We offer style, comfort and privacy in a modern home less than 100 m to beach. This property is ideal for couples but unsuitable for children under 10. All rooms have ensuites, television plus air-conditioning. We offer a generous tropical/cooked breakfast – tea/coffee-making facilities with cake/biscuits are available at all times. Dining room facilities available for use of guests. Internet and Pay TV is also available. Laundry facilities are availble on request. We will do our best to ensure you enjoy your stay in this area.

Lois and Richard Michel

  Easy access

  Children welcome

  Pets welcome

  Facilities for horses

  Couples or adults

  Outstanding garden

  Special location

  Winery nearby

  Restaurant nearby

  Eco friendly

  Onsite activities

  Swimming pool

  Tennis court

  Function facilities

  Wedding facilities

  Internet access

  Cable or satellite TV

  No smoking

Recommended Accommodation

Airlie Beach

☙ Whitsunday Heritage Cane Cutters Cottage
4 Braithwaite Court, Airlie Beach
cottage@whitsunday.net.au
whitsundaycottage.com

☙ Whitsunday Moorings B&B
37 Airlie Crescent, Airlie Beach
(07) 4946 4692
info@whitsundaymooringsbb.com.au
whitsundaymooringsbb.com.au

Ayr – Burdekin

☙ Ayr B&B on McIntyre
8 McIntyre Place, Ayr
(07) 4783 6401
stay@ayrbnb.com.au
ayrbnb.com.au

Boonah – Kalbar – Scenic Rim

☙ Wiss House B&B
7 Ann Street, Kalbar
(07) 5463 9030
reception@wisshouse.com.au
wisshouse.com.au

Brisbane – Ashgrove

☙ Ashbourne House B&B
21 Ashbourne Street, Ashgrove
(07) 3366 6889
bnb@ashbournehouse.com.au
ashbournehouse.com.au

Brisbane – Birkdale

☙ Birkdale B&B
3 Whitehall Avenue, Birkdale
(07) 3207 4442
glentrace@bigpond.com

Brisbane – Chapel Hill

☙ Chapel Woods B&B
7 Candlebark Crescent, Chapel Hill
(07) 3378 9246
diannelange1@gmail.com
chapelwoodsbandb.com

Brisbane – Milton

☙ Brisbane Milton B&B
12 Haig Road, Milton
(07) 3368 3787
info@brisbanemiltonbedandbreakfast.com.au
brisbanemiltonbedandbreakfast.com.au

Brisbane – Thornbury

☙ One Thornbury
1 Thornbury Street, Spring Hill
(07) 3839 5334
info@onethornbury.com
onethornbury.com

Brisbane – West End

☙ Eskdale B&B
141 Vulture Street, West End
0419 487 393
enquiries@eskdale.com.au
eskdale.com.au

Cairns

☙ Machans Beach B&B
167 O'Shea Esplanade, Machans Beach
0405 481 089
gabrille.gelly@bigpond.com
bnbnq.com.au/machansbeach

Cairns – Bayview Heights

☙ Cairns Reef and Rainforest B&B
176 Sydney Close, Bayview Heights
0417 771 291
info@cairnsreefbnb.com.au
cairnsreefbnb.com.au

Cairns – Clifton Beach

☙ South Pacific BnB
18 Gibson Close, Clifton Beach
(07) 4059 0381
southpacificbnb@gmail.com
southpacificbnbcliftonbeach.com.au

☙ Warrawong Lodge
20–24 Alexandra Street, Clifton Beach
(07) 4055 3194
karen@warrawonglodge.com
warrawonglodge.com

Cairns – Edge Hill

☙ Kookas B&B
40 Hutchinson Street, Edge Hill
(07) 4053 3231
kookas@kookas-bnb.com
kookas-bnb.com

Daintree – Cow Bay

☙ Cow Bay Homestay
160 Wattle Close, Cow Bay
(07) 4098 9151
marion@cowbayhomestay.com
cowbayhomestay.com

Dayboro

☙ Dayboro Cottages
3229 Mt Mee Road, Dayboro
(07) 3425 2774
dayborocottages@bigpond.com
dayborocottages.com.au

Gold Coast Hinterland – Nerang

☙ Rumbalara B&B
72 Hoop Pine Court, Advancetown
(07) 5533 2211
denise@rumbalarabnb.com.au
rumbalarabnb.com.au

Gold Coast Hinterland – Tamborine Mountain

☙ Tamborine Mountain B&B
19–23 Witherby Crescent, Eagle Heights
(07) 5545 3595
info@tmbb.com.au
tmbb.com.au

Goomburra

☙ Goomburra Forest Retreat
Forestry Reserve Road, Goomburra
(07) 4666 6058
jgmrcairns@iinet.net.au
goomburraforestretreat.com.au

Hervey Bay

☙ Bay B&B
180 Cypress Street, Hervey Bay
(07) 4125 6919
baybedandbreakfast@bigpond.com
baybedandbreakfast.com.au

☙ Villa Cavour B&B
15 Banksia Street, Hervey Bay
(07) 4124 5454
reception@villacavour.com.au
villacavour.com.au

The Chamomile B&B

☙ The Chamomile B&B
65A Miller Street, Urangan
(07) 4125 1602
info@chamomile.com.au
chamomile.com.au

Hervey Bay – Howard

☙ Montrave House B&B Home and Pet Stay
20 Pacific Haven Drive, Howard
(07) 4129 0183
montrave@bigpond.com
montrave.com

Kilcoy

☙ Kilcoy Upper Sandy Creek B&B
82 Cedarvale Road, Kilcoy
(07) 5498 1285
pandmc@activ8.net.au

Kingaroy

☙ Rock-Al-Roy B&B
15 Kearney Street, Kingaroy
(02) 6657 2536
rockalroybb@burnett.net.au
rockalroy.southburnett.com.au

Malaney – Montville

☙ Secrets on the Lake
207 Narrows Road, Montville
(07) 5478 5888
aldy@secretsonthelake.com.au
secretsonthelake.com.au

Mossman

☙ Mossman Gorge B&B
Lot 15 Gorge View Crescent, Mossman
(07) 4098 2497
mossgorg@bigpond.net.au
bnbnq.com.au/mossgorge

Port Douglas

☙ Frangipani B&B
13 Andrews Close, Port Douglas
0437 410 646
bookings@frangipaniportdouglas.com.au
frangipaniportdouglas.com.au

Rockhampton – The Range

☙ Hazel Cottage
13 Kennedy Street, Rockhampton
0424 846 235
lizandcolpatrick@yahoo.com.au

Stanthorpe

☙ Honeysuckle Cottages and The Rocks Restaurant
15 Mayfair Lane, Stanthorpe
(07) 4681 1510
reservations@honeysucklecottages.com.au
honeysucklecottages.com.au

Sunshine Coast Hinterland – Maleny

☙ Maleny Country Cottages
347 Corks Pocket Road, Reesville Via Maleny
(02) 4441 5511
reception@malenycottages.com.au
malenycottages.com.au

Sunshine Coast Hinterland – Mapleton

☙ Eden Lodge
97 Flaxton Drive, Mapleton
0414 424 045
charlie@bevan.net.au
edenlodge.com.au

Recommended Accommodation

✆ Included in book

Sunshine Coast Hinterland – Montville

✆ **Narrows Escape Rainforest Retreat**
78 Narrows Road, Montville
(07) 5478 5000
reception@narrowsescape.com.au
narrowsescape.com.au

Tamborine Mountain

✆ **Avocado Sunset B&B**
186 Beacon Road, North Tamborine
(07) 5545 2365
stay@avocadosunset.com.au
avocadosunset.com.a

Tamborine Mountain – Boyland

✆ **Clandulla Cottages**
312 Boyland Road, Boyland
(07) 5543 0990
info@clandullacottages.com.au

Tamborine Mountain – Clagiraba

✆ **Fairy Wren Lodge B&B**
24 Henri Robert Drive, Clagiraba
(07) 5533 7427
fairywrenlodgebb@gmail.com
fairywrenlodgebb.com.au

✆ **Mountain Edge Studios**
387 Henri Robert Drive, Clagiraba
(07) 5545 3437
jean@mountainedge.com.au
mountainedge.com.au

Toowoomba

✆ **Beccles on Margaret B&B**
25 Margaret Street, Toowoomba
(07) 4638 5254
acton1@bigpond.com
becclesonmargaretbandb.com.au

Warwick

✆ **Abbey of the Roses Guesthouse**
8 Locke Street, Warwick
(07) 4661 9777
office@abbeyoftheroses.com
abbeyoftheroses.com

Warwick – Yangan

✆ **R on the Downs B&B**
295 Swanfels Road, Yangan
(07) 4664 8587
Info@r-onthedowns.com
r-onthedowns.com

Yeppoon

✆ **While Away B&B**
44 Todd Avenue, Yeppoon
(07) 4939 5719
whileaway@bigpond.com
whileawaybandb.com.au

South Australia

SA

South Australia is the perfect place to visit with warm, dry summers and mild winters. Some of Australia's most famous wine regions and found in South Australia. Today it is also home to the Santos Tour Down Under, The Adelaide Fringe festival, WOMADelaide and Clipsal 500 V8 supercar race. The magnificent South Australian coastline is almost 4000km long with outstanding natural features, great sandy beaches, magnificent cliff formations. Many coastal regions offer a brilliant blend of wine and fresh produce, including local seafood. Kangaroo Island is a must visit with exceptional wildlife and stunning scenery.

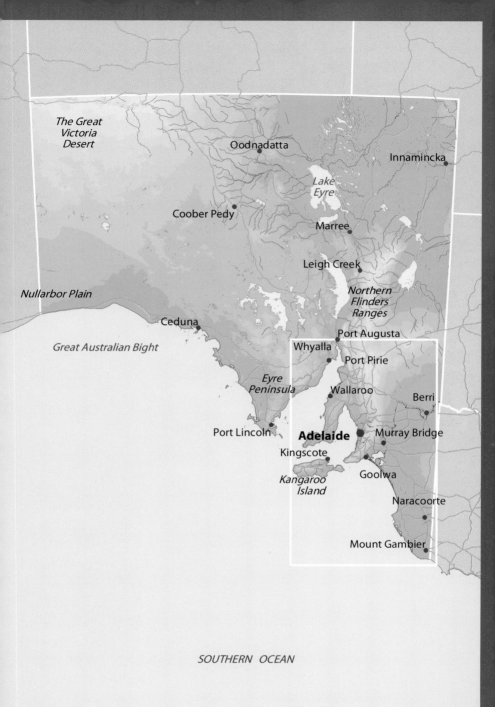

The Great
Victoria
Desert

Oodnadatta

Innamincka

Lake
Eyre

Coober Pedy

Marree

Leigh Creek

Nullarbor Plain

Northern
Flinders
Ranges

Ceduna

Great Australian Bight

Port Augusta

Whyalla

Port Pirie

Eyre
Peninsula

Wallaroo

Berri

Port Lincoln

Adelaide

Murray Bridge

Kingscote

Goolwa

Kangaroo
Island

Naracoorte

Mount Gambier

SOUTHERN OCEAN

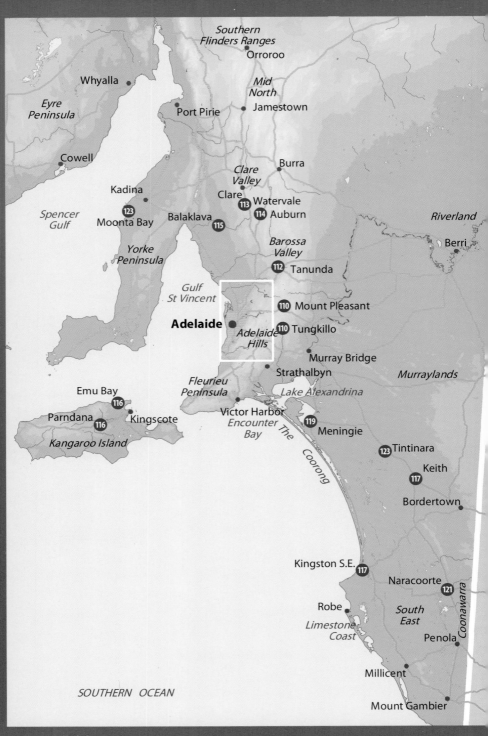

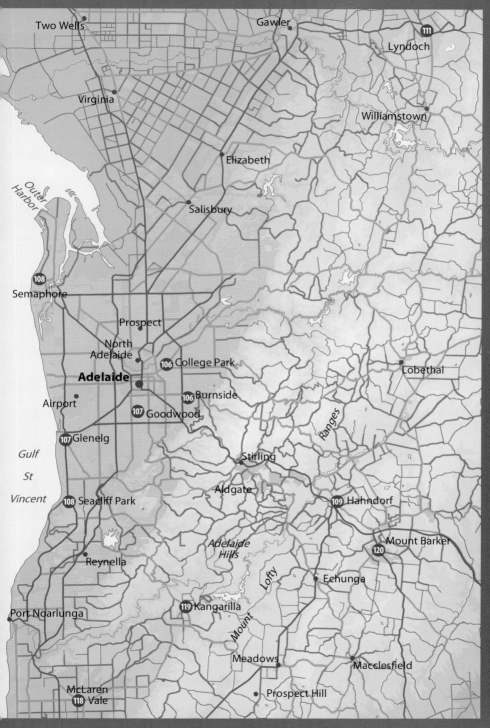

Adelaide – Burnside – Glenunga

Heidi's Bed and Breakfast

B&B Self-Contained
5 km SE of Adelaide CBD

hgoeldi@senet.com.au
39 Queen Street
Glenunga SA 5064
(08) 8379 7126
www.heidisbedandbreakfast.com

Double: $140–$150

VISA MasterCard

Accommodation for 2
1 Bedroom: 1Q
Bathrooms: 1 ensuite

• Full breakfast provisions

Heidi's Bed and Breakfast is ideally located in the eastern suburbs, close to the city centre and the Adelaide Hills. Accommodation is modern and self-contained. A warm and friendly place, tucked away in a quiet garden setting. Fully equipped kitchen ideal for longer stays at special rate. A perfect location for business or holidays, a peaceful place to stay when visiting relatives. Easy walking distance to shops, the Burnside Village shopping centre, restaurants and public transport. Off-street parking is available.

Heidi Goeldi

Guest comment: *'We could not have picked a lovelier place to stay.' V&D UK*

Adelaide – College Park

Possums Rest B&B

Separate Suite
2 km NE of Adelaide CBD

possumsrest@gmail.com
8 Catherine Street
College Park SA 5069
(08) 8362 5356 or 0412 092 881
www.possumsrestbedandbreakfast.com.au

Double: $149
Single: $135
2 night minimum stay

Accommodation for 2
1 Bedroom: 1Q
Bathrooms: 1 ensuite

• Special breakfast

Possums Rest Bed and Breakfast is ideally located in the leafy heritage area of Adelaide. Accommodation is quiet and luxurious, yet only 2 km from the CBD. within walking distance of Adelaide events such as WOMAD, Clipsal 500, Fringe Festival and Festival of Arts. Walk to the Adelaide Zoo, Museum, Art Galleries and numerous shopping and restaurant precincts. Guests are welcome to enjoy the pleasant garden and inground swimming pool in summer. Home cooked breakfasts cater for special dietary requirements. Comfortable fully air conditioned accommodation, has wireless internet connection, television, DVD and cooking facilities. Laundry facilities are available.

Sue and Phil Ogden

Guest comment: *'Exceptional hospitality. A wonderful peaceful home away from home.' S&K, UK.*

Water Bay Villa B&B

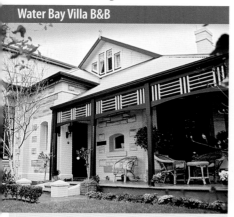

Luxury B&B – Self Contained Suite
11 km SW of Adelaide

glenelg@waterbayvilla-bnb.com.au
28 Broadway
Glenelg South SA 5045
0412 221 724
www.waterbayvilla-bnb.com.au

Double: $250–$300
Single: $210
Children: $20–$45

VISA

Accommodation for 6
2 Bedrooms: 2Q 2S
Bathrooms: 1 ensuite

• Full breakfast provisions

Indulge! Experience the luxury of this historic 1910 Queen Anne Villa in seaside Glenelg. 'The Attic' – your upstairs 4 room suite with private entry and off street parking available. Welcoming bottle of wine, fresh flowers, fruit and chocolates. Antiques, open fire, claw foot bath and laundry. Kitchenette with cooking facilities. Living area with tourist info, TV, DVD and CD Player/Radio. A few minutes stroll via the award winning garden to the nearby beach, Jetty Road, trams, restaurants, 7-day shopping, The Beachouse fun park and marina. Close to airport and public transport. Come and enjoy!

Kathy and Roger Kuchel

Guest comment: *'Thank you for a really comfortable stay. Your facilities are fantastic and the location is second to none. I'll be staying next time I come!' BW London, UK.*

Rose Villa

Luxury B&B Homestay
2 km S of Adelaide

doreen@rosevilla.com.au
29 Albert Street
Goodwood SA 5034
(08) 8271 2947
www.rosevilla.com.au

Double: $150
Single: $140

Accommodation for 2
1 Bedroom: 1K
Bathrooms: 1 ensuite

• Continental breakfast

Treat yourself to a romantic candle lit breakfast in my newly decorated Tea Rose salon. Rose Villa offers an elegant private suite (own entrance) overlooking the garden. Stroll to trendy Hyde Park Road with its delightful cafés and coffee shops, boutiques and flower shops. Close by are buses and trams (to the Bay) and city and The Ghan Terminal. Free wireless internet. 'Rose Villa' is roses, romance and caring hospitality. You are most welcome.

Doreen Petherick

Guest comment: *'We'll never forget the joy of being your guest in the quiet and peaceful Rose Villa. Thanks for sharing some beautiful moments of your life with us.' Mario and Denis, Paris, France.*

Adelaide – Seacliff Park – Brighton

Homestay Brighton

B&B and Homestay
2 km S of Brighton

rimbnb@gmail.com
PO Box 319
Brighton SA 5048
(08) 8298 6671 or 0417 800 755
www.bbbook.com.au/brighton.html

Double: $80–$90
Single: $60–$70
Children: Welcome by arrangement

Accommodation for 4
2 Bedrooms: 1D 2S
Bathrooms: 1 guest share, 1 private

• Full breakfast

Spacious home and grounds in quiet suburb close to Brighton/Seacliff beach. Public transport to the city and nearby large Westfield Shopping Centre. Ideal for day trips to the Fleurieu Peninsula with its picturesque wine areas and southern vales and coast. Guest rooms are upstairs including a television lounge with heating and cooling. Laundry and off-street parking are available. Sascha, our friendly Border Collie dog, stays outside the house.

Ruth and Tim

Guest comments: *'Great value in a relaxing suburb of Adelaide. Outstanding host, helpful, supportive and friendly.' J and GB, UK.*

'Home from Home.' LJ, UK.

'Our stay was wonderful' IB and MR, Spain.

Adelaide – Semaphore

Time and Tide Beach Apartment

Self Contained Beach Apartment
12 km NW of Adelaide CBD

timeandtidebeachapartment@gmail.com
8 Newman Street
Semaphore SA 5019
(08) 8449 7727 or 0410 088 831
www.timeandtidebeachapartment.com.au

AAA Tourism
★★★★

Double: $180–$220
VISA MasterCard

Accommodation for 2
1 Bedroom: 1KT
Bathrooms: 1 ensuite

• Breakfast provisions first night

With panoramic views of the Semaphore coastline, this modern private self-contained one-bedroom apartment will provide you with peace and tranquillity. Good proximity to AAMI Stadium. Walking trails, swimming (a picnic pack is available), shopping and restaurants are all at your doorstep. Return to Time and Tide and relax in the elegantly appointed living area, and watch the sun set with your favourite drink. The perfect place for some relationship maintenance, a quiet business trip or your own place to stay while you visit relatives. Time and Tide waits for you.

Naomi Myers

Adelaide Hills – Hahndorf

Amble at Hahndorf

Self Contained Bed and Breakfast
In Hahndorf

bookings@amble-at-hahndorf.com.au
10 Hereford Avenue
Hahndorf SA 5245
(08) 8388 1467 or 0408 105 610
www.amble-at-hahndorf.com.au

AAA Tourism
★★★★

Double: $150–$220
Single: $150–$220

VISA MasterCard

Accommodation for 14
7 Bedrooms: 4K 3Q
Bathrooms: 5 ensuite

• Full breakfast

Nestled in the Adelaide Hills region of South Australia, amongst cool climate vineyards/cellar doors, great restaurants/cafés located in Historic Hahndorf. Amble at Hahndorf Bed and Breakfast is perfectly located for an enjoyable and peaceful escape, set in lovely gardens, it offers tranquillity, romance and seclusion. This beautiful Hahndorf accommodation is offered in either 'Amble INN', 'Amble Wren', 'Amble Fern' or 'Amble Over'.

'Amble at Hahndorf is life at your own pace'.

Di and Roger

Adelaide Hills

The Adelaide Hills is blessed with many great attractions that can keep you entertained for days. Our most famous attraction is the town of Hahndorf, which has plenty of quality gift and specialty shops, craft outlets and galleries. Local restaurants include Bistro 25, the Mustard Seed and the Hahndorf Inn. Also you could visit The Cedars, the historic home and studio of famous Australian artist, Sir Hans Heysen. Other great Adelaide Hills attractions include Mount Lofty Summit, Cleland Wildlife Park, National Motor Museum, Warrawong Wildlife Sanctuary and the Big Rocking Horse.

Di and Roger
Amble at Hahndorf

Adelaide Hills – Mt Pleasant

Saunders Gorge Sanctuary

B&B • Self Contained Family Cottage and Four Buildings for Couples   *18 km E of Mt Pleasant*

nature@saundersgorge.com.au
18km east of Mt Pleasant
Mt Pleasant SA 5237
(08) 8569 3032
www.saundersgorge.com.au

AAA Tourism
★★★✈

Double: $120–$220
Single: $100–$180
Children: Family cottage suitable for children extra cost $10 per night
Family Cottage $20 extra adult per night sleeps 6
Dinner: Restaurant available on the property

VISA MasterCard

Accommodation for 14
6 Bedrooms: 4K 2Q 2S
Two Bedroom Cottage and Four single room buildings
Bathrooms: 4 ensuite, 1 family share
1 bathroom in family cottage, ensuite in all others

• Continental provisions supplied

ECO Tourism accredited Saunders Gorge Sanctuary is a private property of 1364 ha on the rugged Eastern slopes of the Mt Lofty Ranges (Adelaide Hills). Offering visitors the opportunity to experience the rugged Australian landscape, learn about and enjoy the natural environment. The property is a combination of conservation and sheep grazing. Relax in self contained accommodation. Experiance the tranquility and beauty of the property. Explore the many scenic walks or drive the 4WD trail. Enjoy an evening meal in the licensed restaurant.

Brenton and Nadene Newman

Adelaide Hills – Tungkillo

Sunnybrook B&B

B&B and Self Contained
Tungkillo

relax@sunnybrookbnb.com.au
Mannum Road
Tungkillo SA 5236
(08) 8568 2159
www.sunnybrookbnb.com.au

Double: $180
Extra adults $70 per person
Dinner: Available by request

Accommodation for 6
3 Bedrooms: 3Q
Bathrooms: 2 ensuite

• Special breakfast

SunnyBrook Bed and Breakfast is located in the beautiful Adelaide Hills, a comfortable hour's drive from the City. Choose from either self-contained or hosted. The self-contained accommodation offers complete privacy overlooking the Baker Creek, which meanders through the 20-acre property. Enjoy a delicious 3-course breakfast served in our guest's private dining room (only available on weekends and by prior arrangement) or hide away within your accommodation and cook at your leisure from the provisions supplied. Generous provisions for a hearty breakfast are supplied together with a welcome basket of home baked goodies, chocolates and a bottle of wine. Devonshire tea served on arrival.

Janet and David Hamilton

Barossa Country Cottages

B&B and Country Cottages
1 km SE of Lyndoch

enquiries@barossacountrycottages.com
55 Gilbert Street
Lyndoch SA 5351
(08) 8524 4426 or 0431 924 214
www.barossacountrycottages.com

Double: $195
Single: $195
Children: 2–11 years $25.00. Under 2 years no Charge
Complementary port and chocolates and fresh fruit bowl on arrival.

Accommodation for 10
4 Bedrooms: 2Q 2D 2T
Jacaranda 1 Queen, 1 Double, Geranium 1 queen, 1 Twin, 1 Double sofa-bed
Bathrooms: 2 private
1 separate bathroom in each cottage

• Full breakfast provisions

Barossa Country Cottages at Lyndoch are tucked away in an Australian bush garden in this rural location, yet are close to the heart of the Barossa Valley. They have been a landmark since 1992. Both cottages are fully self-contained, with 2 bedrooms each, full kitchens and reverse cycle air conditioning. Children and pets (outside) are welcome. Private large 6 person spa. Generous provisions for hearty breakfasts of local farm eggs, bacon, hash browns and tomatoes. Juice, bread, milk, cereals and jams and teas and coffees.

Carole Ronayne and Michael Broermann

Barossa Valley

The Barossa is one of the world's great wine regions, acclaimed for food, wine and a rich European heritage. The old hills of the Barossa Ranges look down on a colourful patchwork of vineyards and picture book villages.

Mandy Creed
Bellescapes

Barossa Valley – Lyndoch – Tanunda

Bellescapes

Self Contained B&B Cottages
In town

escape@bellescapes.com
PO Box 481
Lyndoch SA 5351
(08) 8524 4825 or 0412 220 553
www.bellescapes.com

Double: $220–$395
Children: Children Welcome in properties with more than one bedroom
Only Daisybelle accepts dogs
Dinner: Platters and BBQ packs can be arranged at some properties

Accommodation for 9
6 properties, ranging from 1 bedroom to 4 bedrooms
Each property has its own bathroom facilities some with spas

• Full breakfast provisions

Bellescapes properties are exclusively yours, private and self – contained, properties can accommodate between 2–9 guests. Indulge in one of our stunning B&B's designed to spoil, all located within the beautiful Barossa Valley. Choose from either heritage or contemporary properties, 3 with spas and 4 with cosy log fires. Your choice between the townships of Lyndoch, Tanunda or Rosedale. We pride ourselves on providing quality service and accommodation with a very personalised touch.

Mandy and Mark Creed

Barossa Valley – Tanunda

Goat Square Cottages

Cottage with Kitchen
75 km NE of Adelaide

goatsquare@bnbbookings.com
33 John Street
Tanunda SA 5352
1800 227 677 or (08) 8524 5353
www.goatsquarecottages.com.au

AAA Tourism
★★★✦

Double: $210
Children: We can provide a baby's cot at no extra cost
Extra Couple $140.
Dinner: Walking distance to 1918 Restaurant

Accommodation for 8
4 Bedrooms: 3K 1Q
3 separate but joined cottages (one 2 bedroom)
Bathrooms: 3 private
Underfloor heated, with modern double spa and shower over.

• Full breakfast provisions

Set in the historic centre of Tanunda, these 3 adjoining cottages date from 1867, incorporating features from an original structure built in the 1840s, including the old baker's oven. Recent renovations include: modern spa baths in each cottage, under-floor heating and well appointed kitchens. You are welcomed with warm country hospitality and a selection of local products for your breakfast. Very close to some of SA's most famous wineries – a great chance to visit this historic area and then relax sitting in the flowery garden, where you can pick your own fruit in season.

Ngaire Ingham

Barossa Valley – Tanunda – Nuriootpa

Barossa House B&B

B&B
3 km N of Tanunda

admin@barossahouse.com.au
Barossa Valley Way
Tanunda SA 5352
(08) 8562 4022
www.barossahouse.com.au

Double: $170–$235
Single: $120–$150
Children: under 3 free. Extra person $80.
Half and full day personal tours of Barossa Valley from $80

Accommodation for 8
4 Bedrooms: 1K 3Q
Bathrooms: 4 ensuite

• Full breakfast

Barossa House Bed and Breakfast where you will find friendly, personal service, charming country accommodation and the convenience of modern amenities. Four beautiful guest rooms each with ensuite bathroom, air conditioning, colour TV/DVD, heating and electric blankets, bathrobes, hairdryers, tea and coffee making facilities, complimentary chocolates and Port, wireless Internet and bicycles available on request. Barossa House is one of the few traditional hosted accommodation B&B's, located within the heart of the Barossa Valley close to the region's best wineries and restaurants. We have 2 Kia Grand Carnival cars to take you on one of our personalised tours.

Judi and Lee Prettejohn

Clare – Watervale

Stanley Grammar Country House

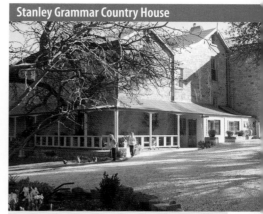

Luxury B&B
Watervale

info@oldstanleygrammar.com.au
Lot 25 Commercial Road
Watervale SA 5452
(08) 8843 0224 or 0412 716 795
www.oldstanleygrammar.com.au

Double: $235–$265

Accommodation for 8
4 Bedrooms: 2K 2Q
4 suites with private bathroom ensuites and TV
Bathrooms: 4 ensuite

• Full breakfast provisions

Experience the grandeur of a 150 year historic old grammar school in the heart of the Clare Valley. A truly magnificent Georgian country mansion, offering relaxed luxury accommodation, overlooking vineyards, rolling lawn gardens; and close to wineries, restaurants, shopping and historic towns. The suites are beautifully decorated with a choice of French provincial, Oriental and contemporary themes. One particular huge classroom is grand, and used as the formal dining and lounge room – with spit balls over 100 years old' on the ceiling. There's a billiard room, a gentleman's library, fully equipped kitchen, BBQ and garden areas. All rooms are filled with paintings, antiques, books, magazines and eclectic pieces which adds so much character.

Denise and Frank Kuss

Clare Valley

Clare has many walking and cycling trails that crisscross the valley between towns and villages and past wineries and vineyards. Clare was settled in the 1840s and named after County Clare in Ireland. Today it is world famous for its outstanding wines particularly Riesling. There are over 40 cellar doors to enjoy along the narrow 40 kilometre corridor between Auburn and Clare.

Dennis Cottage

Luxury B&B Cottage
Auburn

neil@denniscottage.com.au
St Vincent Street
Auburn SA 5451
(08) 8843 0048 or 0417 550 691
www.denniscottage.com.au

AAA Tourism
★★★★✓

Double: $300
Local wine and olive oil also supplied

VISA MasterCard eftpos

Accommodation for 4
2 Bedrooms: 2Q
Bathrooms: 2 ensuite

- Full breakfast provisions

Dennis Cottage is a double storey house, set in a large quiet, peaceful and beautiful garden, walking distance to Cygnets restaurant, Pyes Café and The Rising Sun Hotel, Auburn Gallery, antique shops, cafés and wineries. The start of the Riesling Trail is just a few minutes away. Bedrooms overlook the garden, are bright with Queen Size beds, fully air-conditioned, with en-suites, a dressing room and walk in robes. First class bed linen, towels and dressing robes. Downstairs is a kitchen, separate dining room, laundry, large spa room, and lounge room. The kitchen is fully equipped with under bench oven, glass cook-top, microwave, dishwasher, the finest European glassware and crockery, Esteel cooking pots, everything you would want to cook a banquet.

Neil and Deborah

Clare Valley – Balaklava – Auburn

The Matchbox House

Heritage Listed B&B
In town

thematchboxhouse@gmail.com
2 George Street
Balaklava SA 5461
0406 270 019
www.thematchboxhouse.com.au

Double: $150–$170
Pefect for families/group bookings

Accommodation for 8
3 Bedrooms: 1K 2Q
Plus sofa bed
Bathrooms: 1 guest share, 1 private
We are heritage listed so no ensuite bathrooms

• Breakfast by arrangement

Built in 1906, The Matchbox House is a
contemporary Bed and Breakfast in the heart of
South Australia's art and wine country. Walk to the
shops, close to the Auburn, Watervale and Clare
Valley wineries, restaurants and art galleries and
the popular Balaklava races. King or queen size bed
(plus sofa bed) and own private bathroom. Facilities
include split system heating and cooling, use of
fully equipped kitchen with provisions for breakfast,
Complimentary tea, coffee and biscuits, iron and
ironing board, lounge with flat screen TV and DVD
and CD, antique furniture and original local art,
balconies with rural views, landscaped gardens
with entertaining area and off-street parking.

Inta Depers

Kangaroo Island

Parndana is the business hub
for the "Heartland Region" of
Kangaroo Island, renowned for
spotting wildlife and provides a real
spectacle in late winter/early spring
when the wildflowers come out.
Parndana makes and ideal base
from which to explore the rest of
the island, providing convenient
access to the Island's north and
south coasts. The Parndana
community is well known for its
friendly and welcoming spirit.

Sue Florance
Ficifolia Lodge

Kangaroo Island – Emu Bay

Seascape Lodge on Emu Bay

Small Luxury Lodge
1 km N of Emu Bay

info@seascapelodge.com.au
Bates Road, Emu Bay
Kangaroo Island SA 5223
(08) 8559 5033
www.seascapelodge.com.au

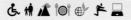

Double: $750–$750
Single: $575–$575
Children: For child rates please contact us for a quote.
Luxury 4WD island tours available
Dinner: 3 course set menu using local produce, quality local wines

Accommodation for 7
3 Bedrooms: 3K 2KT
Spacious, king beds and sensational ocean views
Bathrooms: 3 private
Private bathroom in each suite

• Full breakfast

Explore Australia's premier wildlife destination on one of our exclusive 4WD tours. Our hosted dinner, bed and breakfast property provides an intimate, homely experience whilst Enjoying stunning beach, sea and rural views from every room in the house. Sit back on the open deck in summer, nestle up against the fire in winter or simply relax with a wine in the privacy of your room and soak up the quiet tranquillity. This together with Mandy's elegant home-style cooking will make for a memorable experience.

Mandy and Paul Brown

Kangaroo Island – Parndana

Ficifolia Lodge

3 two-bedroom and 1 deluxe apartments
Parndana

enquiries@accommodationkangarooisland.com.au
45 Cook Street
Parndana SA 5220
(08) 8559 6104 or 0428 828 400
www.ficifolialodge.com.au

AAA Tourism
★★★♦

Double: $140–$175
Linen supplied. Accommodation and B&B packages

Accommodation for 14
7 Bedrooms: 4Q 4S
Bathrooms: 4 private

• Accommodation only

Ficifolia Lodge, offers 3.5 and 4 Star accommodation. Off-street undercover parking, outdoor smoking areas, onsite BBQ and laundry facilities.

1 and 2 Bedroom Apartments.

All are well equipped with full style kitchens, and open plan dining and lounge areas, plus private bathroom facilities. Each apartment is modern and well equipped with quality furnishings, bedding and linen. Reverse cycle air-conditioning. Flat Screen Digital televisions with DVD and CD players. We also offer a FREE DVD library service for in-house guests. A variety of bedding combinations can be catered for. Suitable for singles, couples traveling together, families, or group of up to 14.

Queen, single and bunk bedding arrangements.

Sue and Colin Florance

Keith

20 Hill Avenue

Beautiful Country Bed and Breakfast
Keith

roberetreats@gmail.com
20 Hill Avenue
Keith SA 5267
(08) 8757 8224 or 0417 898 584
www.20hillavenue.com.au

Double: $180
$20 for each addtional adult and room

VISA (mastercard)

Accommodation for 6
3 Bedrooms: 2Q 1T
Bathrooms: 1 ensuite

- Breakfast provisions first night

Beautiful Country Bed and Breakfast located in Keith, South Australia. Ideal stop over when travelling from Melbourne to Adelaide. A wonderful spot to catch up with friends while discovering the Limestone coast. Beautifully appointed with everything to make your stay special.

Large bedrooms – 2 Queen and 1 Twin. Fully equipped kitchen with cooker, dishwasher, microwave, coffee machine. Large living room with LCD TV, DVD player, IPod dock, Pot belly heater, RC Air conditioner, leather lounge. Fresh bathroom with large relaxation bath tub, separate shower. Laundry with front loading washer, office area. Set in a large parkland style garden with off street parking.

Cot and high chair available. Regional breakfast hamper included for the first morning.

Sonya Chalk

Limestone Coast – Kingston SE

Agnes Cottage Bed and Breakfast

B&B
Kingston SE

info@agnescottage.com.au
95 Agnes Street
Kingston SE SA 5275
0447 620 984
www.agnescottage.com.au

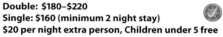

Double: $180–$220
Single: $160 (minimum 2 night stay)
$20 per night extra person, Children under 5 free

Accommodation for 6
3 Bedrooms: 2Q 2S
Bathrooms: 1 family share
Consists of shower, vanity and toilet. 2nd toilet outside.

- Breakfast provisions first night

Capture that Character and Charm of the 1940's era, perfectly complimented by modern conveniences and touches of luxury to make this private 3 bedroom self contained cottage with R/C air conditioning a 'Home Away From Home' experience within walking distance of shops, hotels and coffee shops.

Set in a private garden with fully enclosed paved outdoor entertaining area and BBQ. Fully equipped kitchen, lounge open living room, colour TV, DVD player, iPod dock, laundry.

Offering privacy and relaxation, it is perfect for couples and comfortably accommodates up to six people. All linen and towels provided.

It is only a short stroll to the beach.

Wendy

McLaren Vale

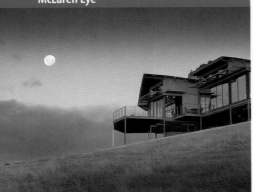

Luxury Retreat
3.5 km S of Kangarilla

stay@mclareneye.com.au
36a Peters Creek Road
Kangarilla SA 5157
(08) 8383 7122 or 0409 430 949
www.mclareneye.com.au

Double: $450
$100 for each additional guest

Accommodation for 4
2 Bedrooms: 2K
Bathrooms: 2 ensuite, 1 guest share

- Full breakfast

Welcome to the McLaren Eye, a billion star luxury retreat for up to four people. Fully equipped with everything you need, and with stunning views all around, the choice is yours whether you simply stay in, indulge and relax, or venture out to explore the region with its world-class wineries, sumptuous food and stunning beaches. Facilities include two double bedrooms with ensuite and private balcony, Galley kitchen with dishwasher, oven, stove, fridge and microwave, Romantic free standing bath surrounded by glass in master bedroom, Flat screen TVs in the living area and both bedrooms, Ducted heating and cooling, Stereo / CD, DVD player. There is access to third bathroom from living area plus a fully equipped separate laundry with washing machine and dryer. Plus a helicopter pad.

Joylene and Rob Edwards

McLaren Vale – Fleurieu Peninsula

Peppermint Farm Cottage B&B

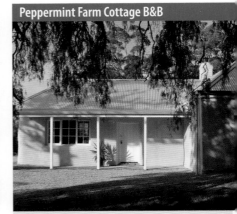

Self Contained Cottage
3 km SE of McLaren Vale township

stay@pfcbandb.com.au
148 Strout Road
McLaren Vale SA 5171
0417 816 475
www.pfcbandb.com.au

Double: $240
Children: Babies and toddlers stay free if guests supply bedding

Accommodation for 4
2 Bedrooms: 2Q
Bathrooms: 1 private
Bathroom includes spa

- Full breakfast provisions

The Peppermint Farm Cottage Bed and Breakfast, McLaren Vale South Australia is fitted with ducted reverse cycle air conditioning for year round comfort. There are two large bedrooms, a luxury bathroom with a spa bath and a fully equipped, modern kitchen. The lounge room has an entertainment centre. A BBQ area with an outdoor setting overlooks the Turra Parri Creek. Imagine cooking a BBQ while sipping local wine and listening to the bird life. You may even see a kangaroo hop by! McLaren Vale offers exceptional wines, regional produce and beautiful scenery nestled between the Mount Lofty Ranges and beaches of Gulf St Vincent.

Paul and Diane Witt

McLaren Vale – Kangarilla

Amanda's Cottage 1899

Romantic Cottage
4 km S of Kangarilla

stay@amandascottage.com.au
54 Peters Creek Road
Kangarilla SA 5157
(08) 8383 7122 or 0409 430 949
www.amandascottage.com.au

Double: $200–$245
Additional guests $90 per person

Accommodation for 4
2 Bedrooms: 1Q 1T
Twin can be converted to a double
Bathrooms: 1 ensuite

- Full breakfast provisions

Amanda's Cottage offers beautiful self contained Accommodation nestled amongst some of Australia's most famous wineries in Mcaren Vale. The cottage features private lounge with open fire, living area with dining table with views to the outdoor entertaining area. The bathroom has been beautifully restored and features an antique claw footed deep bathtub. The master bedroom has a queen bed and the second bedroom has a twin bed, (which can be converted into a double bed), in a cosy setting. All of this along with polished jarrah floors and set on 55 acres of beautiful countryside. Watch the wrens in the garden, or sheep around the cottage with McLaren Vale Wineries and restaurants only minutes away.

Joylene and Rob Edwards

Meningie

Dalton On The Lake

Luxury B&B and Apartment and Cottage
0.5 km SW of Meningie

admason@lm.net.au
30 Narrung Road
Meningie SA 5264
0428 737 161
www.bbbook.com.au/4510.html

Double: $140–$175
Single: $130

Accommodation for 8
2 Bedrooms: 2K 2KT 1Q
Bathrooms: 1 ensuite, 1 private
Studio ensuite; wheel chair friendly Cottage has spa bath and separate toilet and hand basin.

- Full breakfast provisions

You can watch pelicans dancing on the breeze while enjoying absolute luxury self contained accommodation for couples and small groups.

You can indulge with a generous breakfast of fresh home made bread, farm eggs, plunger coffee and much more in either the modern and airy Studio or cosy comfort of the Cottage.

Dalton on the Lake is positioned on Lake Albert just 90 mins easy drive from Adelaide.

While in Meningie you can enjoy the tranquility and mystery of the Coorong, the abundant birdlife, one of South Australia's finest country golf courses or strolls along the Lake.

Denice and Ashley

Mount Barker

3 bedroom house
Mount Barker

bookings@amble-at-hahndorf.com.au
1 / 1 Symonds Drive
Mount Barker SA 5245
(08) 8388 1467 or 0408 105 610
www.amble-at-hahndorf.com.au/summit/

Double: $190

Accommodation for 6
3 Bedrooms: 3KT
Six single beds or three king beds
Bathrooms: 1 ensuite

• Accommodation only

The Summit offers pet friendly air conditioned accommodation in Mt Barker. The summit offers three king beds or six single beds or variations of these as required and would be suitable for families or small gatherings. Cots and roll away beds are also available. It is ideally situated within walking distance of the local golf course. There are many walking trails in the vicinity or you may decide to take a trip to the top of Mt Barker to view the rolling Adelaide Hills or the sweeping plains towards the River Murray.

You can sit in the outside entertaining area and relax with a drink or prepare a meal on the gas BBQ.

Di and Roger

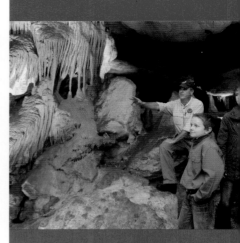

Naracoorte

See magnificent limestone formations in the World Heritage listed Naracoorte Caves National Park. Naracoorte is in the heart of the Limestone Coast and is famous for the Naracoorte Caves National Park – South Australia's only site on the World Heritage List. You can tour four caves, see fossils, go adventure caving and visit a Bat Centre. Naracoorte is also surrounded by premium wine regions producing superior red and white wines.

Richard Peake and Judith Barton
Naracoorte Cottages B&Bs

Naracoorte

Willowbrook Cottages B&Bs

2 Self Contained B&B Cottages
1 km E of Post Office

stay@willowbrookcottages.com.au
3 and 3A Jenkins Terrace
Naracoorte SA 5271
(08) 8762 0259 or 0419 802 728
www.willowbrookcottages.com.au

AAA Tourism
★★★★

Double: $145–$160
Single: $110
Children: $15 per child

VISA · MasterCard · AMERICAN EXPRESS

Accommodation for 6
3 Bedrooms: 2Q 1T
Per cottage
Bathrooms: 1 private
Per cottage

• Full breakfast provisions

The allure and charm of bygone years combined with all the modern conveniences expected by today's traveller – that's the brilliant blend of Willowbrook Cottages B&Bs. Centrally located in Naracoorte, within walking distance to shops and eateries, Willowbrook Cottages are the ideal base for exploring the Limestone Coast including World Heritage Fossil site, Coonawarra and Padthaway wine regions.

Lynette and John Lauterbach

Easy access

Children welcome

Pets welcome

Facilities for horses

Couples or adults

Outstanding garden

Special location

Winery nearby

Restaurant nearby

Eco friendly

Onsite activities

Swimming pool

Tennis court

Function facilities

Wedding facilities

Internet access

Cable or satellite TV

No smoking

Naracoorte Cottages

4 Self Contained B&B Houses
All in town of Naracoorte

info@naracoortecottages.com.au
PO Box 1088
Naracoorte SA 5271
0408 810 645
www.naracoortecottages.com.au

AAA Tourism   AAA Tourism
★★★↗ − ★★★★↗

Double: $168–$187
Single: $132
Children: Aged 2–17 with adult $20 each, $40 at MacHouse; under 2 free
Extra adult $60, $70 at MacDonnell House.

VISA   MasterCard   AMERICAN EXPRESS

Accommodation for 8
4 Bedrooms: 1K 3Q
Bathrooms: 1 ensuite, 2 family share
• Full breakfast provisions

Naracoorte Cottages has four choices of ideal places to stay and explore the World Heritage listed Naracoorte Caves and the Coonawarra, Padthaway and Wrattonbully premium wine regions.
Pinkerton Hill: 5 bedrooms, 3 bathrooms incl 1 spa; MacDonnell House: 4 bedrooms, 3 bathrooms incl 1 spa; Smith Street Villa: 5 bedrooms, 2 bathrooms;

Limestone View: 3 bedrooms, 2 bathrooms incl 1 spa. The B&Bs are in the heart of a town noted for its free swimming lake, The Sheep's Back wool industry museum and Mini Jumbuk woollen bedding factory, thriving shopping centre with hotels, restaurants and takeaway places. Naracoorte Cottages has been in the 'people friendly' B&B business since 1995 and its four houses are rated from 3.5 to 4.5 stars and offer comfort and convenience with all modern amenities. Ideal for singles, couples, families and groups for overnight stopover or longer stay. Plasma TVs, DVD players, local call telephones, access to wireless broadband (BYO computer) and reverse cycle air conditioning.

Richard Peake and Judith Barton

Tintinara – Culburra – Limestone Coast

O'Deas Cottage B&B

Self Contained Cottage
4 km S of Tintinara

stay@odeascottage.com.au
9297 Dukes Highway
Tintinara SA 5266
(08) 8575 8023 or 0409 575 023
www.odeascottage.com.au

Double: $140–$200
Single: $120
Children: $25. Extra adult $55.

VISA MasterCard

Accommodation for 6
2 Bedrooms: 1Q 2T
Bathrooms: 1 private

• Full breakfast provisions

Imagine acres of farmland, clean fresh air, big skies, bright starry nights, drinks on the verandah, the spell of the open fire, a warm country welcome – that's O'Deas Cottage. A relaxed and convenient stopover on a working sheep/cattle property. The original limestone home, built in the early 1900's, has accommodation for 2–6 people. Wool quilts, feather pillows and crisp linen for a good nights sleep. A new fresh bathroom, reverse cycle A/C, a kitchen – cook as much or as little as you like, a BBQ for summer cooking, a large open fire and shady verandahs overlooking the paddocks. Stretch the legs, let the family unwind. Pets outside by arrangement.

O'Deas cottage – 'A taste of country.'

Prin Twelftree

Yorke Peninsula – Moonta Bay – Port Hughes

Amelia's Bed and Breakfast

Luxury Self Contained Stone Cottage
Moonta Bay

ameliasbandb@bigpond.com
31 Bay Road
Moonta Bay SA 5558
0447 528 040
www.ameliasbandb.com.au

AAA Tourism
★★★★✓

Double: $195–$225
Extra person $40/nt

VISA MasterCard

Accommodation for 4
2 Bedrooms: 2Q
Bathrooms: 2 ensuite
two-person spa

• Full breakfast provisions

Luxury, luxury, luxury.

Amelia's is a fully renovated 1870s stone cottage with olde worlde charm but modern amenities.

Attention to detail is fantastic. This bed and breakfast caters for romantic getaways, or just a peaceful getaway – or is a perfect place to 'pop that all important question'.

You can have a 3 course in house dinner cooked by a qualified chef.

Elaine and Tim Love

Recommended Accommodation

✦ Included in book

Adelaide – Blackwood

The Gallery B&B
29 Hannaford Road, Blackwood
(08) 8278 6387
thegallerybnb@iprimus.com.au
thegallerybnb.com.au

Adelaide – Burnside

Petts Wood Lodge
542 Glynburn Road, Burnside
(08) 8331 9924
pettswood@adelaide.on.net
pettswood.com.au

Adelaide – Burnside – Glenunga

✦ **Heidi's Bed and Breakfast**
39 Queen Street, Glenunga
(08) 8379 7126
hgoeldi@senet.com.au
heidisbedandbreakfast.com

Adelaide – College Park

✦ **Possums Rest B&B**
8 Catherine Street, College Park
(08) 8362 5356
possumsrest@gmail.com
possumsrestbedandbreakfast.com.au

Adelaide – Glenelg

✦ **Water Bay Villa B&B**
28 Broadway, Glenelg South
0412 221 724
glenelg@waterbayvilla-bnb.com.au
waterbayvilla-bnb.com.au

Adelaide – Goodwood

✦ **Rose Villa**
29 Albert Street, Goodwood
(08) 8271 2947
doreen@rosevilla.com.au
rosevilla.com.au

Adelaide – Hackney

Athelney Cottage
7 Athelney Avenue, Hackney
0417 707104
athelney@chariot.net.au
athelneycottage.com.au

Adelaide – Mclaren Vale

McLaren Vale Apartments
222 Main Rd, McLaren Vale
(08) 8323 9536
indulge@vintage.net.au
mvsa.com.au

Adelaide – Myponga Beach

Brooklyn Farm
490 Sampson Road, Myponga Beach
(08) 8558 3808
stay@brooklynfarm.com.au
brooklynfarm.com.au

Adelaide – North Adelaide

Adelaide Heritage Cottages
various locations in North Adelaide, North Adelaide
08 82672020
res@adelaideheritage.com
adelaideheritage.com

Adelaide – Salisbury Heights

Cooinda View B&B
3 Cooinda Court, Salisbury Heights
0417 870 231
info@cooindaview.com.au
cooindaview.com.au

Adelaide – Seacliff Park

✦ **Homestay Brighton**
PO Box 319, Brighton
(08) 8298 6671
rimbnb@gmail.com

Adelaide – Semaphore

✦ **Time And Tide Beach Apartment**
8 Newman Street, Semaphore
(08) 8449 7727
timeandtidebeachapartment@gmail.com
timeandtidebeachapartment.com.au

Adelaide Hills – Aldgate

Aldgate Creek Cottage
3 Rugby Road Cottage located on Strathalbyn Rd., Aldgate
(08) 8339 1987
doug@tmorganics.com
aldgatecreekbnb.com

Aldgate Lodge
27 Strathalbyn Road, Aldgate
(08) 8370 9957
stay@aldgatelodge.com.au
aldgatelodge.com.au

Cladich Pavilions
27–29 Wilpena Terrace, Aldgate
(08) 8339 8248
stay@cladichpavilions.com
cladichpavilions.com

Adelaide Hills – Balhannah

Hannah's Cottage
44 Jones Road, Balhannah
(08) 8388 4148
dream@hannahscottage.com.au
hannahscottage.com.au

Adelaide Hills – Basket Range

Burdett's Waratah Cottage
92 Burdetts Road, Basket Range
(08) 8390 0296
amburdett@bigpond.com
burdetts.net.au

Adelaide Hills – Callington

Callington Railway Stay
1149 Back Callington Road, Callington
0448 452 409
info@callingtonrailwaystay.com.au
callingtonrailwaystay.com.au

Adelaide Hills – Hahndorf

✦ **Amble At Hahndorf**
10 Hereford Avenue, Hahndorf
(08) 8388 1467
admin@amble-at-hahndorf.com.au
amble-at-hahndorf.com.au

Adelaide Hills – Macclesfield

Mirrabooka
Strathalbyn Road, Macclesfield
(08) 8388 9733
info@mirrabookabnb.com.au
mirrabookabnb.com.au

Adelaide Hills – Mount Barker

Dumas House
11 Druids Avenue, Mount Barker
0417 445 663
enquiries@dumashouse.com
dumashouse.com

Little Undermount
Springs Road, Mount Barker Springs
(08) 8391 1031
denical@bigpond.com

Adelaide Hills – Mount Pleasant

Stoneybank Settlement Cottages
Lot 100 Stoneybank Lane, Mt Pleasant
(08) 8568 2075
relax@stoneybankcottages.com.au
stoneybankcottages.com.au

Adelaide Hills – Oakbank

Adelaide Hills Country Cottages
229 (Lot 17) Oakwood Road, Oakbank
(08) 8388 4193
relax@ahcc.com.au
adelaidehillscountrycottages.com.au

Adelaide Hills – Palmer

✦ **Saunders Gorge Sanctuary**
Saunders Gorge, Palmer
(08) 8569 3032
nature@saundersgorge.com.au
saundersgorge.com.au

Adelaide Hills – Stirling

Adelaide Hills B&B
35 Garrod Crescent, Stirling
0412 844 676
booking@adelaidehillsbedandbreakfast.com
adelaidehillsbedandbreakfast.com

Castle Keep B&B
2 Glenside Lane, Stirling
(08) 8339 6748
thekeep@thorngrove.com.au
thorngrove.com.au

Adelaide Hills – Summertown

Lorikeet Lane B&B
1 Lorrikeet Way, Summertown
(08) 8390 1712
linger@lorikeetlane.com
lorikeetlane.com

Adelaide Hills – Tungkillo

✦ **Sunnybrook B&B**
Mannum Road, Tungkillo
(08) 8568 2159
relax@sunnybrookbnb.com.au
sunnybrookbnb.com.au

Barossa – Angaston

Acorn Cottage
7 French Street, Angaston
0419 188 974
walnutcottage@activ8.net.au
acorn-cottage.com.au

Walnut Cottage
8 French Street, Angaston
0419 188 974
enquiries@walnut-cottage.com
walnut-cottage.com.au

Recommended Accommodation

🅱 Included in book

Barossa – Gilberton

🅱 **Goat Square Cottages**
70 Gilbert Street, Gilberton
1800 227 677
info@goatsquarecottages.com.au
goatsquarecottages.com.au

Barossa – Greenock

Greenock's Old Telegraph Station
11 Murray Street, Greenock
0429 090 055
booking@oldtelegraphstation.com
oldtelegraphstation.com

Barossa – Lyndoch

🅱 **Barossa Country Cottages B&B**
55 Gilbert Street, Lyndoch
(08) 8524 4426
enquiries@barossacountrycottages.com
barossacountrycottages.com

Barossa Shiraz Estate
1246 Barossa Valley Way, Lyndoch
0422 030 303
bookings@barossashirazestate.com.au
barossashirazestate.com.au

🅱 **Bellescapes**
PO Box 481, Lyndoch
(08) 8524 4825
escape@bellescapes.com
bellescapes.com

Barossa – Seppeltsfield

The Lodge Country House
Seppeltsfield Rd, Seppeltsfield
(08) 8562 8277
stay@thelodgecountryhouse.com.au
thelodgecountryhouse.com

Barossa – Tanunda

🅱 **Barossa House**
Barossa Valley Way, Tanunda
(08) 8562 4022
admin@barossahouse.com.au
barossahouse.com.au

Miriam's Cottage
22 College Street, Tanunda
(08) 8562 8103
miriamsbb@ozemail.com.au

Stonewell Cottages
Stonewell Road Stone Well, Tanunda
0417 848 977
relax@stonewellcottages.com.au
stonewellcottages.com.au

Barossa – Williamstown

Queen's Cottage Barossa Valley
41 Queen Street, Williamstown
0425 177 713
Stay@QueensCottageBnB.com.au
queenscottagebarossavalley.com.au

Tungali Cottage
Williamstown to Springton Rd, Williamstown
(08) 8524 6251
tungali@hotmail.com.au

Barossa – Mallala

Audreys Accommodation
9 Aerodrome Rd, Mallala
0448 654 459
enquiries@audreysaccommodation.com.au
audreysaccommodation.com.au

Barossa – Marananga

Treetops B&B
506 Seppeltsfield Road, Marananga
(08) 8562 2522
gnadenfrei@activ8.net.au
treetopsbnb.com.au

Barossa – Seppeltsfield

Seppeltsfield Vineyard Cottage
27 Gerald Roberts Road, Seppeltsfield
(08) 8563 4059
stay@seppeltsfieldvineyardcottage.com.au
seppeltsfieldvineyardcottage.com.au

Beltana

Beltana Station
Beltana Station, Beltana
(08) 8675 2256
beltanastation1@bigpond.com
beltanastation.com.au

Clare

Brice Hill Country Lodge
56–66 Warenda Road, Clare
(08) 8842 2925
getaway@bricehill.com.au
bricehill.com.au

Bungaree Station
431 Bungaree Road, Clare
(08) 8842 2677
info@bungareestation.com.au
bungareestation.com.au

Clare – Balaklava

🅱 **The Matchbox House**
2 George Street, Balaklava
0406 270 019
thematchboxhouse@gmail.com
thematchboxhouse.com.au

Clare – Watervale

🅱 **Stanley Grammar Country House**
Lot 25 Commercial Road, Watervale
(08) 8843 0224
info@oldstanleygrammar.com.au
oldstanleygrammar.com.au

Clare Valley – Auburn

Annabelle's Cottage
15 Henry Street, Auburn
(08) 8849 2081
stay@annabellescottage.com.au
annabellescottage.com.au

Daisy Manor
4 King Street, Auburn
(08) 8849 2134
daisy@capri.net.au

🅱 **Dennis Cottage**
St Vincent Street, Auburn
(08) 8843 0048
neil@denniscottage.com.au
denniscottage.com.au

Lavender Blue
Main North Road, Auburn
0417 804 965
relax@lavenderblue.com.au
lavenderblue.com.au

Lyreen's Apartment
28a St Vincent Street, Auburn
0448 965 881
stay@lyreensapartment.com.au
lyreensapartment.com.au

One Tree B&B
Lot 2 and 3 Church Street, Auburn
0417 351 052
onetreebandb@gmail.com
onetreebandb.com.au

Clare Valley – Balaklava

Balaklava B&B
3 Fisher Street, Balaklava
0438 886 210
wehry@bigpond.com
bandbfsa.com.au

Clare Valley – Brady Creek

Hallelujah Hideaway
Stock Route, Brady Creek
0403 043 522
Lynda.kutek@optusnet.com.au

Clare Valley – Burra

Burra Creek Cottage
2 Bridge Street East, Burra
0412 987 219
burracreekcottage@yahoo.com.au
australianbedandbreakfast.com.au

Clare Valley – Laura

Smith's Farmstay
227 Smith Road [PO Box 38], Laura
(08) 8663 2576
smithsfarmstay@internode.on.net
australianbedandbreakfast.com.au

Clare Valley – Leasingham

Ethel's Cottage
Main North Road, Leasingham
(08) 8342 0406
ask@ethelscottage.com.au
ethelscottage.com.au

Clare Valley – Snowtown

Hummocks Station
Barunga Homestead Road, Snowtown
0418 811 573
enquiries@hummocksstation.com.au
hummocksstation.com.au

Clare Valley – Watervale

Battunga B&B
326 Upper Skilly Road, Watervale
08 88430120
battunga@chariot.net.au
battunga.com.au

Granmas B&B
Main North Road, Watervale
0408 828 459
denyse@granmas.com.au
granmas.com.au

Fleurieu – Carrickalinga

Dee's Villa
468 Smith Hill Road, Carrickalinga
0409 124324
dees@gotalk.net.au
dees.com.au

Fleurieu – Christies Beach

Christies Seahorse
1 The Esplanade, Christies Beach
0437 133 500
johnwyk@iprimus.com.au
christiesseahorse.com.au

Recommended Accommodation

Fleurieu – Deep Creek Conservation Park

Southern Ocean Retreats
Deep Creek Conservation Park, Deep Creek Conservation Park
(08) 8598 4169
enquiries@southernoceanretreats.com.au
southernoceanretreats.com.au

Fleurieu – Delamere

Nowhere Else Cottage
8449 Main South Rd, Delamere
(08) 8598 0221
gfhodge@activ8.net.au
nowhereelsecottage.com

Fleurieu – Goolwa

Rose-Eden House
27 Cadell Street, Goolwa
0448 752 012
bookings@rose-edenhouse.com.au
rose-edenhouse.com.au

Vue de M B&B
11 Admiral Terrace, Goolwa
(08) 8555 1487
admin@vuedemerde.com.au
vuedemerde.com.au

Fleurieu – Inman Valley

Corinium Roman Villa
160 Nosworthy Road, Inman Valley
0415 694 013
enquiries@crvilla.com.au
crvilla.com.au

Rattleys At Pear Tree Hollow
157 Nosworthy Road, Inman Valley
(08) 8558 8234
enquiries@rattleys.com.au
rattleys.com.au

Fleurieu – Kangarilla

👓 Amanda's Cottage 1899
Peters Creek Road, Kangarilla
(08) 8383 7122
stay@amandascottage.com.au
amandascottage.com.au

McLaren Eye
36a Peters Creek Road, Kangarilla
(08) 8383 7122
stay@mclareneye.com.au
mclareneye.com.au

Fleurieu – Kyeema

Chamel Fields Farmstay
499 Blackfellows Creek Road, Kyeema near Prospect Hill
(08) 8556 7442
chamel.fields@activ8.net.au
chamelfields.com.au

Fleurieu – Maslin Beach

Bott's Beach Retreat
79 Gulf Parade, Maslin Beach
0401 838 641
bottrill@chariot.net.au
bottsbeachretreat.com.au

Fleurieu – Mclaren Vale

👓 Peppermint Farm Cottage B&B
148 Strout Road, McLaren Vale
0417 816 475
stay@pfcbandb.com.au
pfcbandb.com.au

Bellevue B&B McLaren Vale
12 Chalk Hill Road, McLaren Vale
0432 868 402
stay@bellevuebnb.com.au
bellevuebnb.com.au

Jessica's Place
14 Vine Street, McLaren Vale
(08) 8323 8233
jessicasplace@iinet.net.au
jessicasplacemv.blogspot.com

The Linear Way B&B
41 Caffrey Street, McLaren Vale
(08) 8323 7328
barnowl3@bigpond.com
thelinearway.com.au

Fleurieu – Middleton

Wenton Farm Holiday Cottages
63 Burgar Road, Middleton
(08) 8555 4126
bookings@wentonfarm.com.au
wentonfarm.com.au

Fleurieu – Normanville

Santai Villas
4 Cheeseman Street, Normanville
0452 257 477
info@santaivillas.com.au
santaivillas.com.au

Yankalilla Bay Homestead
39 Jetty Road, Normanville
(08) 8558 3223
marg@yankalillabay.com.au
yankalillabay.com.au

Fleurieu – Port Elliot

Brooklands Heritage B&B
60 Heysen Road, Port Elliot
(08) 8554 3808
unwind@brooklands.net.au
brooklands.net.au

Trafalgar Premium Vintage Suites
25 The Strand, Port Elliot
(08) 8554 3888
bookings@trafalgarhouse.com.au
trafalgarhouse.com.au

Fleurieu – Port Noarlunga South

Briny View
Esplanade, Port Noarlunga South
0414 391 349
brinyview@gmail.com
brinyview.com.au

Fleurieu – Port Willunga

Saltaire
4 Marlin Road, Port Willunga
08 83394151
james_baker@merck.com
craferscottages.com.au

Fleurieu – Strathalbyn

Callistemon Cottage
400 Stirling Hill Road, Strathalbyn
0438 789 357
raelenegaffney@hotmail.com

Osborne House Apartment
1 Stones Lane, Strathalbyn
0417 861 435
jandjphelps@yahoo.com.au

Fleurieu – Victor Harbor

Breakaway Farmstay
790 Waitpinga Road, Victor Harbor
(08) 8552 9317
breakawayfarmstay@skymesh.com.au
breakawayfarmstay.com.au

Morgan Park B&B
1 Shetland Court, Victor Harbor
(08) 8552 8781
aclittle@sa.chariot.net.au
morganparkbnb.com.au

Fleurieu – Willunga

Anchor Cottage
PO Box 580, Willunga
(08) 8557 8516
enquiries@portwillungacottages.com.au
portwillungacottages.com.au

McCaffrey Cottage
21 St James Street, Willunga
(08) 8556 2902
bookings@mccaffreycottage.com.au
mccaffreycottage.com.au

Mulberry Lodge
202 Main Road, Willunga
0424 825 965
hazel@mulberrylodgewillunga.com
mulberrylodgewillunga.com

Willunga House
1 St. Peters Terrace, Willunga
(08) 8556 2467
willungahouse@internode.on.net
willungahouse.com.au

Kangaroo Island – Baudin Beach

The Fig Tree B&B
107 Leander Avenue, Baudin Beach
(08) 8553 1326
bookings@thefigtree.com.au
thefigtree.com.au

Kangaroo Island – Parndana

👓 Ficifolia Lodge
45 Cook Street, Parndana
(08) 8559 6104
enquiries@accommodationkangarooisland.com.au
ficifolialodge.com.au

Keith

👓 20 Hill Avenue
20 Hill Avenue, Keith
(08) 8757 8224
roberetreats@gmail.com
roberetreats.com

Kingston

👓 Agnes Cottage B&B
95 Agnes Street, Kingston SE
0447 620 984
info@agnescottage.com.au
agnescottage.com.au

Limestone Coast – Bordertown

Haven on Haynes
25 Haynes St, Bordertown
0419 854 317
havenonhaynes@internode.on.net
havenonhaynes.com.au

Recommended Accommodation

Limestone Coast – Glencoe

Little Yakka B&B
491 Mile Hill Road, Glencoe
(08) 8739 4070
skmaxwell@skymesh.com.au
littleyakkabandb.com.au

Limestone Coast – Meningie

ⓘ **Dalton On The Lake**
30 Narrung Road, Meningie
0428 737 161
admason@lm.net.au

The Cottage No.12 On North
12 North Terrace, Meningie
(08) 8575 1250
kbcoorong@lm.net.au
bandbfsa.com.au

Limestone Coast – Mount Gambier

Mackenzie's on Jardine
9 Jardine Street, Mount Gambier
0409 420 864
robyn@mackenziesonjardine.com.au
mackenziesonjardine.com.au

Limestone Coast – Naracoorte

ⓘ **Naracoorte Cottages**
PO Box 1088, Naracoorte
0408 810 645
info@naracoortecottages.com.au

ⓘ **Willowbrook Cottages B&B's**
5 Jenkins Terrace, Naracoorte
(08) 8762 0259
stay@willowbrookcottages.com.au
willowbrookcottages.com.au

Limestone View Naracoorte
44 Freeling Street, Naracoorte
0408 810 645
info@naracoortecottages.com.au
naracoortecottages.com.au

Limestone Coast – Penola

Georgie's Cottage
1 Riddoch Street, Penola
0427 100 767
georgiescottage@georgiescottage.com
georgiescottage.com

Limestone Coast – Robe

Cricklewood Cottage
24 Woolundry Road, Robe
(08) 8768 2137
info@cricklewood.com.au
cricklewood.com.au

Robe House
1A Hagen Street, Robe
(08) 8768 2770
info@robehouse.com.au
robehouse.com.au

Mount Barker

ⓘ **Amble Summit Mount Barker**
1 / 1 Symonds Drive, Mount Barker
(08) 8388 1467
admin@amble-at-hahndorf.com.au
amble-at-hahndorf.com.au

Murraylands – Loxton

Mill Cottage Loxton
2 Mill Road, Loxton
0439 866 990
info@millcottage.com.au
millcottage.com.au

Murraylands – Lyrup

Pike River Luxury Villas
8 Pike Creek Rd, Lyrup
0428 831 045
caire@pikeriver.com.au
pikeriver.com.au

Pike River Woolshed
Lot 5 Pike Creek Road, Lyrup
(08) 8583 8196
caire@pikeriverwoolshed.com
pikeriverwoolshed.com

Port Pirie

Sampson's Cottage
66 Ellen Street, Port Pirie
(08) 8632 3096
portpirient@westnet.com.au
bandbfsa.com.au

Tintinara

ⓘ **O'Deas Cottage**
9297 Dukes Highway, Tintinara
(08) 8575 8023
stay@odeascottage.com.au
odeascottage.com.au

Wirrabara

Taralee Orchards
Forest Road, Wirrabara
(08) 8668 4343
info@taralee.com.au
taralee.com.au

Yorke Peninsula – Moonta Bay

ⓘ **Amelia's Bed And Breakfast**
31 Bay Road, Moonta Bay
0447 528 040
ameliasbandb@bigpond.com
ameliasbandb.com.au

Tasmania

Discover Tasmania today with awe inspiring coastlines, diverse wilderness, spectacular mountain trekking, rainforests and rivers, endless world heritage wilderness, jaw dropping beaches, exciting sites and cuisine, tantalising wines, artistic cosmopolitan vibe and with a great history and heritage.

King Island

Flinders Island

Bass

Straight

Smithton 140

Burnie

Beauty
Point

Devonport 134 130

Pt Sorell 138 Dilston

St Helens

132 137 Launceston

Deloraine

*Cradle
Mountain*

*Central
Plateau*

Queenstown 139

131

Derwent
Bridge

Swansea 141

Strathgordon

*Lake
Gordon*

Hobart

Pt Arthur

*Storm
Bay*

SOUTHERN OCEAN

Southport

*Tasman
Sea*

Bridgewater

Richmond

Rosetta

Risdon Vale

Lindisfarne

Glebe 137 Rose Bay

135 136 Bellerive

Hobart

Acton Park

Sandy Bay

Easy access

 Children welcome

 Pets welcome

 Facilities for horses

 Couples or adults

 Outstanding garden

 Special location

 Winery nearby

 Restaurant nearby

 Eco friendly

 Onsite activities

 Swimming pool

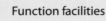 Tennis court

 Function facilities

 Wedding facilities

 Internet access

 Cable or satellite TV

 No smoking

Beauty Point

Pomona Spa Cottages

Luxury and Cottage with Kitchen and Luxury Self Contained Cottages   *40 km N of Launceston*

relax@pomonaspacottages.com.au
77 Flinders Street
Beauty Point TAS 7270
(03) 6383 4073
www.pomonaspacottages.com.au

AAA Tourism
★★★★⯪

Double: $170–$280
Single: $170–$280

VISA MasterCard eftpos

Accommodation for 10
4 Bedrooms: 4K 2S
Spacious bedrooms with river views in 2 one bedroom cottages and 1 two bedroom 2 ensuites cottage.
Bathrooms: 4 ensuite
Spa and separate showers

· Breakfast provisions first night

Relax and enjoy a wine or a delicious breakfast in your private Rotunda, overlooking beautiful views of the Tamar River/valley, a travellers retreat. Spoil yourself in the new luxurious, spacious, sunny 1 and 2 bedroom/2 ensuite S/C Spa Cottages. Water views from your king bed or in front of your cosy wood fire. Stroll in the rambling gardens, orchard, vines and along river to Restaurants, Seahorses, Platypus House. Explore the Tamar Valley Scenic Wine Route, National Parks, Penguins. Ferry and Airport: within 1 hour. Ideally located between Freycinet and Strahan. B.B.Qs. Visit our website for rates for longer stays.

Paula and Bruce Irvin

Derwent Bridge

Derwent Bridge Chalets and Studios

Self Contained Quality Accommodation
0.5 km E of Lake St Clair Turnoff

info@derwent-bridge.com
15478 Lyell Highway
Derwent Bridge TAS 7140
(03) 6289 1000
www.derwent-bridge.com

AAA Tourism
★★★�½

Double: $155–$245
Single: $155–$245
Children: 11 years and younger $25; 12 years and over $40

 VISA MasterCard Diners Club AMERICAN EXPRESS eftpos

Accommodation for 31
14 Bedrooms: 2K 2KT 7Q 1T 4S
10 in Chalets, 4 in studios. All with kitchen or kitchenette
Bathrooms: 10 ensuite, 3 family share

• Continental breakfast

Edged by a snow gum forest and the Derwent River, 5km (10mins) from the World Heritage listed Cradle Mountain, Lake St Clair National Park – half way between Hobart, Strahan, Launceston and Cradle Mountain, this quality 3½ star property is 'simply magic' in summer or winter. Featuring 6x Chalets (2x spa bath) and 4x Studios, with complimentary port wine, chocolate mints and ground plunger coffee. All with TV, DVD, microwave, free Wi-Fi access, etc.

Check-in from 3–7pm.

John and Louise

Deloraine

Deloraine is a charming classified historic riverside town with a café culture and a bohemian, 'arts and crafts' feel. Locally produced taste sensations such as raspberries, cheeses, honey, salmon, chocolates and a great steak are available for the traveller to feast on. Deloraine is a great base for exploration of the surrounding areas including over 200 limestone caves, trout fishing in streams and lakes, water falls, wilderness walks/hiking, wineries, cycling trails, and wildlife parks. Centrally located only 30 minutes to Devonport and Launceston (Airports and Ferry)

Anne and JD
Bowerbank Mill, Deloraine

Deloraine

Self Contained Cottage and Holiday Retreat *50 km SW of Launceston*

info@bowerbankmill.com.au
4455 Meander Valley Road
Deloraine TAS 7304
(03) 6362 2628
www.bowerbankmill.com.au

Cottage: $248 (includes 3 persons)
Children: $29–$39 (conditions apply)
Extra adult $49. Discounts for extra nights

VISA MasterCard

Accommodation for 6 in retreat and 8 in cottage
Bathrooms: 1 family share in each cottage
Bathroom in each (bath, shower, separate toilet)

• Special breakfast

Two sleeping beauties from different styles and eras but offering the same high standard in décor, hospitality and comfort. Situated in the historic and artistic village Deloraine, they are centrally located in quiet streets and walking distance to shopping, restaurants, galleries and river walks. Gourmet Breakfast of home produce for first morning.

DELORAINE HOLIDAY RETREAT is a self-contained spacious four-bedroom retreat with full kitchen, dining room, separate lounge, laundry and outdoor eating area. The Retreat offers spectacular 180 degree views over pretty Deloraine and the magnificent Mountain Range. (sleeps 8)

DELORAINE 60's COTTAGE with its scenic outlook exudes style and appeal. It is newly renovated and offers the cosiness of a cottage but the spaciousness of a self-contained 3 bedroom house with a dining room, laundry, separate lounge. The new stream-line kitchen is a chef's delight! (sleeps 6).

Anne and JD

Deloraine

Bowerbank Mill

Heritage Accommodation
In town

info@bowerbankmill.com.au
4455 Meander Valley Road
Deloraine TAS 7304
(03) 6362 2628
www.bowerbankmill.com.au

Double: $179–$209
Single: $159–$189
Children: $29–$39
Extra adults $49. Discounts for extended stays

VISA **MasterCard**

Accommodation for 17
8 Bedrooms: 6Q 1D 3S
1: 3 bedroom suite, 1: 2 bedrom suite, Chimney Cottage and Meander Cottage.
Bathrooms: 4 ensuite, 1 guest share

- Full breakfast

In a postcard perfect setting, with the backdrop of the hauntingly beautiful Great Western Tiers Mountains, is Bowerbank Mill B&B. This amazing 160 year old converted Mill offers an exceptional stay in its Cottages and Suites.

Antiques, memorabilia and the Mill's original architectural features of stone walls, gigantic beams, six storey chimney, create a charming repose. Beautiful details include quality linen, fresh flowers, delicious treats and gourmet breakfasts from home produce. See tripadvisor.com for reviews.

Anne and JD

Guest comment: *'Our stay at Bowerbank Mill was brilliant. We stepped back in time, relaxed in front of the fire, played Frank Sinatra and drank port in fantastic style. The bed was very comfortable, the linen fresh. All the attention to detail made our stay delightful. If you want ambiance, if you want genuine hospitality and an experience to remember, stay a Bowerbank Mill.'*

Port Sorell

A sweep of golden beaches, sheltered inlets, a seaside holiday haven and magnificent outlooks – that's Port Sorell. Protected by hills and with Bass Strait to the north, the district enjoys a particularly mild climate with low rainfall and a high average of sunshine.

Tranquilles

Luxury B&B
14 km E of Devonport

reservations@tranquilles.com
9 Gumbowie Drive
Port Sorell TAS 7307
(03) 6428 7555 or 0407 933962
www.tranquilles.com

AAA Tourism
★★★★✦

Double: $145–$310

VISA

Accommodation for 6
3 Bedrooms: 1K 2Q
2 queen bedrooms, 1 king suite
Bathrooms: 3 ensuite
1 shower, 2 double spas

- Full breakfast

A unique blend of elegance and relaxation, with three beautifully appointed bedrooms (two with double spas), log fire, conservatory and enclosed courtyard, set in two acres of sweeping gardens. 15 minutes from Devonport, an hour to Launceston. Port Sorell is renowned for beaches, walking tracks and the Narawntapu National Park. A perfect location to unpack once, and explore the many highlights of the region e.g. Cradle Mountain, Stanley, Tamar Wine Route. The meals we serve include fresh Tasmanian produce. For breakfast you can enjoy our own free range eggs, our homemade bread rolls and jams. We are fully licensed and have an Art Gallery for you to enjoy.

Gary Knowles and Margaret Cody

Hobart

The Lodge on Elizabeth

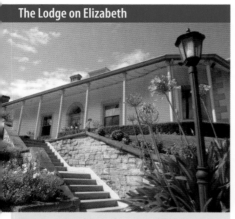

Heritage Listed Guesthouse and S/C Cottage
0.6 km N of Hobart CBD

reservations@thelodge.com.au
249 Elizabeth Street
Hobart TAS 7000
(03) 6231 3830
www.thelodge.com.au

AAA Tourism
★★★★

Double: $135–$210
Extra person $30 per night.

VISA MasterCard AMERICAN EXPRESS eftpos

Accommodation for 31
14 Bedrooms: 11Q 1D 2T
Bathrooms: 14 ensuite

• Continental breakfast

Gracious Heritage Accommodation, C1829 convict built Georgian mansion.

Antique furnishings with ambience and opulence of a Grand manor. All rooms featuring ensuites, with the larger luxurious rooms featuring spas. Guest lounge with complimentary port, coffee or tea. Located a short stroll to Hobart CBD or North Hobart gourmet restaurants. Enjoy a hearty buffet continental breakfast in our dining room each morning.

Our self-contained 'Convict Cottage' package is available for that special occasion or to just relax and unwind. Enjoy sparkling wine, chocolates, fresh fruit and full breakfast provisions. Personalised service and warm hospitality as you would expect.

Jeff and Julie Suffolk

Hobart

Rose Bay is a delightful and quiet suburb overlooking the River Derwent with views to the city of Hobart and Mount Wellington. Enjoy the serenity of this leafy suburb with scenic foreshore walks and the convenience of Hobart city with its historic buildings and Salamanca Market only five minutes away. Stay with friendly locals and enjoy the ease of travel to nearby picturesque Richmond, the vineyards of the Coal River Valley and places further afield such as Port Arthur, The Tasman Peninsula and the Huon Valley.

The King Family
Clovelly House Bed and Breakfast

Hobart – Bellerive

The historic village of Bellerive on Hobart's eastern shore is perhaps best known for its international cricket ground. It also boasts the remnants of the Kangaroo Bluff Fort, enjoyable foreshore walks and cycle paths along the River Derwent as well as several cafés and restaurants. All this and only 6 kilometres from Hobart's CBD.

Jacqueline and David Grant
Bellerive House

Bellerive House

Heritage Listed Luxury B&B
6 km E of Hobart

bb@bellerivehouse.com.au
89–91 Cambridge Road
Bellerive TAS 7018
(03) 6244 7798 or 0404 259 899
www.bellerivehouse.com.au

AAA Tourism
★★★★✦

Double: $195–$265

VISA MasterCard AMERICAN EXPRESS Diners Club eftpos

Accommodation for 6
3 Bedrooms: 3Q
Bathrooms: 3 ensuite

• Full breakfast

Built in 1905 as a gentleman's residence, Bellerive House is a Heritage-listed property that has been beautifully transformed into a luxury Bed and Breakfast. The three guestrooms combine an ensuite bathroom, antique furniture, queen-size beds, fresh white linen and feather duvets. A wood fire in the guest lounge makes it the perfect place to relax after a long day's sightseeing. Guests are offered individually prepared breakfast dishes from an innovative menu that focuses on using the freshest Tasmanian produce.

Jacqueline and David Grant

Guest comment: *'David and Jacqueline weave "magic" for their guests at Bellerive House. We enjoyed our time here enormously and can guarantee no better breakfast in Hobart.' Christine and Ivan Head.*

Hobart – Rose Bay

Clovelly House

B&B and Self Contained Studio
3.5 km NE of Hobart CBD

info@clovellyhouse.com.au
20 Kaoota Road
Rose Bay TAS 7015
(03) 6243 6530 or 0459 243 653
www.clovellyhouse.com.au

Double: $135–$165
Single: $115–$165

Accommodation for 10
5 Bedrooms: 2KT 1Q 2D
Traditional B&B rooms with ensuites
Bathrooms: 5 ensuite
2 rooms have baths, 1 spa, 5 showers

• Full breakfast

Nestled in the leafy suburb of Rose Bay, Clovelly House offers luxurious accommodation situated just 5 minutes from the centre of Hobart and 10 minutes from the airport. A family run bed and breakfast, your hosts, the King Family, look forward to sharing their local knowledge and extending their Tasmanian hospitality to you. Choose from a self-contained studio (kitchenette) or in-house accommodation with ensuites (1 spa). Clovelly House offers the following facilities – guest lounge with log fire; guest conservatory; dining room; spacious gardens; complimentary Wi-Fi access and guest computer with Internet access; continental or full cooked breakfast; off street parking.

The King Family

Launceston

Alice's Cottages and Spa Hideaways

Cottage with Kitchen and Cottages and Spa Hideaways   *0.5 km SW of Launceston*

info@alicescottages.com.au
129 Balfour Street
Launceston TAS 7250
(03) 6334 2231
www.alicescottages.com.au

Double: $170–$200
Single: $130–$170
Children: Can be accommodated in fold out beds
Dinner: All cottages have their own cooking facilities

Accommodation for 12
6 Bedrooms: 6Q
Queen and Double. 6 cottages: Queen.
Bathrooms: 6 ensuite
4 with spas and 2 with showers and baths

• Continental provisions supplied

A wickedly wonderful romantic retreat awaits for lovers in one of Alice's Spa Hideaways tucked away in the historic heart of Launceston is fully self-contained for your privacy and welcomes pets and children by arrangement. Roaring log fires and bubbling spas warm the bodies and stir the passion whilst being cocooned in a different world with all the modern comforts. Launceston's finest restaurants and fabulous Cataract Gorge are a pleasant stroll away, or you may decide to prepare and enjoy dinner in the intimacy of your own fireside. Saviour the complimentary bedtime port, chocolate truffles, brewed coffee and sweet treats which all just tops a tremendous experience.

Rob and Louise Widdowson

Launceston

Launceston, Tamar Valley, the largest regional centre in Tasmania, is the third oldest city in Australia. Visit its many varied attractions and include some of our great food and cool climate wines for a perfect stay.

Carl Gledhill and Helen Hale
The River House

The River House

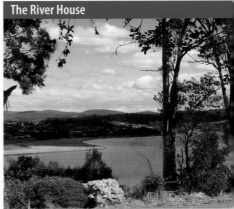

Luxury traditional in-house B&B Suites and S/C Apartment   *14 km N of Launceston*

stay@riverhouselaunceston.com.au
39 Rostella Road
Dilston TAS 7252
0409 701 972 or (03) 6328 1319
www.riverhouselaunceston.com.au

AAA Tourism
★★★★↙

Double: $190–$230
BBQ packs, cheese and meat platters, local wines and beer. Reduced rates from the second night.

VISA MasterCard

Accommodation for 9
4 Bedrooms: 1K 3Q
All in-house with gorgeous ensuites.
Bathrooms: 4 ensuite
Rooms with spas available

• Full breakfast

The River House is in the cool-climate wine growing region of the Tamar Valley, 12 minutes from Launceston CBD. We are a boutique 4.5 star river-front adult retreat, waiting to surround you with country luxury, tranquil privacy and captivating river views. Four elegant ensuited in-house rooms, from deluxe B&B, to a chic self-catering one bedroom apartment. All rooms provide the inclusions you have come to expect with luxury B&B accommodation including gorgeous roomy ensuites with double shower and/or spa bath. Start the day with a sumptuous cooked breakfast, enjoy the open wood fire in winter, dip into the heated pool in summer.

Carl Gledhill and Helen Hale

Queenstown

Penghana

Luxury B&B
Queenstown

info@penghana.com.au
32 Esplanade
Queenstown TAS 7467
(03) 6471 2560
www.penghana.com.au

Double: $160–$175
Single: $150
Dinner: By prior arrangement

Accommodation for 13
6 Bedrooms: 5Q 3S
Bathrooms: 4 ensuite, 2 family share

• Full breakfast

Penghana is an imposing Queen Anne Federation Mansion built for the General Manager of Mt Lyell Mining and Railway Company in 1898. Located high on a knoll above Queenstown the mansion set amongst 2.5 acres of rambling gardens and Tasmanian rainforest has been carefully restored and renovated to offer you the finest accommodation in the region. The four spacious suites all feature queen size beds, ensuites and antique furnishings. The Jukes guest wing comprises two rooms with shared bathroom that is ideal for family groups. All rooms have TV/ DVD with a selection of DVDs available and wireless internet. A guest kitchen is available with tea/coffee facilities and a mini bar.

Maureen and William Kerr

Stanley

There are many things to see and do in Stanley and the surrounding area, such as the Nut Chairlift, Stanley Seaquarium, Stanley Seal Cruises and Highfield Historic Site. Stanley is the perfect place to base yourself for a couple of days to explore close by attractions such as the Tarkine Wilderness, Arthur River Cruises and The Woolnorth Wind farm.

Rose Walker
Rosebank Cottage Collection

Rosebank Cottage Collection

Self Contained Cottages and Apartment
7 km E of Smithton

rose@rosebankcottages.com
46 Brooks Road and 40 Goldie Street
Smithton TAS 7330
(03) 6452 2660 or 0418 505 658
www.rosebankcottages.com

Double: $170–$180
Extra person $35 per night

VISA MasterCard

Accommodation for 15
4 Bedrooms: 4Q 7S
2 two-bedroom cottages, 1 apartment, 1 studio
spa cottage
Bathrooms: 4 ensuite

• Continental provisions supplied

Visit beautiful North-West of Tasmania to stay
at Rosebank Cottages. Choose from two luxury
cottages in a large country garden just ten minutes
from Stanley or stay in the heart of Smithton at
a modern character cottage or the brand new
modern Townhouse. Cottages feature cosy wood

heating, some double spas, queen beds, barbeque
facilities, flat screen television and DVDs.

Complementary breakfast provisions including
Hot Crusty Bread. Rosebank Cottages are central
to the many surrounding attractions including the
quaint fishing village of Stanley where you will find
excellent cafés, restaurants craft and gift shops.

Rose Walker

Swansea

Schouten House

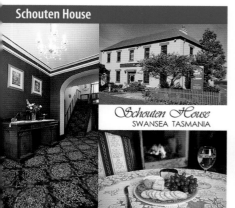

Heritage Listed B&B
0.5 km E of Swansea

enquiries@schoutenhouse.com
1 Waterloo Road
Swansea TAS 7190
(03) 6257 8564
www.schoutenhouse.com.au

Double: $175–$210
Single: $150–$180
Children: Welcome, additional charge applies
Dinner: Authentic Indian curries, by arrangement

Accommodation for 12
6 Bedrooms: 5Q 1T
Antique/Four Poster Queen Beds
Bathrooms: 6 ensuite

- Full breakfast

Schouten House is c1844 Georgian Bed and Breakfast Accommodation. A landmark Heritage Listed property in the seaside town of Swansea, overlooking Great Oyster Bay and Freycinet Peninsula on the East Coast of Tasmania. Your hosts, Cameron and Jodie, welcome you to this gracious home. The house offers six suites, all with queen sized beds and private ensuites.

Guests can enjoy two lounge areas, one with open fire, and a dining room where a generous full cooked breakfast is served.

Enquire about meals by arrangement.

Cameron and Jodie Finlayson

Swansea – Freycinet Coast

The historic township of Swansea encompasses a charming collection of heritage homes. Visit world class restaurants or shuck oysters and sip local wines on sandy, unspoiled beaches. Wineglass Bay in the beautiful Freycinet National Park with white sandy beaches and pure clear turquoise waters is perfect for sea kayaking, swimming and scuba diving.

Cameron and Jodie Finlayson
Schouten House

Recommended Accommodation

Arthur River

Arthur River Holiday Units
2 Gardiner Street, Arthur River
(03) 6457 1288
arreflections@bigpond.com
arthurriver.com.au

Beauty Point

✦ **Pomona Spa Cottages**
77 Flinders Street, Beauty Point
(03) 6383 4073
relax@pomonaspacottages.com.au
pomonaspacottages.com.au

Bicheno

Greenlawn Cottages
16999 Tasman Highway, Bicheno
(03) 6375 1114
greenlawncottages@bigpond.com
greenlawncottages.com

Burnie

Glen Osborne House
9 Aileen Crescent, Burnie
(03) 6431 9866
info@glenosbornehouse.com.au
glenosbornehouse.com.au

The Duck House
26–28 Queen Street, Burnie
(03) 6431 1712
lynne.ferencz@bigpond.com
duckhousecottage.com.au

Coles Bay

Sheoaks on Freycinet
47 Oyster Bay Court, Coles Bay
(03) 6257 0049
sheoaks.bandb@bigpond.com
sheoaks.com

Deloraine

✦ **Bowerbank Mill**
4455 Meander Valley Road, Deloraine
(03) 6362 2628
info@bowerbankmill.com.au
bowerbankmill.com.au

✦ **Deloraine Accommodation**
4455 Meander Valley Road, Deloraine
(03) 6362 2628
info@bowerbankmill.com.au
bowerbankmill.com.au

Derwent Bridge

✦ **Derwent Bridge Chalets and Studios**
15478 Lyell Highway, Derwent Bridge
(03) 6289 1000
info@derwent-bridge.com
derwent-bridge.com

Devonport – Port Sorell

✦ **Tranquilles**
9 Gumbowie Drive, Port Sorell
(03) 6428 7555
reservations@tranquilles.com
tranquilles.com

Hobart

✦ **The Lodge on Elizabeth**
249 Elizabeth Street, Hobart
(03) 6231 3830
reservations@thelodge.com.au
thelodge.com.au

Hobart – Bellerive

✦ **Bellerive House**
89–91 Cambridge Road, Bellerive
(03) 6244 7798
bb@bellerivehouse.com.au
bellerivehouse.com.au

Hobart – Crabtree

Crabtree House
130 Crabtree Rd, Crabtree
0429 626 640
bookings@crabtreehouse.com.au
crabtreehouse.com.au

Hobart – Richmond

Laurel Cottage
9 Wellington Street, Richmond
(03) 6260 2397
jmwilt@southernphone.com.au
laurelcottages.com.au

Hobart – Rose Bay

✦ **Clovelly House**
20 Kaoota Road, Rose Bay
(03) 6243 6530
info@clovellyhouse.com.au
clovellyhouse.com.au

Launceston

✦ **Alice's Cottages and Spa Hideaways**
129 Balfour Street, Launceston
(02) 4575 5250
info@alicescottages.com.au
alicescottages.com.au

Edenholme Grange
14 St Andrews Street, Launceston
(03) 6334 6666
sales@edenholme.com
edenholme.com

Launceston – Ross

Ross Bakery Inn
15 Church Street, Ross
(03) 6381 5246
enquiries@rossbakery.com.au
rossbakery.com.au

Launceston – Bridport

Platypus Park Country Retreat
20 Ada Street, Bridport
(03) 6356 1873
platypuspark@tassie.net.au
platypuspark.com.au

Launceston – Dilston

✦ **The River House**
39 Rostella Road, Dilston
0409 701 972
stay@riverhouselaunceston.com.au
riverhouselaunceston.com.au

Launceston – Jackeys Marsh

Forest Walks Lodge
669 Jackeys Marsh Road, Jackeys Marsh
(03) 6369 5150
forestwalkslodge@me.com
forestwalkslodge.com

Launceston – Lilydale

Plovers Ridge Country Retreat
132 Lalla Road, Lilydale
(03) 6395 1102
ploversridge@gmail.com
ploversridge.com.au

Launceston – Longford

The Racecourse Inn
114 Marlborough Street, Longford
(03) 6391 2352
innbaker@vision.net.au
racecourseinn.com

Launceston – Windermere

Windermere Cabins
302 Windermere Road, Windermere
(03) 6328 1666
admin@windermerecabins.com.au
windermerecabins.com.au

Queenstown

✦ **Penghana**
32 The Esplanade, Queenstown
(02) 6775 1277
info@penghana.com.au
penghana.com.au

Mt Lyell Anchorage
17 Cutten Street, Queenstown
(03) 6471 1900
stay@mtlyellanchorage.com
mtlyellanchorage.com

Penghana B&B
32 Esplanade, Queenstown
(03) 6471 2560
info@penghana.com.au
penghana.com.au

Richmond

✦ **Mulberry Cottage B&B**
23a Franklin Street, Richmond
(07) 4154 4003
miriam23@bigpond.net.au
mulberrycottage.com.au

Smithton – Stanley

✦ **Rosebank Cottage Collection**
32 Smith Street, Smithton
(03) 6452 2660
rose@rosebankcottages.com
rosebankcottages.com

Swansea

✦ **Schouten House**
1 Waterloo Road, Swansea
(03) 6257 8564
enquiries@schoutenhouse.com
schoutenhouse.com.au

Wynyard

Alexandria B&B
1 Table Cape Road, Wynyard
(03) 6442 4411
manager@stayalexandria.com.au
stayalexandria.com.au

Victoria

Melbourne was the capital city of Australia from federation in 1901 until 1927 and many Melbournian's still see Melbourne as Australia's number one city. Well known for its shopping, and lanes with boutique wine bars and wonderful restaurants Melbourne is also home to great sporting venues, galleries and theatres. Many of Victoria's iconic regions are close to the city, including The Dandenong Ranges, Mornington Peninsula wine region, Gippsland, The Great Ocean Road and The Grampians.

Mildura

Ouyen

175

Swan Hill

Big
Desert

Charlton

Echuca

Horsham

Bendigo

Heathcote 160

Wartook

Mount Avoca

Seymou

Halls Gap 159

149

Castlemaine

Pomonal

Smeaton

Daylesford

Grampians

156

Cavendish 158

Ballarat

Dunkeld

Hamilton

Geelong

167

Melbour

157

Torquay

163

Otway
Range

147

Allansford

162

159

Aireys
Inlet

Warrnambool

Lorne

173

Princetown

172

148

Apollo Bay

SOUTHERN OCEAN

Bass

Straight

© 2012 Carto Tech Services

Canberra

Rutherglen
174
Wodonga
Wangaratta
Cudgewa 152
...parton 176 Corryong
151 150 Beechworth
Benalla Bright
Baddaginnie

High
Country
Omeo

Marysville 164
177
Narbethong
...nong
Bairnsdale Sarsfield
149
Gippsland Lindernow Lakes Entrance
Nilma North South Wilderness Coast
157
West Gippsland Sale

Warratah North

Wilsons
Promontory

Tasman

Sea

© 2012 Carto Tech Services

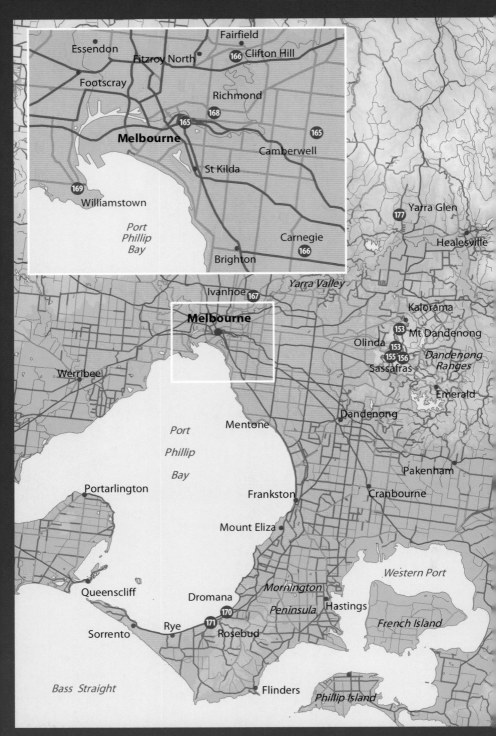

Aireys Inlet – Anglesea – Great Ocean Road

Overboard Seaside Cottages

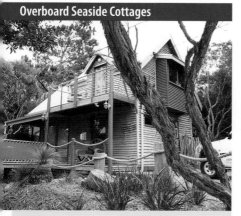

Luxury Self Contained Boutique Cottages
Aireys Inlet

stay@overboardcottages.com.au
Barton Court
Aireys Inlet VIC 3231
0417 341 367 or (03) 5289 7424
www.overboardcottages.com.au

Double: $195–$275
$35 per extra person per night. Minimum booking
two nights.

Accommodation for 7
3 Bedrooms: 2Q 1D 1S
Aireys Overboard: 1 Queen, 1 trilogy. Anglesea
Overboard: 1 Queen.
Bathrooms: 2 ensuite

• Accommodation only

Relax by the sea in one of our 2 stylish cottages.
One rustic, nautical and enchanting, the other,
modern chic and sexy, both private, unique and
indulgent. Both cottages are fully self-contained
with log fires, spas and just 300m to beach. Ideal
for couples but Aireys Overboard, our 'flagship'
cottage, does have a second 'bunk room'. Anglesea
Overboard, with one large bedroom sleeps 2 and is
pet friendly, (by arrangement). Designed and set up
especially for a memorable and indulgent weekend
or midweek retreat, honeymoon, special occasion
or just a luxurious getaway for longer periods.

Bohdan Philippa

Aireys Inlet

Situated on the famous Great
Ocean Road just a 90 minute, no
traffic light drive, from Melbourne.
Aireys' is a town for all seasons
without the hustle and bustle of
busier coastal towns. Marked by
the historic 'Split Point Lighthouse'
and with its new marine park and
the Great Otway National Park
there's a myriad of things to do,
from bird watching and beach
walking to surfing and fishing and
everything in between.

Arcady Homestead

B&B and Homestay and Farmstay
10 km N of Apollo Bay

arcadyhomestead@fastmail.fm
925 Barham River Road
Apollo Bay VIC 3233
(03) 5237 6493
www.bbbook.com.au/arcadyhomestead.html

AAA Tourism
★★★

Double: $120–$130
Single: $75–$85
Children: 50%
Dinner: B/A

Accommodation for 9
4 Bedrooms: 2Q 1D 3S
Bathrooms: 1 guest share

• Special breakfast

Set on sixty scenic acres, part farmland and part natural bush. Share breakfast with our Kookaburras, explore the Otway Forest trails, tree-fern and glow worm gullies and waterfalls, see some of the tallest trees in the world or visit Port Campbell National Park, which embraces Australia's most spectacular coastline. The Otway Ranges are a bushwalkers paradise. Bird-watchers? We have identified around thirty species in the garden alone! Many visit our kitchen window! Our home has wood fires and spring water. Our beds are cosy, our meals country-style, and our atmosphere relaxed and friendly.

Marcia and Ross Dawson

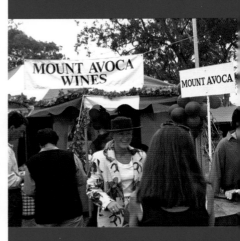

Avoca

Pyrenees – ssshhh . . .Victoria's best kept secret, the Pyrenees provides a relaxing getaway two hours from Melbourne with numerous wineries, a rich gold mining heritage and natural beauty. With Sovereign Hill, the Grampians, Castlemaine and Daylesford 45 minutes away, The Pyrenees is perfect to enjoy a day or a week of quality time with friends or family.

Lisa and Matthew Berry
eco-Luxe @ Mount Avoca

Avoca

eco-Luxe @ Mount Avoca

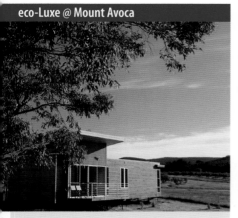

Homestead and Luxury Eco Lodges
8 km SW of Avoca

stay@eco-luxe.com.au
Moates Lane
Avoca VIC 3467
(03) 5465 3282 or 1300 797 363
www.eco-luxe.com.au

AAA Tourism
★★★★

Double: $260–$390
Children: $40
Extra adult $50, Homestead min 2 nights

Accommodation for 23
2 Bedrooms: 3K 2Q 4T 1S
1 King 1 Bunk per lodge, 2 King, 2 Queen 4 singles
in Homestead
Bathrooms: 1 ensuite, 1 guest share, 3 private
5, 1 per Lodge with spa, 2 in Homestead

• Continental breakfast

Nestled amongst the picturesque vineyard and
olive grove at Mount Avoca, eco-luxe @ mount
avoca are three newly completed lodges that
blend a balance of luxury with an eco sensibility.
Designed for couples with tranquillity in mind, each
self-contained lodge has an additional small bunk
room that sleeps two. Or, if your group is large, you
can stay in the original Barry family home (sleeps
up to eleven) situated on the highest point of the
property. Relax in two large living areas in comfort
and style and enjoy the magnificent backdrop of
Mt Avoca and the Pyrenees Range.

Lisa and Matthew Barry

Bairnsdale

Tara House

B&B
1.2 km NW of town centre

enquiries@tarahouse.com.au
37 Day Street
Bairnsdale VIC 3875
(03) 5153 2253
www.tarahouse.com.au

AAA Tourism
★★★★

Double: $120–$170
Single: $120–$130
Children: fold out bed in parents room, extra $60
Dinner by arrangement

Accommodation for 6
3 Bedrooms: 2KT 1Q
traditionally decorated
Bathrooms: 3 ensuite
one ensuite with claw foot bath

• Full breakfast

Enjoy a relaxing and rejuvenating time forgetting
your worries. Three double rooms in renovated
Victorian homestead on 2.3rds acre with secluded
garden for sitting and contemplating.

Sit on the verandah and enjoy a wine or read
a book. Full cooked breakfast and dinner by
arrangement Each room has TV/DVD, heating and
ceiling fans and electric blankets.

Guest lounge with fire, TV/cable and DVDs. Come
smell the roses. Two hours from snow, 30 minutes
to ocean, 15 minutes to lake. Lots of bicycle tracks
and bush walking.

Phillip

Beechworth

Freeman on Ford

5 Star Luxury B&B
35 km E of Wangaratta

info@freemanonford.com.au
97 Ford Street
Beechworth VIC 3747
(03) 5728 2371 or (03) 5728 2055
www.freemanonford.com.au

AAA Tourism
★★★★★

$275–$395

Accommodation for 12
6 Bedrooms: 2K 3Q 1T
Bathrooms: 6 ensuite

• Full breakfast

Currently Freeman on Ford is the only 5 star and Eco Star Accredited B&B in Beechworth with environmentally friendly policies and luxury appointments. It stands alone in quality and furnishings. The hosts have paid much attention to detail with Victorian décor to match its historical significance. Built in 1866, a former bank it was once the second Brigidine Convent in Australia.

Freeman on Ford features an a private inground swimming pool and spa in landscaped gardens. There is onsite covered secure parking. The B&B is situated in the main street, near the Post Office, Historical Precinct, restaurants and quality shops. If you enjoy being pampered this the place for you.

Award winning Freeman on Ford has received national awards for 'excellence' and has outstanding recommendations on Trip Advisor.

Heidi Freeman and Jim Didolis

Beechworth

Beechworth continues to attract attention because of its quality mix of old world charm from its well-presented main streets and its high standard of culinary, accommodation and shopping experiences.

Birgit Shonafinger
Freeman on Ford

Beechworth

Foxgloves

Luxury B&B and Separate Suite
0.3 km N of PO

foxgloves1@westnet.com.au
21 Loch Street
Beechworth VIC 3747
(03) 5728 1224
www.foxgloves.com.au

Double: $185–$230
Single: $160–$230
Twin share $205.00

Accommodation for 9
4 Bedrooms: 4Q 1S
2 Queen, 1 Queen/twin, 1 Queen private suite upstairs
Bathrooms: 4 ensuite

• Full breakfast

Welcome to our tastefully restored Victorian cottage (c 1897) in the heart of historic Beechworth. We offer country hospitality in quietly elegant surrounds with all the delights of contemporary comforts. Our personal attention includes traditional cooked breakfast, homemade afternoon teas and complimentary port/sherry in our cosy lounge or on the plant-filled patio. All fully serviced bedrooms have heating/cooling, electric underblankets and quality linen. The guest lounge/dining room has TV/DVD, log fire in winter and cooling in summer for your comfort.

John and Sheila Rademan

Bright – Mt. Buffalo

The Buckland – Studio Retreat

Luxury Self Contained Chalets
12 km SW of Bright

stay@thebuckland.com.au
116 McCormacks Lane
Buckland Valley VIC 3740
0419 133 318
www.thebuckland.com.au

AAA Tourism
★★★★✓

Double: $300–$360
Children: only small babies travelling with own port-a-cot or similar

Accommodation for 10
5 Bedrooms: 1K
5 Luxury one bedroom Chalets
Bathrooms: 5 ensuite
Bathrooms with double rainwater shower or shower and bath

• Full breakfast

The Buckland – Studio Retreat features luxury accommodation tucked away in the picturesque Buckland Valley close to Bright, Mt. Buffalo and the wineries of the Victorian High Country. Each of the 5 individual studios has an open plan lounge/kitchen area, king size bedroom and funky bathroom with double rainwater showers and private bush outlook. The décor is contemporary and stylish and creature comforts are well catered for: goosedown doonas, espresso coffee machine, seductive mood lighting, plush robes and 'Occitane' aromatherapy products.

Sabine Helsper and Eddie Dufrenne

Easy access

 Children welcome

 Pets welcome

 Facilities for horses

 Couples or adults

 Outstanding garden

 Special location

 Winery nearby

 Restaurant nearby

 Eco friendly

 Onsite activities

 Swimming pool

 Tennis court

 Function facilities

 Wedding facilities

 Internet access

 Cable or satellite TV

 No smoking

Cudgewa – Corryong

Elmstead Cottages

Cottage with Kitchen
12 km SW of Corryong

manager@elmsteadcottages.com.au
61 Ashstead Park Lane
Cudgewa VIC 3705
(02) 6077 4324
www.elmsteadcottages.com.au

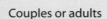 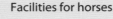 

AAA Tourism
★★★

Double: $100
Single: $100
Extra person $10

Accommodation for 8
3 Bedrooms: 2Q 4S
1 in Elmstead Cottage, 2 in Arthur's Cottage. Cottages are not near each other.
Bathrooms: 2 private

• Breakfast by arrangement

Elmstead Cottage: A one room cottage set amongst magnificent elm trees on a working farm, cute cosy and affordable.

Arthur's Cottage: An eco-friendly, historic two bedroom cottage (circa 1887). Secluded location on the banks of the Cudgewa Creek where platypus and trout abound. Fully equipped kitchen.

Marja and Tony Jarvis

Dandenong Ranges – Mount Dandenong

Observatory Cottages

Luxury Self Contained Cottages
2 km N of Mt Dandenong

enquiries@observatorycottages.com.au
8 Observatory Road
Mt Dandenong VIC 3767
(03) 9751 2436
www.observatorycottages.com.au

Double: $590
Single: $205
Children: $35
Weekend Minimum 2 night stay Fri/Sat or Sat/Sun Cost $590.

VISA (MasterCard) eftpos

Accommodation for 16
8 Bedrooms: 8Q 3S
Family 4b/r home and 4 couples cottages
Bathrooms: 2 family share, 4 private
All Single cottages have full Bathrooms with shower/sink/toilet double spa's are seperate from the main Bathroom. Family four bedroom home has two full bathrooms, spa's have overhead showers.

• Accommodation only

With stunning views of Port Phillip Bay and the surrounding Suburbs at Observatory Cottages, you feel as though you can touch the stars. Always looking for ways to improve your stay yet keeping with the feel of yesteryear we take great pride and pleasure from seeing our guests return over and over again.

'Where your peace and privacy is respected, your senses soothed and lasting memories created…'

Leeanne and Daniel Gazzola

Dandenong Ranges – Olinda

Candlelight Mountain Retreats

Self-contained stylish accommodation
0.3 km N of Olinda

stay@candlelightmountainretreats.com.au
7–9 Monash Avenue
Olinda Village VIC 3788
(03) 9751 2464
www.candlelightmountainretreats.com.au

Double: $295–$400
Single: $295–$400
Children: 0–3 yrs $15, 4–11 yrs $25p/n
Extra couple $100 p/n. A generous Continental hamper and free range eggs are included.
Dinner: Platters available.

VISA (MasterCard) DC AMEX eftpos

Accommodation for 13
7 Bedrooms
One 3 b/r cottage, Two 1 b/r cottages, Two Studio apts
Bathrooms: 5 ensuite

• Special breakfast

A collection of stylish classic cottages and studios scattered throughout the Dandenong Ranges, with fresh modern interiors and all the lifestyle luxuries you have come to expect. The cottages offer you deep spa baths, open wood fires, luxurious beds, coffee machines and breakfast provisions. Two cottages and one studio near Olinda village in ferny garden settings. One cottage with open fire and spa in a mountain bush setting. The new Blackwood studio in Sassafras Village created by interior designer provides hi-tech music, luscious king bed, deep spa and gas log fire. The beautiful little Folly studio offers a king bed and is an affordable option for short stays.

Peta and Laurie Rolls

Dandenong Ranges

Kalorama, Olinda and Sassafras are picturesque villages set in the beautiful Dandenong Ranges where you can wander through walking trails and enjoy William Ricketts Sanctuary, Healesville Sanctuary, Puffing Billy, and Yarra Valley Wineries. And all less than an hour from Melbourne.

Peta Rolls, Candlelight Cottages Retreat
Image Andrew Chapman

Dandenong Ranges – Olinda

Folly Farm Rural Retreat

Luxury B&B Cottage and Farmstay
Olinda

enquiries@follyfarm.com.au
192 Falls Road
Olinda VIC 3788
(03) 9751 2544
www.follyfarm.com.au

AAA Tourism
★★★★✦

Double: $240–$270
Two night minimum stay on weekends Fri/Sat or Sat/Sun
Dinner: Wonderful restaurants in Olinda and Mt. Dandenong Villages

VISA MasterCard

Accommodation for 2
1 Bedroom: 1Q
,Four poster bed.
Bathrooms: 1 ensuite
Ensuite with Double spa bath If required a separate Access Bathroom built to Australian Standards is available.

• Full breakfast provisions

Folly Farm was established to escape the bustle of city life in 1912, today the Hill Station property still makes the perfect getaway. Situated on private ten acres, the open plan cottage sits above the blueberry fields with views to Mt. Dandenong and our Edna Walling gardens. After a day exploring the mountain, relax in a bubbling double spa, dream in front of the fire and sleep peacefully in the romantic, queen sized four poster bed. Say hello to our alpaca. Exclusively for one couple…casual elegance… simple pleasures…

Belinda and Robert Rooth

Dandenong Ranges – Olinda

Gracehill Accommodation

Luxury B&B and Cottage
1.5 km E of Olinda

stay@gracehill.com.au
28 Chalet Road
Olinda VIC 3788
(03) 9751 1019
www.gracehill.com.au

AAA Tourism
★★★★⌐

Double: $160–$380
Children: 0–3 years $10, 4–12 years $25p/n
Extra Couple $70 p/n

VISA MasterCard eftpos

Accommodation for 6
3 Bedrooms
Bathrooms: 3 private

• Full breakfast provisions

The Gracehill property was established in 1970 and has been running as a family business for the last 13 years offering unique accommodation for couples and families with children in a safe and tranquil environment in Olinda the heart of the Dandenong Ranges.

Gracehill has three unique accommodation settings situated on six acres of established gardens and bushland with magnificent views over the Dandenong Ranges.

Gracehill offers all the modern comforts with luxurious linen and beds, double spa baths, coffee machines, wood fire and cosy gas log fires.

Betty Heinrich

Dandenong Ranges – Sassafras

Clarendon Cottages

Luxury Self Contained Cottages
1 km S of Sassafras

pam@clarendoncottages.com.au
11 Clarkmont Road
Sassafras VIC 3787
(03) 9755 3288 or 0438 529 220
www.clarendoncottages.com.au

Double: $240–$295
Single: $240–$295
Children: Extra bedroom $40 per person

VISA MasterCard eftpos

Accommodation for 6
3 Bedrooms: 3Q
1 Two bedroom cottage and 1 One bedroom cottage
Bathrooms: 2 ensuite
Both cottages have double spas.

• Full breakfast provisions are provided for the first two mornings of your stay

Clarendon's boutique guest accommodation consists of two charming cottages in a secluded, peaceful and romantic setting. Two acres of English country gardens and meadow nestle amongst a huge variety of beautiful century old trees. The cottages are within easy walking distance of Sassafras Village and Sherbrooke Forest. Two cosy 1 & 2 bedroom cottages each with its own individual charm are located separately on the two acre property. Gas log fires, spas, fully equipped kitchens, air conditioning and private decks are just some of the many features. LCD TV, DVD and CD in both cottages. Full breakfast provisions are provided for the first two mornings stay.

Pam and Ian Hankey

Dandenong Ranges – Sassafras

Luxury B&B
40 km SE of Melbourne GPO

risik@bigpond.net.au
2 Ellis Avenue
Sassafras VIC 3787
0414 699 818
www.sassafrasromanticretreat.com

Double: $245–$255
Single: $245–$255

Accommodation for 2
1 Bedroom: 1D
Super comfortable double bed, with luxury
Sheridan bedding
Bathrooms: 1 ensuite

• Full breakfast provisions

Luxury Self Contained cottage in Sassafras, set
on 5 acres of immaculate gardens is designed
specifically to cater for couples looking for tranquil
comfortable and private surroundings for their
getaway. The cottage includes a light filled lounge,
dining area for two overlooking the French private
gardens, a fully equipped luxury kitchenette, tasteful
well appointment bedroom and en suite bathroom
and walk in robe. The cottage has its own private
entrance through ornate wrought iron gates, with
private parking and spacious private decking. Your
cottage is set on 5 acres of immaculate gardens,
and a short stroll to sassafras village. Although our
home is also on the property, it is far enough to give
you privacy, but close enough to cater to anything
you may require during your stay with us.

Renee

Daylesford – Smeaton

Tuki Retreat

Stone Cottages
20 km NW of Daylesford

info@tuki.com.au
60 Stoney Rises Road
Smeaton VIC 3364
(03) 5345 6233
www.tukiretreat.com.au

AAA Tourism
★★★★

Double: $200–$280

Accommodation for 18
9 Bedrooms: 2K 6Q 2S
1 and 3 bedroom cottages
Bathrooms: 7 ensuite, 1 private
Bathrooms with spas

• Full breakfast provisions

A unique rural retreat, offering tranquillity, 70km
views. Tuki Retreat is situated on historic 'Stoney
Rises', a traditional sheep grazing property. The
cottages offer a wonderful view of the Loddon-
Campaspe Valley and are surrounded by dry
stonewalls, landscaped gardens and established
trees. There is a private lake in front of the stone
cottages. All have open fireplaces, cathedral
ceilings and a veranda to watch the sunset on.
The master bedroom has a Queen size bed, with
electric blankets and linen and towels are all
provided. There is a double sofa bed in the lounge
room for additional guests.

Robert and Jan Jones

Geelong

Ardara House

B&B
0.5 km S of Geelong

ardara@bigpond.net.au
4 Aberdeen Street
Geelong VIC 3218
(03) 5229 6024
www.ardarahouse.com.au

Double: $130–$160
Single: $80–$110
Children: $20

Accommodation for 9
5 Bedrooms: 1Q 2D 2S
Bathrooms: 4 ensuite, 1 guest share

- Continental breakfast

Built in the Edwardian period (circa 1900) as a large family home, Ardara House offers the grace and homeliness of a bygone era. Guests can enjoy the relaxed and friendly atmosphere of fine Irish hospitality close to the heart of Geelong and on the beginning of the Great Ocean Road. Four spacious guest rooms feature luxurious beds and old world décor but with all the modern comforts and conveniences. Many of Geelong's finest restaurants, entertainment facilities as well as the shopping centre are only a stroll away.

Owen and Maureen Sharkey

Gippsland – Nilma North

Springbank B&B

Luxury B&B and Cottage
8 km E of Warragul

bookings@springbankbnb.com.au
240 Williamsons Road
Nilma North VIC 3821
(03) 5627 8060 or 0437 350 243
www.springbankbnb.com.au

AAA Tourism
★★★★↙

Double: $165–$175
Single: $125–$135
Cottage: Double $140–$165 Single from $115
Dinner: Dinner, massage by arrangement.

Accommodation for 6
3 Bedrooms: 3Q
2 in House, 1 in Cottage
Bathrooms: 3 ensuite
Includes claw foot bath

- Full breakfast

Springbank, a delightful 1890's Victorian Homestead offers luxury and boutique accommodation for a maximum of 3 couples set on 20 acres close to Warragul. Quiet, private and restful with extensive cottage gardens provides the perfect setting. Gourmet breakfasts, BBQ and outdoor cooking facilities, warm and friendly atmosphere. Open fires in the winter and reverse cycle airconditioning. Superb dining by arrangement.

Kaye and Chris Greene

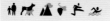

South Mokanger Farm Cottages

Farmstay, Self Contained Cottages
10 km E of Cavendish

info@smfarmcottages.com.au
728 Mokanger Road
Cavendish VIC 3314
(03) 5574 2398
www.smfarmcottages.com.au

Double: $180–$295
Children: Extra persons from $40
Stoneycroft: Sleeps 6 (plus 8 in bunkhouse). Mountain
Duck sleeps 8.

VISA MasterCard

Accommodation for 22

• Accommodation only

Welcome to South Mokanger Farm Cottages,
two beautiful self contained cottages on our pet
friendly farmstay at the southern edge of the
Grampians National Park. You are invited to watch
seasonal farm activities on our beautiful 4,500 acre
property with wide open spaces. Stoneycroft for
6 guests in two bedrooms, 1 Queen Bedroom,
1 with 2 bunks plus Shearers quarters if your
party is larger. Mountain Duck for 8 guests in
four bedrooms. Each cottage has full kitchens,
dishwasher, laundry, BBQ facilities with outdoor
furniture, wood fires (wood supplied), linen and
towels, electric blankets, fans and reverse cycle air
conditioning in Mountain Duck Cottage, electric
heating, television, CD, ipod dock and DVD player
with selection of DVDs.

Jill and Rob Gardner

Grampians – Halls Gap

Halls Gap is the heart of
Victoria's most spectacular
wilderness region. The Grampians
National Park.

Hidden within this view with the
dramatic horizon rising a half
kilometre above and where the
mornings are slow and lazy, you
will find specialty shops, adventure
guides, restaurants and cafés.

Don Calvert
Mountain Grand Boutique Hotel

Grampians – Halls Gap

Mountain Grand Hotel

Guest House
Halls Gap

don@hallsgap.net
Main Road Town Centre
Halls Gap VIC 3381
(03) 5356 4232 or 1800 192 110
www.mountaingrand.com

AAA Tourism
★★★✦

Double: $166–$333
Options from B and B to Indulgence Getaways with all meals

Accommodation for 30
10 Bedrooms: 3K 7Q
Most rooms can become twin/triple
Bathrooms: 10 ensuite
Spa Rooms available

• Full breakfast

This is one of country Victoria's last remaining traditional guesthouses, now refurbished into a very comfortable small hotel in the heart of Halls Gap. With its balconies and unique facade, the Mountain Grand has been well upgraded and is a place to call home after a big day exploring the Grampians. There are ten warm, cosy guest bedrooms with fresh décor and ensuite bathrooms – some with spas. No pretentious luxury, just homely country comfort with wood fire lounge rooms, big screen TVs and Club Bar. Full breakfasts and 3 course dinners are included in the tariff. 'The Balconies' Restaurant and 'Café Grand' are so popular, especially on Saturday nights with mellow 30s to 70s live music.

Kay and Don Calvert

Great Ocean Road – Warrnambool

Merton Manor Exclusive B&B

Luxury Heritage Listed B&B and Separate Suites   *1 km N of Warrnambool PO*

merton@ansonic.com.au
62 Ardlie Street
Warrnambool VIC 3280
(03) 5562 0720 or 0417 314 364
members.datafast.net.au/merton

AAA Tourism
★★★★✦

Double: $160–$180
Single: $130–$150
Extra person $35

Accommodation for 12
6 Bedrooms: 1K 5Q 1T
Private Bedrooms
Bathrooms: 6 ensuite
6 double spas

• Full breakfast

Merton Manor is a traditional B&B with mews style accommodation set within an historic Victorian villa. It features antiques, open fires, billiard and music rooms and grand dining room and is located mid way between Adelaide and Melbourne. All suites feature private entrances, climate control heating and air conditioning, private lounge rooms and ensuites with double spas. Merton Manor is situated within walking distance to the cultural attractions and restaurants of Warrnambool. The 12 Apostles, whale viewing, Tower Hill State Game Reserve and the Maritime Museum are all close by. AAAT 4.5 stars. Beach and Botanical Gardens nearby.

Pamela and Ivan Beechey

Heathcote

Once a gold mining region, Heathcote's new gold is Shiraz. Quickly becoming the Shiraz capital of Australia, winemakers and locals alike are keen to talk about the Cambrian soil and the big, beautiful red wines that come from grapes grown here.

Leslye Thies
Emeu Inn B&B

Emeu Inn Bed and Breakfast

Luxury B&B and Self Contained Cottage with mini kitchen   *45 km SE of Bendigo*

info@emeuinn.com.au
187 High Street
Heathcote VIC 3523
(03) 5433 2668
www.emeuinn.com.au

Double: $200–$270
Single: $150–$220
Children: $40 per person per night
Cottage $540/couple: two nights. Extra person $40/nt

Accommodation for 19
7 Bedrooms: 7Q
Cottage sleeps four in queen-size bed and double sofa bed.
Bathrooms: 7 ensuite
Deluxe cottage with double spa and separate shower

• Continental breakfast

Indulge yourself in luxury at the Award-winning Emeu Inn. Relax in the spacious suites with queen beds, private ensuites with spas and all the extras gourmet travellers expect. Homemade fruitcake, port and nibbles await you.

Contemporary restaurant serving modern regional food on-site, where local produce and wines are standard fare. Enjoy some golf, Lake Eppalock, the forests, the shops or the wine! Part of the Goldfields, Heathcote's an easy weekend getaway!

Fred and Leslye Thies

Heathcote – Goldfields

Luxury Self Contained Rural Retreat
120 km NE of Melbourne

bookings@hutonthehill.com
720 Dairy Flat Road
Heathcote VIC 3523
(03) 5433 2329 or 0417 315 880
www.hutonthehill.com.au

Double: $250–$300
You're the only guests in the property. Gift
Vouchers available. Wine tours available.

VISA MasterCard

Accommodation for 4
2 Bedrooms: 1K 1Q
Choice of King or Queen or both
Bathrooms: 1 ensuite
Spa bath. Separate shower and separate toilet

• Full breakfast provisions

Heathcote's only luxury self contained cottage on
a sheep farm, offering cosy wood fire in winter and
solar heated swimspa in summer. You're the ONLY
guest, not another house in sight for miles on the
horizon. Totally private, utterly unique, serenely
beautiful. A gem in the Goldfields offering you
secluded quiet. Enjoy stunning views at Hut on the
Hill from every room even the spabath. See eagles
soar and kangaroos graze. Close to many wineries.
Deluxe packages available. Check website for
more details.

David and Astrid

Lakes Entrance

Self Contained Cottages
2 km SW of PO

info@kalimnawoods.com.au
30 Kalimna Jetty Road
Lakes Entrance VIC 3909
(03) 5155 1957 or 0421 499 373
www.kalimnawoods.com.au

Double: $99–$225
Children: $15 per night
Extra adults $20 per night. Breakfast hampers available
for additional charge

VISA MasterCard eftpos

Accommodation for 27
13 Bedrooms: 8Q 11S
3 x 1 bedroom cottages 5 x 2 bedroom cottages
Bathrooms: 8 ensuite

• Breakfast by arrangement

Romantic Spa and Woodfire Cottages set in a
wonderful rainforest and garden setting on the
edge of Australia's largest inland lake system.
Bellbirds, King parrots and Lorikeets are just some
of the abundant birdlife. At night watch the Sugar
Gliders and Possums feed. Explore the lakes, see
the Koalas at Raymond Island or visit the nearby
Buchan Caves. Only 300 metres to the Kalimna
Jetty and 2 km to the town centre. Kalimna Woods
cottages are self catering. Breakfast hampers
are available.

Carole and Arthur

La Perouse Lorne

Luxury and Guest House
140 km SW of Melbourne

email@laperouselorne.com.au
26A William Street
Lorne VIC 3232
0418 534 422
www.laperouselorne.com.au

Double: $225–$375
Breakfast served Parisian style in our kitchen
Dinner by arrangement excluding Saturday evenings

Accommodation for 8
4 Bedrooms: 2KT 2Q
4 suites: All rooms have flat screen TV/DVDs with
Apple TV, tea and coffee making, mini fridge, fireplace,
verandah, ensuite, ocean views
Bathrooms: 4 ensuite
Double bath

• Special breakfast, free Wi-Fi

La Perouse is an informal, relaxed small boutique
hotel with a very friendly approach. The style is
French inspired which feels more like you are
staying with old friends and having breakfast in their
kitchen rather than an inpersonal hotel restaurant.

The house is full of prints, books, furniture and
memorabilia that remind you of France. La Perouse
provides luxury accommodation and is the ideal
spot to relax after walking along the surf coast walk.
The location is in Lorne an area of outstanding
natural beauty, near the 12 Apostles and on the
doorstep of the Otway rainforest. You can check
rates and availability and/or book online. We look
forward to welcoming you to La Perouse.

Laurel and Sue

Guest Comment: *The whole impression we got from
our stay is summed up in two words: charm
and attention.*

Lorne – Aireys Inlet

Lorneview B&B

B&B and Separate Suite
14 km E of Lorne

lorneview@bigpond.com
677 Great Ocean Road
Eastern View VIC 3231
(03) 5289 6430
www.lorneview.com.au

 AAA Tourism
★★★★

Double: $150–$180
Single: $140–$170

VISA (MasterCard)

Accommodation for 4
2 Bedrooms: 2Q
Bathrooms: 2 ensuite

• Continental breakfast

Lorneview has two spacious guest rooms, separate from main house, one with beach and bush views and the other overlooking the bush. Each room has QS bed, ensuite, TV, CD/DVD player, heating, air conditioning, refrigerator, iron, ironing board, tea and coffee facilities. Delicious breakfast of fresh fruit, homemade muesli, muffins and croissants is served in the separate breakfast room or on the front balcony of the main house overlooking the beach. Dinner is unavailable, but there are many excellent restaurants nearby. Barbecue and Games Room provided. Enjoy walks along the beach and go to sleep listening to the waves.

Nola and Kevin Symes

Lorne – Otway Ranges – Birregurra

Elliminook Homestead

Luxury B&B, Heritage Homested, and
Apartment   *38 km N of Lorne*

enquiries@elliminook.com.au
585 Warncoort Birregurra Road
Birregurra VIC 3242
(03) 5236 2080
www.elliminook.com.au

 AAA Tourism
★★★★♪

Double: $160–$240
Country continental breakfast

VISA (MasterCard) (AMERICAN EXPRESS)

Accommodation for 10
5 Bedrooms: 4Q 1D
Antique iron and brass beds. Additional single bed available in three bedrooms
Bathrooms: 4 ensuite

• Continental breakfast

Award winning Elliminook c1865 is a beautifully restored and decorated National Trust classified brick homestead providing a great relaxing getaway. Guests enjoy the historic garden, croquet, tennis court, open fires, liquor service, fresh flowers in your room, and welcoming hospitality. From Elliminook you can explore the Great Ocean Road, Twelve Apostles, Shipwreck Coast, Otway Fly Tree Top Walk, waterfalls and forest of the scenic Otway Ranges. Experience nearby Brae Restaurant and Royal Mail Hotel, Birregurra. Stay in an ensuite bedroom or our 2 bedroom self contained south wing with private entrance. For a unique accommodation experience be our welcome guest.

Jill and Peter Falkiner

Marysville

Spectacular views, sparkling streams, fresh mountain air and beautiful no matter what time of the year. Only 95 Km north east of Melbourne travelling through the beautiful Yarra Valley Wine regions and magnificent tall timbers of the Black Spur.

Sharen and Terry Donovan
Darymples

Dalrymples Guest Cottages

Quality B&B Self Contained Cottages
Marysville

info@dalrymples.com.au
18 Falls Road
Marysville VIC 3779
(03) 5963 3416 or 0419 103 834
www.dalrymples.com.au

Double: $210–$260
$245 per couple per night – 2 nights min weekend, mid week specials
Dinner: Ask us about meals

VISA | MasterCard | eftpos

Accommodation for 12
6 Bedrooms: 6K
2 x two-bedroom, 2 x one-bedroom cottages
Bathrooms: 2 ensuite
Spa baths, all bedrooms have full ensuite

• Full breakfast provisions

Luxury self-contained B&B freeform architect designed cottages. An intriguing blend of Japanese and Australian design and décor using bold colours, clean simple lines, beautiful fabrics, luxury king size beds, Jotul real wood fires, two person free standing spa baths and home cooked breakfast hampers give these cottages a special point of difference. In the heart of Marysville and nestled on over an acre of beautiful private gardens. Beautifully furnished with attention to detail we love to give. Only 95km north east of Melbourne traveling through the beautiful Yarra Valley wine region and magnificent tall timbers of the Black Spur.

Sharen and Terry Donovan

Melbourne

Apartment 401

CBD Apartment
Melbourne

email@apartment401.com.au
258 Flinders Lane
Melbourne VIC 3000
(03) 954751007 or 0412 068 855
www.apartment401.com.au

Double: $250–$350
Single: $250

Accommodation for 2
1 Bedroom: 1Q
Bathrooms: 1 ensuite
Bath with shower above.

• Accommodation only

Melbourne CBD apartment. Perfect for art lovers, foodies and shoppers, this stunning 1 bedroom apartment in the historic Majorca House building is located right in the heart of Melbourne's bustling, bohemian arts precinct and laneway area, just one block from the Yarra river. The spacious, light filled lounge-dining room looks down on Degraves Street, famous for its coffee bars and eateries. The bedroom has a queen sized bed and a tiny, Parisian style Juliet balcony. There is a fully equipped, stylish kitchen and a large tiled bathroom complete with bathtub.

Gayle Lamb

Melbourne – Camberwell

Springfields

B&B
9 km E of Melbourne

robynjordan@hotmail.com.au
4 Springfield Avenue
Camberwell VIC 3124
(03) 9809 1681 or 0434 353 750
www.bbbook.com.au/springfields.html

AAA Tourism
★★★✦

Double: $150
Single: $110
Children: Children welcome – contact us for prices.

Accommodation for 4
2 Bedrooms: 1KT 1T
Bathrooms: 1 guest share, 1 private
Guest bathroom is located between the two guest bedrooms.

• Full breakfast

'Springfields' is our attractive and spacious family home in a quiet avenue in one of Melbourne's finest suburbs. Guests comment on the quietness, and the fresh fruit salad at breakfast! Guests can enjoy the peace and privacy of their own lounge – or join us for a friendly chat. Public transport is nearby. Children are most welcome. Make our home your home when you next visit Melbourne. Free Wi-Fi connection.

Robyn and Phillip Jordan

Melbourne – Carnegie

Josephine's B&B

B&B and Homestay
12 km SE of Melbourne CBD

josephinesbb@optusnet.com.au
40 Rosanna Street
Carnegie VIC 3163
(03) 9569 9386 or 0412 458 736
www.josephinesbb.com.au

Double: $130
Single: $100
Children: Children are welcome.
Family: 2 adults and 2 children $150
Cooked breakfast available – small charge. Special dietary needs catered for.

VISA MasterCard altpos

Accommodation for 5
3 Bedrooms: 1Q 1T 1S
Bathrooms: 2 private

• Continental breakfast

Situated in a pleasant garden setting, Josephine's Traditional Hosted Bed and Breakfast is located in Carnegie, in the south eastern suburbs of Melbourne. Serviced by rail, tram and bus, and just off the Monash Freeway, we are just 12km from the central City area. We have three air-conditioned guest rooms, queen, twin and single. A cot and high chair are available. We are perfectly suited for couples, families and holiday makers as well as business travellers with a comfortable guest lounge with tea/coffee, cable TV, DVD and VCR. Enjoy a cooked or continental breakfast in the modern family room or alfresco in the garden.

Jo and Ed Biggs

Melbourne – Clifton Hill

ParkSideStay

Elegant parkside apartment
5 km NE of Melbourne GPO

wendy.teltscher@bigpond.com
109 Walker Street
Clifton Hill VIC 3068
0418 389 074 or (03) 9486 2121
www.parksidestay.com.au

Double: $165
Single: $155
Children: $50

Accommodation for 3
1 Bedroom: 1K 1D
Plus 1 double sofa bed
Bathrooms: 1 ensuite

• Accommodation only

ParkSideStay is an elegantly self-contained apartment that comprises a king size bedroom, kitchenette, large bathroom, living and dining areas that open onto a delightful, sunny northerly private enclosed courtyard garden. ParkSideStay provides a stylish home with excellent space, comfort, parklands outside the property and excellent car parking. ParkSideStay is surrounded by parklands and public transport gives easy access to Melbourne's attractions: MCG, Tennis Centre, Docklands, Federation Square, Concert Hall/, St Kilda Beach and Flemington Race Course. Easy and direct access from Melbourne's International and Domestic Airport: also close to Melbourne's major tertiary institutions and hospitals.

Wendy

Melbourne – Ivanhoe

Magnolia Road Apartment B&B

B&B and Apartment with Kitchen and Apartment B&B *9 km NE of Melbourne CBD*

joy@magnoliaroad.net.au
12 Magnolia Road
Ivanhoe VIC 3079
(03) 9499 6443 or 0414 748 335
www.magnoliaroad.net.au

Double: $180

VISA MasterCard

Accommodation for 2
1 Bedroom: 1Q
Bathrooms: 1 ensuite

• Full breakfast provisions

A modern and stylish one bedroom, self contained apartment in leafy Magnolia Road, Ivanhoe, close to the Ivanhoe shopping strip where great cafés and restaurants are closely located. Features private bedroom with queen size bed, overhead fan, overhead adjustable reading lights, air conditioning, electric blanket and a selection of pillows with crisp white sheets. Separate lounge with plasma TV and Optus channels, surround sound, DVD player with CD, radio and IPod dock. Lounge, kitchen and bedroom have polished timber floors, secluded rear courtyard with outdoor setting that has an old English feel and the tranquillity of magnolia's.

Joy Spain

Melbourne – Keilor

Overnewton Cottage

Self Contained Cottage
21 km N of Melbourne CBD

info@overnewtoncastle.com.au
51 Overnewton Road
Keilor VIC 3036
(03) 9331 6367 or 0417 537 779
www.overnewtoncastle.com.au

Double: $200–$325
Extra Adult $25 per night.
Dinner by arrangement

VISA MasterCard Diners Club AMERICAN EXPRESS eftpos

Accommodation for 6
2 Bedrooms: 1K 2D
1 x King Bed Downtairs 2 x Double Sofa Beds Upstairs
Bathrooms: 2 private

• Full breakfast

Beautifully Designed, Double Storey Cottage for a relaxing night away.

2 Bedroom, shared accommodation for up to 6 guests.

– 1 queen bed – 2 double sofa beds – Fully Equipped Kitchen – Laundry Facilities – Private Balcony overlooking the Maribyrnong Valley.

– Private BBQ Facilities in the comfort of your own retreat – Check-in: 2pm – Check-out: 10am.

Overnewton Castle

 Easy access

 Children welcome

 Pets welcome

 Facilities for horses

 Couples or adults

 Outstanding garden

 Special location

 Winery nearby

 Restaurant nearby

 Eco friendly

 Onsite activities

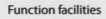 Swimming pool

 Tennis court

 Function facilities

 Wedding facilities

 Internet access

Cable or satellite TV

No smoking

Melbourne – Richmond

Rotherwood

Luxury Self Contained Apartment
1.5 km E of Melbourne Central

rotherwoodbb@bigpond.com
13 Rotherwood Street
Richmond VIC 3121
0431 552 928 or (03) 9428 6758
www.rotherwoodbnb.com

Double: $155–$185
Single: $145–$175
$880 per week. S/C Apt includes breakfast

VISA MasterCard

Accommodation for 3
1 Bedroom: 1Q
Separate Queen sized bedroom plus fold out bed in sitting room.
Bathrooms: 1 private

• Full breakfast provisions

'On the Hill' in Richmond, 'Rotherwood' is at the heart of Melbourne's attractions.

Walking distance of the MCG, Royal Botanic Gardens, National Tennis Centre, shops and cafés. Opposite Epworth Hospital. 5 minute tram ride to City. Easy access to National Gallery, Concert Hall, Crown Casino, and Southbank. Private entrance to Victorian era apartment. Large sitting room leading to terraced garden. Bedroom, private bathroom, and separate dining room with cooking facilities. Special Breakfast provided. Extra fold-out bed.

Airport transport available. TV and Wireless Internet. Short or long term stay.

Flossie Sturzaker

Captains Retreat B&B, Apartments and Cottages

Luxury B&B
Williamstown

admin@captainsretreat.com.au
2 Ferguson Street
Williamstown VIC 3016
(03) 9397 0352 or 0438 358 823
www.captainsretreat.com.au

AAA Tourism
★★★★✩

Double: $140–$260
Single: $130–$245
Delicious full cooked breakfasts. Elegant small functions B/A.

Accommodation for 13
6 Bedrooms: 6Q 1S
Bathrooms: 6 ensuite
2 with double spa, 1 with single spa

• Special breakfast

The award winning 'Captains Retreat' boutique accommodation, just 15 minutes from Melbour's CBD, offers 3 delightful self-contained apartments and 3 cottages as well as the beautiful, refurbished Victorian B&B home in a fabulous location – just one door from the water and walking distance to restaurants, shops and yacht clubs. This charming old home with its somewhat checkered history, (including having been a convent and a brothel!), boasts beautiful décor, very comfortable beds, ensuite bathrooms (3 with spas) digital televisions, free Wi-Fi, gas fireplaces in most bedrooms and one suite even has its own private lounge room! There is also a large guest lounge with fire and french doors to a large north-facing balcony overlooking a walled garden. It's a big house! Winners: RACV People's choice award for Guest Satisfaction, Hobson's Bay Tourism Award, Hobson's Bay Hospitality Award, Hobsons Bay Food Safety Award.

Melissa Meek-Jacobs

Melbourne – Williamstown

Enjoy this unique historical peninsula with glorious parks, yacht clubs, spectacular city views, great walks, beach, galleries, museums, theatres, restaurants only 15 minutes from Melbourne.

Melissa Meek
Captains Retreat B&B

Stand alone Lakeside Villas
6 km N of Dromana

info@lakesidevillas.com.au
25 Harrisons Road
Dromana VIC 3936
(03) 5987 3275
www.lakesidevillas.com.au

AAA Tourism
★★★★✦

Double: $290–$400
Extra guest from $50 pn
Dinner: Stillwater restaurant open daily

Accommodation for 12
3 Bedrooms: 3K
3 villas each with King bedroom plus sofabed
Bathrooms: 3 ensuite
Ensuite bathrooms have twin access and double spa

• Full breakfast provisions

Perched overlooking the vineyards lake these contemporary villas are an oasis of tranquillity. Quality appointments throughout ensure your stay is an experience of relaxation. The open plan living and kitchen, which spills out onto your own private balcony over the lake, creates a feeling of spaciousness and warmth. Amenities include king size beds, double spa baths, open fire and your own laundry. Because Lakeside Villas are family owned and operated we offer the personal services of a small establishment without compromising on the necessary luxuries.

Mornington Peninsula – Rosebud – Hastings

Nazaaray Beach House, Coastal Cottage and Winery

Self Contained Beach House and Coastal Cottage *In Rosebud*

nazaaray@gmail.com
40 Murray Anderson Road
Rosebud VIC 3929
0407 391 991 or 0416 143 439
www.nazaaray.com.au

Double: $160–$200
Children: or adults $50 per person per night
Beach Hse $900–1645/wk dual occupancy 1 boom.
Coastal Cottage 950–1300/wk

VISA MasterCard eftpos

Accommodation for 8
3 Bedrooms: 1K 1KT 3S
Beach House for 6 adults and 2 children. Coastal
Cottage for 2–6 persons
Bathrooms: 1 ensuite, 1 family share
Beach House includes spa room

• Accommodation only

Enjoy the restful atmosphere of a Mornington
Peninsula coastal town just 350 metres to a
swimming beach and to the shops. Located in a
quiet street surrounded by holiday houses this
renovated three bedroom house is a pleasant
surprise. Nazaaray Coastal Cottage is a self-contained
accommodation just a little way back from the
large grassed foreshore area which overlooks the
Westernport Marina. It features open plan living with
polished floor boards. Lounge Room with an open
fire place. The Dining room overlooks outdoor patio
and barbecue area with a mature garden.

Param and Nirmal Ghumman

Easy access

Children welcome

Pets welcome

Facilities for horses

Couples or adults

Outstanding garden

Special location

Winery nearby

Restaurant nearby

Eco friendly

Onsite activities

Swimming pool

Tennis court

Function facilities

Wedding facilities

Internet access

Cable or satellite TV

No smoking

Princetown – Great Ocean Road

Limestone Rock Formations off the south-west coast of Victoria Twelve Apostles are the focal point for travellers on the Great Ocean Road. Majestic rock stacks standing in the southern Ocean, buffeted by huge seas and winds. Not only do they offer wonderful photography but are the start of a journey. Along a unique coastline as the Twelve Apostles are not alone as they lead visitors on to Lochard Gorge, shipwrecks, and more coastal discoveries.

Lynne Boxshall
Arabella Country House

Macka's Farm

Self Contained Lodges and Farmhouse
10 km NW of Princetown

holidays@mackasfarm.com.au
2310 Princetown Road
Princetown VIC 3269
(03) 5598 8261
www.mackasfarm.com.au

AAA Tourism
★★★

Double: $185–$320
Weekly: $1030–$1960

  VISA MasterCard

Accommodation for 35
2x1 and 1x3 bedroom lodges and a
4 bedroom farmhouse

• Accommodation only

Macka's Farm is a working dairy farm with quality, self-contained accommodation with fun activities for kids a scenic 2½ hour drive from Melbourne. Log fires, verandahs with ocean views. Enjoy amazing sunsets and spectacular starry skies around the camp fire. The fabulous 12 Apostles only 6km down the road – Macka's Farm is the perfect choice for that getaway for the whole family or the romantic couple.

Observe the milking and get farm fresh milk and eggs.

Leave with unforgettable memories.

Trudi and Carey

Princetown – Twelve Apostles

Arabella Country House

Luxury B&B and Homestay
6 km E of Princetown

arabellacountryhse@bigpond.com
7219 Great Ocean Road
Princetown VIC 3269
(03) 5598 8169
www.arabellacountryhouse.com.au

Double: $170–$175
Single: $90
Children: $25 under 6 years old
Dinner: $40.00 for 3 courses set menu, please advise
dietary requiremt

VISA MasterCard eftpos

Accommodation for 10
4 Bedrooms: 3Q 1D 2S
Bathrooms: 4 ensuite

- Full breakfast

A Homestead with amazing views, Large Gardens,
Country Hospitality so close to the 12 Apostles
you can see them. Hosts Lynne and Neil invite
you to enjoy their spacious ensuite rooms, which
have Flat Screen TV and sweeping views of the
Southern Ocean. Located in the private guest wing
with Dining Lounge room, assorted drinks always
available. Afternoon Tea is served on arrival. Your
Sumptuous Australian Country Breakfast consists
of a Comprehensive Buffet plus Menu Selections
cooked to order.

Central to Otway Rainforest and Waterfalls, world
renowned Coastline, Scenic Helicopter Flights,
Gourmet Trail, Great Ocean Walk.

Lynne and Neil Boxshall

Rutherglen

Rutherglen is known throughout
Australia as a place with great soul
and home to some of the world's
greatest wines. Rutherglen is also
a place of country lanes, idyllic
pastoral scenes, ancient River Red
Gums and lush vineyards stretching
off to the horizon.

Rutherglen

Cuddle Doon Cottages B&B

Heritage Listed Miner's Cottages
0.7 km SW of Rutherglen

cuddledoon@westnet.com.au
11–13 Hunter Street
Rutherglen VIC 3685
(02) 6032 7107 or 0407 646 569
www.cuddledoon.com.au

AAA Tourism
★★★★

Double: $140–$165
Extra person $40 All prices include GST.

Accommodation for 10
5 Bedrooms: 4Q 1D
Antique Brass Bed, marble wash stand
Bathrooms: 3 guest share
2 corner spa baths, 3 showers 3 toilets

• Full breakfast provisions

Step back in time as you enter our 100 year old Miner's Cottages, beautifully refurbished with some antique furniture, top quality beds and linen. These are very romantic cottages with corner spas, cosy log burning fires, cottage gardens. Breakfast provisions provided. Enjoy fabulous Rutherglen Wines and Gourmet Wine Truffle chocolates.

John can take you on a luxury ride in the 1982 Classic Cadillac to some of our 25 Wineries, maybe have lunch looking over the vines. Rutherglen has several Fine Dining Restaurants, plus many other dining opportunities. Pet friendly and .cyclist friendly.

John and Beryl Lloyd

Swan Hill – Lake Boga

Lake Boga – the jewel in the heart of the Mallee 16km south of Swan Hill, offers unique recreational experiences of Bird watching, a natural wonderland for Fishing, Horticulture, the Arts, all Water Sports, Observatory/Planetarium, Catalina Flying Boat Museum, Fine foods &Wineries, the Pioneer Settlement. Come, stay a while and see our breathtaking sunsets.

Tricia and Bruce Pollard
Burrabliss B&B

Swan Hill – Lake Boga

Burrabliss Farms B&B

B&B, Guesthouse, Cottage and Garden Suite
15 km S of Swan Hill

info@burrabliss.com.au
169 Lakeside Drive
Lake Boga VIC 3584
(03) 5037 2527 or 0427 346 942
www.burrabliss.com.au

AAA Tourism
★★★★

Double: $150–$180
Single: $135–$150
Children: $15
Country style breakfast included. B/F provisions in Villa
Dinner: $50

Accommodation for 19
5 Bedrooms: 1K 2KT 2Q
1 suite, 1 villa, 2 traditional, 1 two storey house
Bathrooms: 3 ensuite, 2 family share, 1 guest share

• Special breakfast

Pamper yourself. After all you deserve it. Luxury accommodation at its best: whether for your honeymoon, a romantic weekend or simply need to get away. Burrabliss is the idyllic location for a nature lover with 6 acres natural habitat. Suite Bliss offers stylish garden setting accommodation with king bed, spa, private lounge. Villa Bliss offers self-contained. Traditional B&B also available. 'Lakeside Retreat' is a two story holiday home ideal for a family or a small group holidaying together. Enjoy yabbying, strolling through our country garden, exploring nearby wetlands with 68 bird species noted in the area. Undercover BBQ facilities and car parking. Complimentary chocolates and wine.

Tricia and Bruce Pollard

Wangaratta

Wangaratta is famous for world class wines, gourmet food, spectacular golf courses and links to Ned Kelly. The Murray to Mountains rail trail and the Great Alpine Road both start at Wangaratta.

Margaret Blackshaw
The Pelican B&B

Wangaratta

The Pelican

B&B and Farmstay
6 km E of Wangaratta

pelicanblackshaw@hotmail.com
606 Oxley Flats Road
Wangaratta VIC 3678
(03) 5727 3240 or 0413 082 758
www.bbbook.com.au/thepelican.html

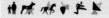

Double: $130–$150
Single: $60–$80
Children: $40
$40 extra person in double room
Dinner: $40 per person by arrangement

Accommodation for 6
3 Bedrooms: 1Q 1T 2S
Bathrooms: 1 guest share, 1 private

• Full breakfast

Our historic homestead, just 6km from Wangaratta, offers secluded accommodation in a private upstairs wing. The main bedroom has a balcony overlooking a lagoon fringed with giant redgums. Birdlife abounds including ducks, waterfowl and pelicans. A twin room overlooks the garden where peacocks roam. A cooked breakfast is served in the elegant dining room and features home grown produce with freshly brewed tea and coffee. We offer our guests a unique experience – walk our 400 acre beef cattle and horse property edged by Maloneys Creek with its sandy beaches, go 'trackside' to watch the harness horses at work, help with the feeding of the mares and foals or simply relax in the garden, on the patio or by an open fire in the lounge.

Margaret and Bernie Blackshaw

Yarra Valley

The Yarra Valley is a world renowned wine region of unspoilt pristine beauty, where the water and the air are clean and crisp, the views spectacular and the friendly ambience invites you to just rest for a while.

Yarra Valley Tourism
Image Andrew Chapman

Yarra Valley – Narbethong

Woodlands Rainforest Retreat

Luxury Rainforest Bungalows
1.5 km SW of Narbethong

relax@woodlandscottages.com.au
137 Manby Road
Narbethong VIC 3778
(03) 5963 7150
www.woodlandscottages.com.au

AAA Tourism
★★★★✓

Double: $325–$410
Dinner: Gourmet Catering on request
(advance booking)

Accommodation for 8
4 Bedrooms: 4K
Bathrooms: 4 ensuite
Therapeutic quality spas in each bungalow

• Full breakfast provisions

At Woodlands Rainforest Retreat we provide a rare combination of genuine privacy, indulgent luxury and nature based experience – just for couples. The four superbly designed split level self contained bungalows are situated on 16 hectares of native forest, overlooking the fern gullies of Hermitage Creek near Narbethong in the Yarra Valley, 80km NE of Melbourne, 30 minute from the ski trails of Lake Mountain and the boating and fishing waterways of Lake Eildon. Each bungalow has huge windows that open on to a wallpaper of living forest with large brick open fireplaces, central heating and cooling, fully equipped kitchens, king beds, sunken spa, full surround iPod enabled sound systems with DVD and CD players.

Gary and Vicky King

Yarra Valley – Yarra Glen

The Gatehouse at Villa Raedward

Luxury Apartment
7 km S of Yarra Glen

info@villaraedward.com.au
26 Melba Highway
Yering VIC 3770
(03) 9739 0822 or 0425 730 624
www.villaraedward.com.au

AAA Tourism
★★★★✓

Double: $230–$345

Accommodation for 4
2 Bedrooms: 1Q
Large, comfortable bedroom
Bathrooms: 2 private
2 person spa, large shower in marble bathroom

• Full breakfast provisions

Formal Italian style complements a lovely Yarra Valley setting in these two architect-designed fully self contained units with undercover parking and private entrance and patio looking out over the Valley. Each self-contained suite has a large bedroom with a queen bed, marble bathroom with large shower and two person spa overlooking a relaxing, private courtyard garden, fully equipped kitchen, reverse cycle air conditioning, DVD/TV. A complimentary bottle of Yarra Valley Bubbly, slippers, bathrobes, port, fresh coffee, sumptuous 3 course breakfast provisions, DVD library are all included. The large semi-formal and extensively planted garden is a wonderful feature of this delightful property.

John and Sandra Annison

Recommended Accommodation

Aireys Inlet

Aireys Overboard Seaside Cottage
1 Barton Court, Aireys Inlet
0417 341 367
stay@overboardcottages.com.au
overboardcottages.com.au

Alexandra

Waverley Guesthouse.
56 Nihil Street, Alexandra
(03) 5772 1146
waverley@ycs.com.au
waverleyguesthouse.com.au

Anglesea

Anglesea Overboard Seaside Cottage
39C O'Donohue Road, Anglesea
0417 341 367
stay@overboardcottages.com.au
overboardcottages.com.au

Ꮼ **Overboard Cottages**
39C O'Donohues Road, Anglesea
(03) 5289 7424
stay@overboardcottages.com.au
overboardcottages.com.au

Apollo Bay

Ꮼ **Arcady Homestead**
925 Barham River Road, Apollo Bay
(03) 5237 6493
arcadyhomestead@fastmail.fm

Apollo Bay B&B
4 Murray St, Apollo Bay
(03) 5237 7153
info@apollobaybandb.com.au
apollobaybandb.com.au

Nelson's Perch B&B
54 Nelson Street, Apollo Bay
0400 590 841
nelsonsperch@optusnet.com.au
nelsonsperch.com

Avoca

Ꮼ **eco-Luxe @ Mount Avoca**
Moates Lane, Avoca
(02) 6230 2046
Leanne@MountAvoca.com
eco-luxe.com.au

Bairnsdale

Ꮼ **Tara House**
37 Day Street, Bairnsdale
(08) 8976 7009
enquiries@tarahouse.com.au
tarahouse.com.au

Bambra

Countrywide Cottages
1205 Deans Marsh Road, Bambra
(03) 5288 7399
stay@countrywidecottages.com.au
countrywidecottages.com.au

Barongarook

Wanawong Retreat
950 Colac-Lavers Hill Road, Barongarook
(03) 5233 8215
info@wanawong.com.au
wanawong.com.au

Beaufort

Mureybet
232 Old Shirley Rd, Beaufort
0400 526 386
w.t.barwick@gmail.com
mureybet.com.au

Beechworth

Ꮼ **Foxgloves**
21 Loch Street, Beechworth
(03) 5728 1224
foxgloves1@westnet.com.au
foxgloves.com.au

Ꮼ **Freeman on Ford**
97 Ford Street, Beechworth
(03) 9421 0248
freemanford@westnet.com.au
freemanonford.com

Bena

Benaway Cottages
810 Anderson Inlet Road, Bena
(03) 5657 2268
barbara@benaway.com.au
benaway.com.au

Benalla – Baddaginnie

Ꮼ **Glen Falloch Farm Cottage**
252 Warrenbayne West Road, Baddaginnie
0403 340 660
stay@glen-falloch.com.au
www, glen-falloch.com.au

Bright

Ellie Mae's B&B
30 Coronation Avenue, Bright
0418 174 131
libby@elliemaes.com.au
elliemaes.com.au

Bright – Myrtleford

Ꮼ **The Buckland – Studio Retreat**
PO Box 533, Bright
(08) 9293 2518
stay@thebuckland.com.au
thebuckland.com.au

Buninyong

Brim Brim Gardens
901 Lal Lal Street, Buninyong
(03) 5341 3096
stephen.falconer@ctemail.net.au
brimbrimgardens.com.au

Carisbrook

Lochinver Farm
245 Baringhup Road, Carisbrook
(03) 5464 2356
info@lochinverfarm.com.au
lochinverfarm.com.au

Colac

Lislea House
61 Corangamite Street, Colac
(03) 5235 8357
info@lisleahouse.com.au

Croydon North

Baringa Villa
15 Baringa Road, Croydon North
0419 344 769
info@baringavilla.com.au
baringavilla.com.au

Cudgewa – Corryong

Ꮼ **Elmstead Cottages**
61 Ashstead Park Lane, Cudgewa
(02) 6077 4324
manager@elmsteadcottages.com.au
elmsteadcottages.com.au

Dandenong Ranges – Olinda

Ꮼ **Folly Farm Rural Retreat**
13 Cards Lane, Olinda
(03) 9751 2544
follyfarm@iprimus.com.au
follyfarm.com.au

Ꮼ **Candlelight Cottages Collection**
7–9 Monash Avenue, Olinda Village
(02) 4751 9270
stay@candlelightcottages.com.au
candlelightcottages.com.au

Dandenong Ranges – Sassafras

Ꮼ **Clarendon Cottages**
11 Clarkmont Road, Sassafras
(03) 9755 3288
pam@clarendoncottages.com.au
clarendoncottages.com.au

Ꮼ **Sassafras Romantic Retreat**
2 Ellis Avenue, Sassafras
0414 699 818
risik@bigpond.net.au
sassafrasromanticretreat.com

Dandenongs

Ꮼ **Gracehill Accommodation**
28 Chalet Road, Olinda
(03) 9751 1019
stay@gracehill.com.au
gracehill.com.au

Daylesford

Balconies Daylesford
35 Perrins Street, Daylesford
(03) 5348 1322
info@balconiesdaylesford.com
balconiesdaylesford.com.au

Daylesford – Smeaton

Ꮼ **Tuki Retreat**
60 Stoney Rises Road, Smeaton
(03) 5345 6233
info@tuki.com.au
tuki.com.au

Don Valley

Hill 'n' Dale Farm Cottages
1284 Don Rd, Don Valley
0488 162 642
admin@hillndalefarmcottages.com.au
hillndalefarmcottages.com.au

Emerald

Fernglade on Menzies
11 Caroline Crescent, Emerald
(03) 5968 2228
info@ferngladeonmenzies.com.au
ferngladeonmenzies.com.au

Fish Creek

Fish Creek B&B
65 Old Waratah Road, Fish Creek
(03) 5683 2599
rest@fishcreekbeds.com.au
fishcreekbeds.com.au

Recommended Accommodation

Forrest

Forrest River Valley B&B
135 Yaugher Road, Forrest
(03) 5236 6322
stay@forrestrivervalley.com.au
forrestrivervalley.com.au

Geelong

✃ **Ardara House**
4 Aberdeen Street, Geelong
(03) 5229 6024
ardara@bigpond.net.au
ardarahouse.com.au

Gelantipy Via Buchan

Karoonda Park
Gelantipy Road, Gelantipy via Buchan
(03) 5155 0220
enquiries@karoondapark.com
karoondapark.com

Gippsland – Nilma North

✃ **Springbank B&B**
240 Williamsons Road, Nilma North
(03) 5763 2262
bookings@springbankbnb.com.au
springbankbnb.com.au

Glenaire

Glenaire Cottages
3440 Great Ocean Rd, Glenaire
(03) 5237 9237
glenairepark@bigpond.com
glenairecottages.com

Glenlyon

Armley Park
1065 Daylesford – Malmsbury Road, Glenlyon
03 53 48 7979
bookings@dayget.com.au
armleypark.com.au

Grampians

Ardwick Homestead
1340 Wimmera Highway, Apsley
(03) 5586 5255
ardwick@me.com
ardwick.com.au

Grampians – Brimpaen

The Grelco Run
Schmidt Road, Brimpaen
(03) 5383 9221
grelco@skymesh.com.au
grampiansgrelcorun.com

Grampians – Cavendish

✃ **South Mokanger Farm Cottages**
728 Mokanger Road, Cavendish
(03) 5574 2398
info@smfcottages.com.au
smfarmcottages.com.au

Grampians – Glenthmpson

Cherrymount Retreat
60 Cherrymount Lane, Glenthompson
(03) 5577 4396
cherrymount@aussiebroadband.com.au

Grampians – Halls Gap

✃ **Mountain Grand Hotel**
Main Road Town Centre, Halls Gap
(03) 9397 0352
don@hallsgap.net
mountaingrand.com

Grampians – Pomonal

Welch's on Wildflower
39 Wildflower Drive, Pomonal
(03) 5356 6311
welchs@netconnect.com.au
welchsonwildflower.com.au

Grampians – Willaura

Hawksview at Mafeking
234 Masons Rd, Willaura
(03) 5354 6244
j.osullivan@uq.edu.au
mafekingfarm.com.au

Harcourt North

MillDuck Strawbale B&B
143 Ford Road, Harcourt North
(03) 5439 6451
bandb@millduck.com.au
millduck.com.au

Heathcote

✃ **Emeu Inn B&B**
187 High Street, Heathcote
(03) 5433 2668
info@emeuinn.com.au
emeuinn.com.au

✃ **Hut on the Hill**
720 Dairy Flat Road, Heathcote
(03) 5433 2329
bookings@hutonthehill.com
hutonthehill.com.au

Hepburn Springs

65 Main
65 Main St, Hepburn Springs
0439 379 450
info@65main.com
65main.com

Hurstbridge

Pine Ridge B&B
40 Schaeffer Road, Hurstbridge
(03) 9719 7677
pineridgebnb@gmail.com
pineridgebnb.com

Jamieson

Emerald Park Holiday Farm
266 Licola Road, Jamieson
(03) 5777 0569
marion.mcrostie2@bigpond.com
emeraldpark-jamieson.com

Johanna

Johanna River Farm and Cottages
420 Blue Johanna Road, Johanna
(03) 5237 4219
johannafarm@bigpond.com
johanna.com.au

Johanna Seaside Cottages
395 Red Road Johanna, Johanna
(03) 5237 4242
info@johannaseaside.com.au
johannaseaside.com.au

Kalorama

Bonza View B&B
26 Bonza View, Kalorama
(03) 9728 8887
bonza@bonzaview.com.au
bonzaview.com.au

Lakes Entrance

✃ **Kalimna Woods Cottages**
30 Kalimna Jetty Road, Lakes Entrance
(03) 5155 1957
info@kalimnawoods.com.au
kalimnawoods.com.au

Waverley House Cottages
205 Palmers Rd, Lakes Entrance
(03) 5155 1257
enquiries@waverleyhousecottages.com.au
waverleyhousecottages.com.au

Lilydale

Murrindindi Executive Retreat
415 Ti-Tree Creek Road, Lilydale
0425 751 477
info@murrindindiretreat.com.au
murrindindiretreat.com.au

Loch

Bellview Hill B&B
270 Soldiers Road, Loch
(03) 5659 7285
enquiries@bellviewhill.com
bellviewhill.com.au

Longford

Frog Gully Cottages
Lot 2419 Rosedale Road, Longford
0439 369 057
ann@froggully.com.au
froggully.com.au

Lorne

✃ **La Perouse B&B**
26a William Street, Lorne
0418 534 422
email@laperouselorne.com.au
laperouselorne.com.au

Lorne – Aireys Inlet

✃ **Lorneview B&B**
677 Great Ocean Road, Eastern View
(03) 5289 6430
lorneview@bigpond.com
lorneview.com.au

Lorne – Otway Ranges

✃ **Elliminook**
585 Warncoort Road, Birregurra
(03) 5236 2080
enquiries@elliminook.com.au
elliminook.com.au

Macks Creek

The Barn at Glenwood Farm
122 Roberts Road, Macks Creek
(03) 5186 1310
glenwoodfarm@bigpond.com
glenwoodfarm.com.au

Maldon

Nuggetty Cottage
30 Nuggetty Road, Maldon
(03) 5475 2472
relax@nuggettycottage.com.au
nuggettycottage.com.au

Mansfield

Alpine Country Cottages
3/2 The Parade, Mansfield
(03) 5775 1694
catwil@bigpond.net.au
alpinecountrycottages.com.au

Burnt Creek Cottages
68 O'Hanlons Road, Mansfield
(03) 5775 3067
burntcreek@bigpond.com
burntcreekcottages.com.au

Wombat Hills Cottages
55 Lochiel Road, Mansfield
(03) 5776 9507
wombathills@bigpond.com
wombathills.com.au

Marysville

❦ **Dalrymples**
18 Falls Road, Marysville
(03) 5963 3416
info@dalrymples.com.au
dalrymples.com.au

Melbourne

❦ **Apartment 401**
258 Flinders Lane, Melbourne
(03) 9428 8104
email@apartment401.com.au
apartment401.com.au

Melbourne – Camberwell

❦ **Springfields**
4 Springfield Avenue, Camberwell
(03) 9809 1681
the.jordans@pacific.net.au

Melbourne – Carnegie

❦ **Josephine's B&B**
40 Rosanna Street, Carnegie
(03) 5952 3616
josephinesbb@optusnet.com.au
josephinesbb.com.au

Melbourne – Clifton Hill

❦ **ParksideStay**
109 Walker Street, Clifton Hill
(03) 9486 2121
wendy@parksidestay.com.au
parksidestay.com.au

Melbourne – Doncaster East

Blue Willow B&B
18 Maxia Rd, Doncaster East
0429 413 980
bluewillowbb@hotkey.net.au
bluewillow.com.au

Melbourne – Eltham

Cantala B&B
62 Henry Street, Eltham
(03) 9431 3374
cantalabnb@bigpond.com
cantalabedandbreakfast.com.au

Eltham South Lodge
58 Kent Hughes Road, Eltham
(03) 9439 4933
lodge@elthamaccommodation.com.au
elthamaccommodation.com.au

Melbourne – Forest Hill

Deanswood B&B
7 Deanswood Road, Forest Hill
0404 736 805
deanswood@optusnet.com.au
deanswood.com.au

Melbourne – Heidelberg

Austin Rise B&B
5 Quinn Street, Heidelberg
(03) 9455 0740
brettnbeverley@bigpond.com
austinrise.com.au

Melbourne – Ivanhoe

❦ **Magnolia Road Apartment B&B**
12 Magnolia Road, Ivanhoe
(03) 9499 6443
joy@magnoliaroad.net.au
magnoliaroad.net.au

Melbourne – Keilor

❦ **Overnewton Cottage**
51 Overnewton Road, Keilor
(03) 9331 6367
info@overnewtoncastle.com.au
overnewtoncastle.com.au

Melbourne – Kensington

Kensington B&B
97 McConnell St, Kensington
0423 926 020
enquiry@kensingtonbb.com.au
kensingtonbb.com.au

Melbourne – Kooyong

Carlisle B&B
400 Glenferrie Road, Kooyong
(03) 9822 4847
carlisle@internex.net.au
melbournesbest.com.au/carlisle

Melbourne – Research

Crestcastle B&B
24 Crest Road, Research
(03) 9437 0603
info@crestcastle.com.au
crestcastle.com.au

Melbourne – Richmond

❦ **Rotherwood**
13 Rotherwood Street, Richmond
0431 552 928
rotherwoodbb@bigpond.com

Melbourne – Southbank

Crown Guest House
274 City Road, Southbank
0413 960 960
alfjim1@gmail.com

Melbourne – St Kilda East

Alrae
7 Hughenden Rd, St Kilda East
(03) 9527 2033
info2@bigpond.com
visitvictoria.com/alrae

Melbourne – West Melbourne

Robinsons in the City
405 Spencer Street (cnr Batman Street), West Melbourne
(03) 9329 2552
robinsons@ritc.com.au
ritc.com.au

Melbourne – Williamstown

❦ **Captains Retreat B&B**
2 Ferguson Street, Williamstown
(02) 9660 5881
admin@captainsretreat.com.au
captainsretreat.com.au

North Haven By the Sea
Merrett Drive, Williamstown
(03) 9399 8399
info@yourhomeaway.com.au
yourhomeaway.com.au

Merrijig

Buttercup Cottage
271 Buttercup Road, Merrijig
(03) 5777 5591
buttercup@mansfield.net.au
buttercup.com.au

Mirboo North

Campbell Homestead B&B
295 Toomeys Road, Mirboo North
(03) 5664 1282
inq@campbellhomestead.com.au
campbellhomestead.com.au

Monbulk

Eagle Hammer Cottages
440 Old Emerald Road, Monbulk
(03) 9756 7700
info@eaglehammer.com.au
eaglehammer.com.au

Mornington – Dromana

❦ **Lakeside Villas at Crittenden Estate**
25 Harrisons Road, Dromana
(03) 5987 3275
info@lakesidevillas.com.au
lakesidevillas.com

Mornington – Flinders

❦ **Nazaaray Beach House**
266 Meekins Road, Flinders
(03) 5989 0126
info@nazaaray.com.au
nazaaray.com.au

Mornington – Langwarrin

Hillcrest on Valley
34 Valley Road, Langwarrin
(03) 9776 8596
george.scerri@optusnet.com.au
langwarrinbedandbreakfast.com.au

Mornington – Rye

Amour Eva Retreats
6 Eva Street, Rye
0411 170 356
amoureva@optusnet.com.au

Ocean Blue Coastal Retreats
12 Blakiston Grove, Rye
(03) 9775 4015
info@oceanbluecoastalretreats.com.au
oceanbluecoastalretreats.com.au

Plantation House at Whitecliffs
33 Maori Street, Rye
(03) 5985 5926
info@PlantationHouse.com.au
plantationhouse.com.au

Mornington – Sorrento

A La Plage
1 Watson Rd, Sorrento
(03) 5984 1280
info@alaplage.com.au
alaplage.com.au

Recommended Accommodation

☙ Tamasha House
699 Melbourne Road, Sorrento
(03) 5984 2413
tamasha@ozemail.com.au
TamashaHouse.com.au

Mornington – Tootgarook

Truemans Cottages
59 Truemans Road, Tootgarook
(03) 5988 6540
bookings@truemanscottage.com.au
truemanscottage.com.au

Mornington – Mount Eliza

Cosy Corner
12 Albatross Avenue, Mount Eliza
1300 880 997
bookings@lahaj.com
hostedaccommodationaustralia.com.au

Mount Beauty

Braeview
4 Stewarts Rd, Mount Beauty
0418 572 834
info@braeview.com.au
braeview.com.au

Mount Dandenong

☙ Observatory Cottages
8 Observatory Road, Mount Dandenong
(03) 5237 6939
enquiries@observatorycottages.com.au
observatorycottages.com.au

Adeline B&B
1462 Mount Dandenong Tourist Road, Mount Dandenong
(03) 9751 1116
adeline4@bigpond.com
adeline.com.au

Linden Gardens Rainforest Retreat
1383 Mt. Dandenong Tourist Road, Mount Dandenong
(03) 9751 1103
relax@lindengardens.com.au
lindengardens.com.au

Newborough

Brigadoon Cottages
108 Haunted Hills Rd, Newborough
(03) 5127 2656
mail@brigadooncottages.com
brigadooncottages.com

Ocean Grove

Ti Tree Village Pty Ltd
34 Orton Street, Ocean Grove
(03) 5255 4433
info@ti-treevillage.com.au
ti-treevillage.com.au

Olinda

Arcadia Cottages
188–190 Falls Rd, Olinda
(03) 9751 1017
arcadia@arcadiacottages.com.au
arcadiacottages.com.au

Woolrich Retreat
20 Woolrich Road, Olinda
(03) 9751 0154
getaway@woolrichretreat.com
woolrichretreat.com.au

Pakenham

Orchard Cottage
485 Toomuc Valley Rd, Pakenham
(03) 5942 7326
hardingsorchard@bigpond.com
orchardcottage.com.au

Phillip Island

Glen Isla House
230–232 Church Street, Cowes
(03) 5952 1882
info@glenisla.com
glenisla.com

Princetown

☙ Arabella Country House
7219 Great Ocean Road, Princetown
(03) 5598 8169
arabellacountryhse@bigpond.com
innhouse.com.au/arabella.html

☙ Macka's Farm
2310 Princetown Road, Princetown
(03) 5598 8261
holidays@mackasfarm.com.au
mackasfarm.com.au

Kangaroobie
Old Ocean Road, Princetown
(03) 5598 8151
kangaroobie@kangaroobie.com
kangaroobie.com

Rutherglen

☙ Cuddle Doon Cottages
12 Hunter Street, Rutherglen
(02) 6032 7107
cuddledoon@westnet.com.au
cuddledoon.com.au

Ready Cottage
92 High Street, Rutherglen
(02) 6032 7407
stay@readycottage.com.au
readycottage.com.au

Sarsfield

Stringybark Cottages
77 Howards Road, Sarsfield
(03) 5157 5245
neil@stringybarkcottages.com.au
stringybarkcottages.com.au

Seville

Redlands
20 Stevenson Lane, Seville
0408 825 293
redlands.seville@gmail.com

Skenes Creek

Heathbrae B&B
47 Great Ocean Road, Skenes Creek
0427 181 715
heathray47@gmail.com
apollobay.nu/heathbrae

Smeaton

Abergeldie B&B
3472 Creswick-Newstead Rd, Smeaton
(03) 5345 6223
abergeldie@netconnect.com.au
daylesford.net.au/abergeldie

Strath Creek

Halls on Falls Homestead
440–444 Falls Road, Strath Creek
(03) 5784 9232
info@hallsonfallshomestead.com.au
hallsonfallshomestead.com.au

Swan Hill – Lake Boga

☙ Burrabliss Farms B&B
169 Lakeside Drive, Lake Boga
(03) 5037 2527
info@burrabliss.com.au
burrabliss.com.au

The Murray

Tinys B&B
64 Golf Drive, Shepparton
0419 590 466
info@tinysbandb.com
tinysbandb.com

Walkerville South

Bear Gully Coastal Cottages
33 Maitland Court, Walkerville South
(03) 5663 2364
beargully@bigpond.com
beargullycottages.com.au

Wangaratta

☙ The Pelican
606 Oxley Flats Road, Wangaratta
(03) 5727 3240
pelicanblackshaw@hotmail.com

Waratah North

Prom Coast Holiday Lodge
1075 Waratah Road, Waratah North
(03) 5684 1110
pchlodge@dcsi.net.au
promcoastholidaylodge.com.au

Warragul West

Springwood Park Homestead
420 Lardner Road, Warragul West
(03) 5623 1396
spnmjl@dcsi.net.au
springwoodparkhomestead.com.au

Warrnambool

☙ Merton Manor Exclusive B&B
62 Ardlie Street, Warrnambool
(02) 6845 4320
merton@ansonic.com.au
http://members.datafast.net.au/merton

Yanakie

Limosa Rise
40 Dalgleish Road, Yanakie
(03) 5687 1135
relax@LimosaRise.com.au
LimosaRise.com.au

Yanakie Wilsons Promontory

Promhills Cabins
3650 Meeniyan-Promontory Road, Yanakie
Wilsons Promontory
(03) 5687 1469
promhills@yanakie.com.au
promhillscabins.com.au

Recommended Accommodation

Yarck

Glenfield Cottage
145 Middle Creek Road, Yarck
(03) 5773 4304
walsh145@me.com
australianbedandbreakfast.com.au

Yarra Valley – Narbethong

❧ **Woodlands Rainforest Retreat**
137 Manby Road, Narbethong
(03) 5963 7150
relax@woodlandscottages.com.au
woodlandscottages.com.au

Yarra Valley – Yarra Glen

❧ **The Gatehouse At Villa Raedward**
26 Melba Highway, Yering
(03) 9739 0822
info@villaraedward.com.au
villaraedward.com.au

Western Australia

If you're looking to step into a world of great beauty and discover experiences found nowhere else on earth, spend some time in Western Australia – with a vast and untouched outback with fascinating native fauna and flora.

INDIAN
OCEAN

Timor
Sea

Wyndham

Kimberley

Derby

Broome

Halls Creek

Great

Sandy

Desert

Port Hedland

Karratha

Marble Bar

Exmouth

Pilbara

Newman

*Gibson
Desert*

*Little Sandy
Desert*

Carnarvon

Warburton

Meekatharra

Kalbarri

Mount Magnet

Geraldton

Leonora

*Great Victoria
Desert*

Kalgoorlie

Nullarbor Plain

Perth

Eucla

Fremantle

Norseman

Great Australian Bight

Bunbury

Esperance

Albany

SOUTHERN OCEAN

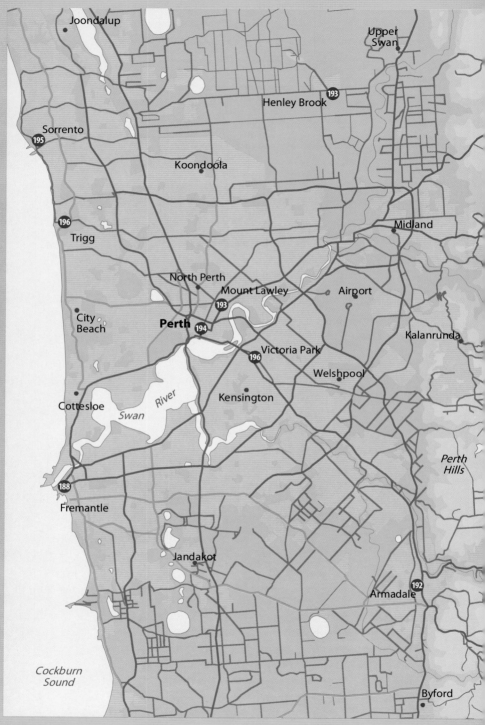

Peppermint Lane Lodge

Luxury B&B
20 km E of Bunbury

peppermintlanelodge@bigpond.com
351 Wellington Mill Road
Wellington Mill 6236
(08) 9728 3138
www.peppermintlanelodge.com.au

Double: $315

VISA MasterCard

Accommodation for 8
4 Bedrooms: 4K
Bathrooms: 4 ensuite

- Full breakfast

Secretly and superbly located, Peppermint Lane Lodge is the ideal place to spend some time away from city life. Our four suites offer wonderful well appointed accommodation. All rooms have king beds and ensuites with double doors opening to a terrace. Soak in the sunshine around the pool or enjoy drinks and aperitifs around the pot belly on the cooler Valley evenings. Ideally placed to explore the Ferguson Valley and Geographe wine region, close to beaches and only 2 hours from Perth. Dinner is available on request.

Kim and Simon Wesley

Easy access

Children welcome

Pets welcome

Facilities for horses

Couples or adults

Outstanding garden

Special location

Winery nearby

Restaurant nearby

Eco friendly

Onsite activities

Swimming pool

Tennis court

Function facilities

Wedding facilities

Internet access

Cable or satellite TV

No smoking

B&B and Hotel
12 km S of Perth

info@terracecentral.com.au
79–85 South Terrace
Fremantle 6160
(08) 9335 6600 or 0428 969 859
www.terracecentral.com.au

AAA Tourism
★★★★

Double: $185–$240
Single: $185–$240
Children: $50
2 night min. weekends

VISA MasterCard D AMERICAN EXPRESS eftpos

Accommodation for 40
18 Bedrooms: 10Q 6D 2T 2S
Air-conditioned En-suite
Bathrooms: 18 ensuite

• Continental breakfast

Heritage Boutique style B&B Hotel in the city centre of Fremantle with 18 air-conditioned en-suite bedrooms and 5 apartments.

Close to rail and bus service. 3 minutes walk to Markets, shops. Close to all tourist attractions and ferry to Rottnest Island. All rooms air-conditioned, en-suite bathroom.

Free wireless broadband, TV and DVD Player, tea and coffee, fridge. Free parking..

Barry White

**B&B and Heritage Listed Luxury
Accommodation**   *0.5 km N of Fremantle*

fothergills@iinet.net.au
18–22 Ord Street
Fremantle 6160
(08) 9335 6784
www.fothergills.net.au

AAA Tourism
★★★★

Double: $160–$275
Children: Free under 5. Cot available

Accommodation for 14
7 Bedrooms: 1KT 6Q
Bathrooms: 6 ensuite

- Full breakfast

Our heritage-listed AAA four star B&B occupies three grand limestone Victorian homes built on the slope of Monument Hill overlooking Fremantle to the Indian Ocean beyond and with Rottnest Island on the horizon – and yet only a 6 minute stroll to the heart of Fremantle.

The elegant, air-conditioned spacious rooms are fitted with TV, DVD, Bose CD and have wireless internet. Our mini fridge offers complimentary welcome snack, mineral water and soft drinks. Enjoy our luxury toiletries and climb into a bed dressed with luxury high thread count linen. In the morning tuck into a wonderful breakfast – cooked and continental – all included as part of Fothergills unique service. Our flowered courtyards are furnished with seating for your use and the whole property is filled with a rich collection of work by local, national and international artists. Of particular interest is the iconic quartet of stunning bronze statues, Iris, depicting human life evolving like a beautiful flower.

David Cooke, Suzy Llewellyn, Paulette Lowe, Kwi Yeon Im

Margaret River Wine Region

Margaret River region is an intricate tapestry of premium wineries, pristine beaches, awe-inspiring natural wonders, spectacular forests and fine restaurants.

Donna Carter
The Noble Grape Guesthouse and Brookwood Estate www. Brookwood.com.au

The Noble Grape Guesthouse

Boutique Motel Style accommodation
12 km N of Margaret River

stay@noblegrape.com.au
29 Bussell Highway
Cowaramup 6284
(08) 9755 5538 or 0418 931 721
www.noblegrape.com.au

AAA Tourism
★★★★♩

Double: $150–$190
Single: $135–$155
Children: $30 per child
Extra adult $30

VISA MasterCard AMERICAN EXPRESS eftpos

Accommodation for 16
6 Bedrooms: 3K 2KT 1Q 3S
Spacious but cosy, well appointed and comfortable
Bathrooms: 6 ensuite
One bathroom with universal access

• Continental breakfast

The Noble Grape is a cosy Guesthouse in the heart of the Margaret River Wine Region. Colonial style charm with quaint antiques nestled in an English cottage garden. Vineyards, beaches, galleries, chocolate and cheese factories minutes away. Enjoy a leisurely breakfast in our dining room overlooking the garden while watching the native birdlife. Spacious country style rooms with ensuite and hairdryer, r.c. air conditioning, TV, DVD, refrigerator, microwave, tea/coffee, electric blanket, comfortable arm chairs and private courtyard. Guest barbecue. Wireless Internet. Room with universal access. Smoking outside only.

Rodney and Donna Carter

Rosewood Guesthouse

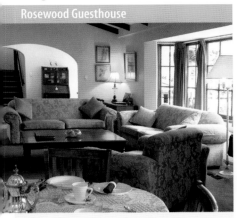

Luxury B&B · Separate Suite and Rolls Royce Tours available   *1 km SW of Post Office*

info@rosewoodguesthouse.com.au
54 Wallcliffe Road
Margaret River 6285
(08) 9757 2845 or 0427 772 911
www.rosewoodguesthouse.com.au

 AAA Tourism ★★★★

Double: $199–$275
Single: $189–$250
Children: We do not have facilities for children
Suite $250–$300 double. Extra guests from $60. Max 4
Dinner: Cheese plates and soup with crusty bread can
be ordered

Accommodation for 12
6 Bedrooms: 4K 2KT 1Q
5 B&B plus 1 spa suite
Bathrooms: 6 ensuite
Suite has 2 person spa bath

• Full breakfast

Rosewood Guesthouse is an award winning B&B
which provides a warm and friendly atmosphere,
welcoming guests from all parts of the globe.
Beautifully appointed rooms with modern
en-suites. Fire in the lounge with complimentary
port, Rosewood breakfasts feature fantastic daily
specials for variety. Just a 700 metre walk to the
main street restaurants, 4 minute drive to wineries,
Rosewood is the ideal base to explore the region
and Jane and Keith will be happy to help plan
your itinerary. Book instantly on our websites
BookNow page.

Jane and Keith Purdie

Loaring Place B&B

Luxury B&B and Guest House
4 km SW of Margaret River

booking@margaretriverbnb.com
15 Loaring Place
Margaret River 6285
(08) 9758 7002
www.margaretriverbnb.com

 AAA Tourism ★★★★

Double: $135–$250
Children: Foldaways by arrangement
Dinner by arrangement

Accommodation for 8
4 Bedrooms: 4Q
Bathrooms: 4 ensuite
Double spa bath in each room.

• Full breakfast

Be treated to the personalised and warm hospitality
of Pam and Dirk Hos. Four fabulous rooms each
with double spa hidden in 9 acres of beautiful
native forest. A brand new boutique, modern and
eco-friendly B&B. In the morning you will enjoy
a gourmet Australian breakfast in the spacious
lounge or outside in the alfresco area overlooking
the tranquil bush landscape. After a day of
indulgence in the Margaret River Wine Region you
can arrange a massage to ease away your cares,
and relax in your own double spa bath. 5 minutes
from the Margaret River mouth and the surf.

Pamela and Dirk Hos

Seclusions of Yallingup

Bali style B&B
10 km N of Yallingup

escape@seclusionsofyallingup.com.au
58 Zamia Grove
Yallingup 6282
(08) 9756 6219 or 0419 861 087
www.seclusionsofyallingup.com.au

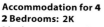

Double: $220–$285
Supper platters available on request at extra cost

VISA MasterCard

Accommodation for 4
2 Bedrooms: 2K
2 bedrooms, ensuite. King bed only not able to split to twin.
Bathrooms: 2 ensuite
Large open shower. Separate toilet.

- Special breakfast

'Seclusions' of Yallingup is luxury B&B on 7 acres of stunning bushland in the Margaret River Wine Region. Situated in Yallingup, we are only a 15 min drive to Dunsborough and 35 min drive to Margaret River.

Make the most of the local attractions the Region has to offer, we are close to many wineries, breweries, art galleries and restaurants, plus magnificent beaches.

'Seclusions' has only 2 King Guest Suites ensuring our personal attention at all times to our very special guests. When your privacy is paramount, ESCAPE to the magic of 'Seclusions' of Yallingup.

Fran and Ken

Armadale Manor B&B

B&B and Self Contained House and Cottage
Armadale

bnb@armadalecottage.com.au
3161 Albany Highway
Armadale 6112
(08) 9497 1663 or 0421 606 597
www.armadalemanor.com.au

AAA Tourism
★★★★↗

Double: $145–$155
Clarence House: S/C, 3b/r, 2 bath/r $250/nt.
Seville House: S/C, 4b/r, 2 bath/r $250/nt

VISA MasterCard

Accommodation for 13
5 Bedrooms: 1K 3Q 5S
Bathrooms: 5 ensuite

- Full breakfast

Armadale Manor is an Award-Winning Bed and Breakfast offering good old-fashioned warmth, comfort and hospitality. Located only 25 minutes from Perth, our 4½ star boutique B&B is situated in the heart of heritage country, with wineries, animal parks, botanic gardens, museums and great shopping within easy reach. Armadale Manor has all the comforts of home, including: private en-suites, comfortable couches, air conditioning, LCD flat screen TVs with Foxtel, tea and coffee making facilities, plus appliances, utensils, toiletries, a private entrance and wireless high-speed Internet access to ensure the perfect stay. Each day at Armadale Manor begins with a delicious full or continental breakfast.

Ruth and Terry Lynam

Park View B&B

B&B
15 km NE of Perth CBD

parkviewbedbreakfast@hotmail.com
6 Exmoor Lane
Henley Brook 6055
(08) 6296 7502
www.parkviewbnb.com.au

Double: $130
10% discount to Seniors card holders if booked
direct. Cooked breakfasts available for additional $15pp.
Special diets catered for.

Accommodation for 4
2 Bedrooms: 2Q
Bathrooms: 2 ensuite

• Continental breakfast

We invite you to stay with us in one of our two
air conditioned, queen-sized ensuite bedrooms
with HD Colour TV/DVD Player, Fridge, Tea/
Coffee facilities, iron and ironing board. Guest
lounge, laundry facilities and short term extra
baggage hold (conditions apply) available. We
are just 10 minutes from the Swan Valley with
great access to wineries, boutique breweries,
restaurants and cafés. Close to the historic town of
Guildford and national parks, 30 minutes to Perth
CBD and 35 minutes to many of Perth's famous
sandy beaches. To fully appreciate the attractions'
hospitality, use our chauffeur service at a small fee
per kilometre.

Morag and Matt Robertson

Durack House B&B

Luxury B&B
3 km N of Perth

durackhouse@westnet.com.au
7 Almondbury Road
Mt Lawley 6050
(08) 9370 4305
www.durackhouse.com.au

Double: $195–$215

Accommodation for 4
2 Bedrooms: 1KT 1Q
Bathrooms: 2 ensuite

• Special breakfast

An elegant Edwardian home situated in the
quiet leafy suburb of Mt Lawley with two ensuite
bedrooms each with reverse cycle air-conditioning,
televisions, DVDs, in house movies, electric
blankets, hairdryers and comfortable beds with
quality linen. The lush gardens at Durack House
offer a tranquil retreat after a busy day. Enjoy a
complimentary drink each evening in the open
courtyard. An elegant and cosy sitting room is
available exclusively to guests at all times. Only 3km
from the City, with bus and train access 300 meters
away. Sightseeing, shopping, the beautiful Swan
River and Kings Park are within easy reach. The
vibrant café strip on Beaufort Street is within
walking distance.

Sandra and Bill Durack

Perth – Northbridge

Enjoy the vibrant nightlife of Northbridge which is a gourmet delight and also the discount shopping haven of Harbourtown. Northbridge is only a 5 minute drive from Perth CBD with regular buses into the city. Perth, built on the Swan River, is the fastest growing city in Australia.

Sarah Rossetti
Above Bored B&B

Above Bored Bed and Breakfast

Luxury B&B and S/C Guest Wing Suite
5 km N of Perth

stay@abovebored.com.au
14 Norham Street
North Perth 6006
(08) 9444 5455 or 0419 838 282
www.abovebored.com.au

AAA Tourism
★★★★

Double: $190–$200
Single: $180–$190
Children: Free in existing bedding. $30 extra in Master or King/twin room.
Stay A Week Get 8th Night Free

VISA MasterCard

Accommodation for 7
3 Bedrooms: 1K 2Q 1T 2S
Bathrooms: 2 ensuite, 1 private

• Full breakfast provisions

Above Bored Bed and Breakfast is an exclusive non-intrusive boutique hotel in a 1927 Federation home in a quiet street, just 5 minutes north of Perth CBD, the night life of Northbridge, and the discount shopping hub of Harbourtown. Equally suited to the lone traveller, couples seeking a romantic getaway, or families where the children and/or pets aren't frowned upon, this B&B suits all. Choose between the luxuriously appointed en-suited Master bedroom, the spacious King or Twin bedroom, with its own fabulous underwater fresco ceiling bathroom, or the en-suited Garden room, in its own cottage, kitchenette and remote controlled lock up garage. Free Wi-Fi and Parking.

Dr Sarah Rossetti

Albacore B&B

B&B
Sorrento

stay@albacorebnb.com.au
18 Albacore Drive
Sorrento 6020
(08) 9448 2238 or 0417 182 358
www.albacorebnb.com.au

Double: $150
Minimum 2 night stay

VISA MasterCard eftpos

Accommodation for 4
2 Bedrooms: 1KT 1Q
Bathrooms: 2 ensuite

- Full continental breakfast

Two beautifully appointed air conditioned on Perth's sunshine coast. Choose either a queen double bed or two king single beds, each with private verandah and en suite bathroom. Situated just 20 minutes from Perth CBD and five minutes from Hillarys Boat Harbour and Sorrento Quay. With over 20 shops, cafés and restaurants Hillarys Boat Harbour is a destination in itself. The gorgeous sunset coast tourist drive connects Sorrento Quay in the north with Fremantle in the south. You can expect traditional, friendly service and fine attention to detail. Bill and Meriel will be happy to give advice on transport, tours and some of the best places to see around Perth.

Bill and Meriel Falconer

Perth – Trigg – Scarborough

Exquisite beaches and walking/bike riding paths. Excellent beachside cafés/restaurants. Enjoy Hillarys Marina and AQWA underwater world or ferry to Rottnest.

Sue Stein
Trigg Retreat B&B

Trigg Retreat B&B

B&B
15 km N of Perth

sue@triggretreat.com
59 Kitchener Street
Trigg 6029
(08) 9447 6726 or 0417 911 048
www.triggretreat.com

AAA Tourism
★★★★✦

Double: $195
Single: $195

Accommodation for 6
3 Bedrooms: 3Q
Bathrooms: 3 ensuite

• Full breakfast

Gold Award for Hosted Accommodation WA 2012, 2011, Silver Award 2013, 4½ star, Accredited, tastefully furnished two-storey home with three ensuite queensize rooms, A/C, luxurious queensize beds, flat screen TV/DVD, fridge, tea/coffee, free wi-fi, bedside chocolates. A gourmet, continental breakfast, served in guest breakfast room or garden courtyard. Optional hot selection available from enticing menu.

'Stroll to the beach', exquisite WA coastline, walking, riding paths and cafés. Airport – 30 min direct route. Perth city – 15 min drive. Guest and owners facilities are separate. Certificate of Excellence from Trip Advisor in 2014, 2013, 2012, 2011.

Sue Stein

Durham Lodge B&B

Boutique Accommodation
4 km SE of Perth CBD

guest@durhamlodge.com
165 Shepperton Road
Victoria Park 6100
(08) 9361 8000
www.durhamlodge.com

AAA Tourism
★★★★✦

Double: $150–$350

Accommodation for 6
3 Bedrooms: 1K 2Q
Bathrooms: 3 ensuite

• Continental breakfast

Durham Lodge is a four and a half star property, purpose-built to provide relaxing, private and very efficient, bed and breakfast accommodation in Perth. The elegant guest house is cosy, inviting and well appointed. A sofa and comfy chairs huddle around the fireplace ready for cold winter nights. The lodge has three superior guest rooms each fitted with a quality orthopaedic bed to ensure a comfortable and restful nights' sleep. Two suites are fitted with queen size beds, while the third has a king size bed. Guest rooms are tastefully and elegantly decorated and include ensuites, individual reverse cycle air conditioning, remote control television, bar fridge, tea and coffee facilities and direct dial telephones to each room.

Sonja and Michael

Manuel Towers Boutique B&B

Luxury B&B
50 km S of Perth

info@manueltowers.com.au
32A Arcadia Drive
Shoalwater 6169
(08) 9592 2698 or 0423 124 293
www.manueltowers.com.au

Double: $220
Single: $0–$165
Children: under 12 $55 over.12 $85
From $220 per night

VISA MasterCard Diners Club eftpos

Accommodation for 12
5 Bedrooms: 4Q 1D 1T
Bathrooms: 5 ensuite, 1 family share

• Full breakfast

A stunning Bed and Breakfast Accommodation located on the beautiful Shoalwater Bay Marine Park, overlooking Seal and Penguin Islands in the Rockingham area, only 45 minutes from Perth, an ideal stop on the way to Margaret River. Manuel Towers is a unique rustic and stone building with a Provence / Mediterranean atmosphere. The character filled bedrooms are large, comfortable all with ensuites, some have spas, balconies, sea views, Queen beds, fridges, tea/coffee, TVs, DVDs, clock radios and all standard requisites. Manual Towers is located right across from the Shoalwater Marine Park and access to some the most beautiful wildlife and scenery in the world.

Ali and Manuel

Rockingham – Shoalwater

Discover the magic of Shoalwater Island Marine Park, Penguin and Seal Islands. Home to pelicans, dolphins, seals, penguins and many other birds. Swim, snorkel in safe pristine waters or kayak to the islands. Swim with dolphins. A wind and kite surfing mecca. Ferry tours to islands. Stunning sunsets, coastal walks.

Manuel Nunez
Manuel Towers Boutique B&B

Recommended Accommodation

🅑 Included in book

Albany

Albany – 'Mia Amore'
15 Robert St, Albany
08 92913720
vbostin@bigpond.com
australianbedandbreakfast.com.au

Albany View Street Lodge B&B
35 View Street, Albany
(08) 9842 8820
stay@albanyviewstbb.com.au
albanyviewstbb.com.au

Bridgetown

Lucieville Farm Chalets
RMB 390 South West Highway, Bridgetown
(08) 9761 1733
lucievillefarm@iinet.net.au
lucieville.com.au

Sunnyhurst Chalets
Lot 15 Doust Street, Bridgetown
(08) 9761 1081
enquiries@sunnyhurstchalets.com.au
sunnyhurstchalets.com.au

Broome

BroomeTown B&B
15 Stewart Street, Broome
(08) 9192 2006
info@broometown.com.au
broometown.com.au

Coco Eco
Lot 9 Williams Road Coconut Well Broome,
Broome
(08) 9192 3103
lyndahagan@bigpond.com
cocoeco.com.au

Ochre Moon B&B
13 Goodwit Cres, Broome
(08) 9192 7109
enquiries@ochremoon.com.au
ochremoon.com.au

Reflections B&B
69 Demco Drive, Broome
(08) 9192 6610
info@reflectionsbnb.com.au
reflectionsbnb.com.au

The Bungalow – Broome
3 McKenzie Road, Broome
0417 918 420
info@thebungalowbroome.com.au
thebungalowbroome.com.au

Busselton

Baudins of Busselton
87 Busselton Highway, Busselton
(08) 9751 5576
baudins@iinet.net.au
baudins.com.au

Beds By The Bay
125 Adelaide street, Busselton
(08) 9754 4519
mike@busseltonguesthouse.com.au
busseltonguesthouse.com.au

Broadwater B&B
407 Bussell Highway Broadwater, Busselton
(08) 9751 4545
stay@broadwaterbandb.com.au
broadwaterbandb.com.au

Inn the Tuarts
19 Rushleigh Rd, Busselton
(08) 9754 1444
stay@innthetuarts.com.au
innthetuarts.com.au

Cowaramup

Corwarmup Studios
52 Treeton Road, Cowaramup
0437 776 603
janine@amrex.com.au

Taunton Farm Holiday Park
Bussell Highway, Cowaramup
(08) 9755 5334
enquiries@tauntonfarm.com.au

Donnybrook

Boronia Farm
47 William Rd, Donnybrook
(08) 9731 7154
relax@boroniafarm.com.au
boroniafarm.com.au

Dunsborough

Toby Inlet B&B
2 Backwater Retreat, Dunsborough
(08) 9756 7653
stay@tobyinlet.com.au
tobyinlet.com.au

Esperance

Esperance B&B by the Sea
72 Stewart Street, Esperance
(08) 9071 5640
esperancebb@bigpond.com
esperancebb.com

Ferguson Valley – Bunbury

🅑 **Peppermint Lane Lodge**
351 Wellington Mill Road, Wellington Mill
(08) 9728 3138
peppermintlanelodge@bigpond.com.au
peppermintlanelodge.com.au

Fremantle

🅑 **Fothergills of Fremantle**
18–22 Ord Street, Fremantle
(08) 9335 6784
fothergills@iinet.net.au
fothergills.net.au

🅑 **Terrace Central B&B**
79–85 South Terrace, Fremantle
(02) 4232 2504
info@terracecentral.com.au
terracecentral.com.au

Halls Head

Dolphin Point B&B
26 Bermuda Place, Halls Head
0413 669 387
stay@dolphinpointbandb.com.au
dolphinpointbandb.com.au

Harvey

Harvey Hills Farmstay Chalets
Weir Road, HARVEY
(08) 9729 1434
farmstay@geo.net.au
harveyhillsfarmstay.com.au

Hazelvale

Che Sara Sara Chalets
92 Nunn Road, Hazelvale
(08) 9840 8004
chesara@denmarkwa.net.au

Henty

Ferguson Farmstay
930 Henty Road, Henty
(08) 9728 1392
info@fergusonfarmstay.com.au
fergusonfarmstay.com.au

Kununurra

Bougainvillea Lodge B&B
511 Riverfarm Rd, Kununurra
0400 681 100
judyhughes@activ8.net.au
kununurrabedandbreakfast.com

Manjimup

Karri Rose B&B
14 Karri Street, Manjimup
(08) 9772 4240
vkammann@wn.com.au
karrirose.com.au

Margaret River

🅑 **The Noble Grape**
Lot 18 Bussell Highway, Cowaramup
(08) 9755 5538
stay@noblegrape.com.au
noblegrape.com.au

🅑 **Loaring Place B&B**
15 Loaring Place, Margaret River
(08) 9758 7002
booking@margaretriverbnb.com
margaretriverbnb.com

🅑 **Rosewood Guesthouse**
54 Wallcliffe Road, Margaret River
(08) 9757 2845
info@rosewoodguesthouse.com.au
rosewoodguesthouse.com.au

Llewellins Guesthouse
64 Yates Road, Margaret River
(08) 9757 9516
info@llgh.com.au
llewellinsguesthouse.com.au

Margaret River Guest House
5 Valley Road, Margaret River
(08) 9757 2349
info@margaretriverguesthouse.com.au
margaretriverguesthouse.com.au

Narrogin

Chuckem Farm
1481 Tarwonga Road, Narrogin
(08) 9881 1188
rwiese@westnet.com.au

Perth

Coranda Lodge B&B
73 Twelfth Road Haynes, Perth
0418 943 776
corandalodge@bigpond.com
bedandbreakfastperth.net.au

Perths La Casa Rosa B&B
62B Wittenoom Street, Perth
08 92256868
rose@lacasarosa.com.au
lacasarosa.com.au

Perth – Alexander Heights

Astoria Retreat B&B
62 Avila Way, Alexander Heights
(08) 9247 2436
natalie@astoriabnb.com.au
astoriabnb.com.au

Recommended Accommodation

Perth – Armadale

Armadale Manor B&B
3161 Albany Highway, Armadale
(08) 9497 1663
bnb@armadalecottage.com.au
armadalemanor.com.au

Perth – Bayswater

95 On Roberts B&B
95 Roberts Street, Bayswater
0419 942 123
bandb@95onroberts.com.au
95onroberts.com.au

Perth – Bicton

Annie's Bicton B&B
40 Coldwells Street, Bicton
(08) 9438 2026
annie.bicton@optusnet.com.au
anniesbictonbedandbreakfast.com.au

Perth – Brigadoon

Stocks Country Retreat
26 Boulonnais Drive, Brigadoon
(08) 9296 1945
retreat2stocks@bigpond.com
stockscountryretreat.com

Perth – Burns Beach

Burns Beach B&B
7 Fourmile Avenue, Burns Beach
(08) 9304 7825
contact@burnsbeachbnb.com.au
burnsbeachbnb.com.au

Perth – Como

Como B&B
2A Bickley Crescent, Como
(08) 9450 1442
como-bedbreakfast@bigpond.com.au
como-bedbreakfast.com.au

Como Waters B&B
3 Philp Avenue, Como
0416 105 414
info@comowaters.com.au
comowaters.com.au

Perth – Coogee

Coogee Beach Accommodation
16 Toulon Grove, Coogee
(08) 9434 1691
haste@iinet.net.au
coogeebeachwa.com.au

Perth – Gidgegannup

Lakeview Lodge
131 Lakeview Drive, Gidgegannup
(08) 9578 3009
contact@lakeviewlodge.com.au
lakeviewlodge.com.au

Talleringa B&B
135 Redbrook Circle, Gidgegannup
(08) 9572 9393
talleringa@bigpond.com
talleringa.com.au

Perth – Gooseberry Hill

Grandview B&B
30 Girrawheen Drive, Gooseberry Hill
(08) 9293 2518
geoff@grandviewbandb.com.au
grandviewbandb.com.au

Perth – Gwelup

Lakeside Retreat
6 Salvin Road, Gwelup
(08) 9445 8504
info@lakesideretreat.com.au
lakesideretreat.com.au

Perth – Henley Brook

Park View B&B
6 Exmoor Lane, Henley Brook
(08) 6296 7502
info@parkviewbnb.com.au
parkviewbnb.com.au

Perth – High Wycombe

Jennys Retreat
23 Edwards Road, High Wycombe
0412 680 198
jennysretreat@bigpond.com

Perth – Hillarys

Hillarys Harbour View Retreat
23 Urbahns Way, Hillarys
0428 249 805
info@hillarysharbourview.com.au
hillarysharbourview.com.au

Perth – Lesmurdie

Anapana Ridge
38 Gilchrist Road, Lesmurdie
(08) 9291 7997
nbarnard@bigpond.com
anapanaridge.com

Falls Retreat B&B
45 Falls Road, Lesmurdie
(08) 9291 7609
roza@westnet.com.au
perthbedandbreakfast.com.au

The Good Life B&B
64 George Road, Lesmurdie
08 92913106
cherry@goodlifebnb.com.au
goodlifebnb.com.au

Perth – Moore River

Woollybush Guest House B&B
205 Woollybush Loop, Moore River
(08) 9577 1909
woollybush@westnet.com.au
woollybushguesthouse.com

Perth – Mosman Park

Rosemoore B&B
2 Winifred Street, Mosman Park
(08) 9384 8214
rosemoore@bigpond.com
rosemoore.com.au

Perth – Mount Claremont

Grainger BnB
15 Grainger Drive, Mount Claremont
0422 601 394
graingerbnb@hotmail.com
graingerbnb.com

Mary's B&B
17 Townsend Dale, Mount Claremont
(08) 9286 1134
marysbedandbreakfast@hotmail.com
marysbedandbreakfastperth.com

Perth – Mt Lawley

Durack House B&B
7 Almondbury Road, Mt Lawley
(02) 9949 8487
durackhouse@westnet.com.au
durackhouse.com.au

Perth – Muchea

Enderslie House B&B and Farmstay
15 Peters Road, Muchea
0412 407 648
enderslie@bigpond.com
endersliehouse.com.au

Perth – Nedlands

Exley House B&B
2 Bedford Street, Nedlands
(08) 9386 4452
exleyhse@iinet.net.au
exleyhouse.com.au

Perth – Northbridge

Above Bored B&B
14 Norham Street, North Perth
(08) 9444 5455
stay@abovebored.com.au
abovebored.com.au

Perth – Pinjarra

Lazy River Boutique B&B
9 Wilson Road, Pinjarra
(08) 9531 4550
unwind@lazyriver.com.au
lazyriver.com.au

Perth – Rockingham

Homestead B&B
14 Palm Drive, Warnbro Rockingham
(08) 9593 0928
info@homesteadrockingham.com.au
Homesteadrockingham.com.au

Perth – Scarborough

Beach Manor B&B
196 The Esplanade, Scarborough
(08) 9245 2288
info@bedandbreakfastperth.com
bedandbreakfastperth.com

Perth – Sorrento

Albacore B&B
18 Albacore Drive, Sorrento
08 94482238
stay@albacorebnb.com.au
albacorebnb.com.au

Sorrento Beach B&B
30 Hood Tce, Sorrento
(08) 9447 4871
bookings@sorrentobeachbb.com.au
sorrentobeachbb.com.au

Perth – Stoneville

Chalets on Stoneville
4405 Stoneville Road, Stoneville
(08) 9295 6628
info@chalets.com.au
chalets.com.au

Perth – Success

Parkside Suites B&B
15 Reeves Entrance, Success
0412 952 331
jdennison@westnet.com.au
parksidesuitesbnb.com.au

Recommended Accommodation

✆ Included in book

Perth – Trigg

✆ **Trigg Retreat B&B**
59 Kitchener Street, Trigg
(03) 5348 1535
sue@triggretreat.com
triggretreat.com

Perth – Victoria Park

✆ **Durham Lodge B&B**
165 Shepperton Road, Victoria Park
(08) 9361 8000
guest@durhamlodge.com
durhamlodge.com

Perth – Wilson

Anarina Lodge
15 and 15A Holford Way, Wilson
0439 935 440
patsy@anarinalodge.com
anarinalodge.com

Fern Cove B&B
12 Hyland Way, Wilson
(08) 9451 1374
office@ferncove.com.au
ferncove.com.au

Perth – York

Lavendale Farm
5895 Great Southern Highway, York
(08) 9641 4131
lavendalefarm@westnet.com.au
lavendalefarm.com

Shoalwater

✆ **Manuel Towers**
32a Arcadia Drive, Shoalwater
(08) 9592 2698
manueltowers@dodo.com.au
manueltowers.com.au

South Porongurup

Jilba
338 Millinup Rd, South Porongurup
(08) 9853 1038
jbaily@omninet.net.au
jilba.com.au

Wandering

Millfarm B&B
131 North Wandering Road, Wandering
(08) 9884 1041
millfarmbedandbreakfast@yahoo.com.au
millfarmbedandbreakfast.com

Wellington Mill

Peppermint Lane Lodge
351 Wellington Mill Road, Wellington Mill
(08) 9728 3138
peppermintlanelodge@bigpond.com
peppermintlanelodge.com.au

Yallingup

✆ **Seclusions Of Yallingup**
58 Zamia Grove, Yallingup
(08) 9756 6219
escape@seclusionsofyallingup.com.au
seclusionsofyallingup.com.au

Index by Name
of Accommodation

The New Zealand
Bed & Breakfast Book

Committed to generous hospitality

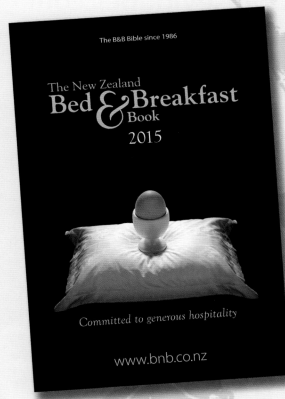

The B&B Bible since 1986

The New Zealand
Bed & Breakfast Book
2015

Committed to generous hospitality

www.bnb.co.nz

Bed & Breakfast in New Zealand means a warm welcome and a unique holiday experience. Most B&B accommodation is in private homes with a sprinkling of guesthouses and small hotels. Each listing in the guide has been written by the host themselves and you will discover their warmth and personality through their writing.

LuggageLock
Tamper evidence for your peace of mind

Tear off and keep number-tab for reference - don't waste time writing down serial numbers!

Remove the lock by hand - no scissors or knives necessary!

Available from selected Australia Post outlets and bag shops.

www.luggagelock.com.au

Notes

Notes